TWO LEGS SUFFICE

LESSONS LEARNED BY TEACHING

TWO LEGS SUFFICE:

LESSONS LEARNED BY TEACHING

JOHN J. VIALL

HOOP SKIRT PRESS

CINCINNATI, OHIO

For Anne, the finest educator I know,
for Abby, Seth, Sarah and Emily
and for the thousands of students who taught me so much.

To Ellora and the next generation of learners.

"Not much is ever gained simply by wishing for it."
Thucydides

TABLE OF CONTENTS

1:	Talk to the Grunts	1
2:	The Quintessential Fact	15
3:	Fantasy of the Fixed School	29
4:	Liberal Yin, Marine Corps Yang	36
5:	Dead Dogs and Milkshake Bets	48
6:	Luke and His Pompoms	58
7:	Frankenstein Gets a Brain	68
8:	Water Buffalo and Rumble Seats	82
9:	Case of the Egg McMuffin	90
10:	Nothing Human is Alien	100
11:	Two "N" Words and a "D" Word	112
12:	Eat What I Serve or Starve	123
13:	Sisyphus Never Quits	138
14:	We All Enter by the Same Rectangle	152
15:	Poison Ivy Dilemma	163
16:	The Iceberg	171
17:	WWAD (What Would Abe Do)	179
18:	The Mom and Pop Effect	188
19:	Think Horses, Not Zebras	197
20:	Two Legs Suffice	209
21:	Not English Class	227
22:	Songhai Trade	245
23:	Pick Up a Broom and Sweep	261
24:	How to Bicycle across America	284
25:	Basics for Tommy, Trevor and Ryan	301
26:	Roger is the Key	317
27:	And His Soul Left His Body	333
28:	Gone, Test, Gone	341
29:	Nuns and Runners	344
30:	Clean Underwear Standards	353
31:	Was Your Father a Teacher?	367

1.

Talk to the Grunts

"Ther is many a man that creith 'Werre! werre!
that woot ful litel what werre amounteth."
Geoffrey Chaucer

I don't drink much. Besides, it's seven a.m. and I'm hardly awake. "Not again," I mutter, rubbing my eyes and adding a string of my favorite expletives.

I hold in my hands another stinging editorial directed at teachers. This one, from *The New York Times*, carries the headline:

TEACHERS: WILL WE EVER LEARN?

The author is assistant professor in the Harvard Graduate School of Education. So you might assume he knows what he's talking about.

You'd be wrong.

He starts by outlining a "tidal wave" of school reforms since 1983. I taught for decades. So I remember them all. The professor lists vouchers, charter schools, state standardized tests, No Child Left Behind and "Race to the Top." With implementation of Common Core in the offing a fresh round of reforms is about to commence.

He leaves out a laundry list of changes veteran educators might include but sums up results. U. S. K-12 education remains "stubbornly mediocre."

I feel myself wavering. Is it too early for bourbon?

✳✳✳

What is it we keep failing to learn? Apparently, the problem with education in this country is teachers.

According to the professor we have too many dumb ones manning the classrooms. Only 23% come from the top third of their college classes. What about Finland, a country whose schools are almost too good to be true? Finland has smart teachers. America needs to find smart teachers, under some rocks or something, and pronto.

As a former teacher, suddenly I feel like such a dolt.

"Well," I wonder, "*will* we ever learn?"

I set the editorial aside and gather my wits. I don't think I'm deluding myself when I say I was a good teacher. I don't think I'm hallucinating when I say I worked with a number of excellent educators and all kinds of good ones during my career. Call me stupid, I guess, but I would argue that teachers come in the same varieties, excellent, good, fair, and poor, as lumberjacks, car mechanics, Congress persons and Harvard professors.

I tell myself: "You can do your bit to answer the professor's question if you do it right."

The dilemma is how? How write a book about education that might offer useful insights? How capture the interest of some fraction of the general reading public? And is there some way to poke all the self-styled "education experts" where it hurts most?

I mean—in the ego.

Perhaps some sleazy sex and the right title might help: *Fifty Shades of Grade Book*? Nope. No way that's going to sell.

All I did was spend my career in a large rectangular room in close company with teens. All I offer is a memoir about life in the classroom, a love story about working with thousands of kids.

Still, I'm compelled to try.

First, I mean this book as a defense of good educators—an explanation of what they do—and a look at the daunting problems they confront. There are plenty of bad books to choose from if you want to read about what teachers do wrong.

I also believe my book has value because of what it's *not*. I won't be offering the latest plan to fix the schools. I'm not an authority in the fixing field. I'm not Steven Brill or Arne Duncan or Michelle Rhee. U. S. Secretary of Education Duncan and former Washington, D. C. School Chancellor Rhee we shall meet again. Brill is the prototypical critic and school fixer—a lawyer—who wrote a book about education, lambasting

2

teachers: *Class Warfare: Inside the Fight to Fix America's Schools*. Brill never bothered to teach. He studied "war" at a safe remove and didn't have to worry about getting killed or maimed.

What do I know? Part of what I know I know because I sat in class as if in a coma during my own misspent youth. Another chunk I know because I dropped out of college in 1968 and joined the Marines. I know what I know, in part, because I've pedaled a bike across the United States.

Most of what I know I learned by teaching: American and Ancient World History, for thirty-three years, at the seventh and eighth grade levels, for Loveland City Schools, near Cincinnati, Ohio. That's not an especially long tenure in the classroom. Nevertheless, it represents more time spent working with kids than Rhee and Brill and all nine U. S. Secretaries of Education combined.

That fact alone ought to tell us something.

***

Naturally, training in history informs my thinking. More than two thousand years ago, when ancient Greeks named their Seven Wise Men, they placed Thales, scientist and philosopher, at the top of their list. Thales was once asked, "What is hard?"

"To know thyself," he replied.

"What is easy?"

"To give advice."

America's teachers know what Thales meant. Since passage of No Child Left Behind (NCLB) in 2002, the focus of school reform has been almost entirely on those at the front of the classroom. *Will* we ever learn, the Harvard professor wonders? I'm not sure. But I suspect you might have asked any of four million U. S. educators and they could have told you the utopian law was flawed from the start.

But the promises of politicians and pronouncements of policy makers were unequivocal. By 2014 every child was going to be proficient in reading and math. Not 88%. Not 96%. Every single one.

In the thirteen years since NCLB was enacted into law, countless editorials and TV reports have bolstered one theme. Google: "education crisis in America" and 300,000,000 results pile up. Don't have time to do all that reading? Here's the capsule version: America's schools are failing. Teachers are at fault.

Ms. Rhee became a brand name in school reform, turning up on television during one stretch as frequently as *Law and Order* reruns. In 2008 she graced the cover of *Time*, broom in hand, promising to clean out all the lousy teachers in Washington, D. C. and fix the biggest problem in education. Sweep! Just like that! Even Oprah gave Rhee, who taught for only three years, some televised love.

Meanwhile, "Fox News and Friends" did an interview with John Legend, the singer, and asked him to comment on school-related issues. The segment, titled "America's Education Crisis," was accompanied by tags like: "The Trouble with Schools," "A Broken System" and "Teachers Behaving Badly," lest viewers miss the point.

On CNN Campbell Brown hosted a series called "America's Schools in Crisis," leading off with talk about "broken" and "failing" schools. When Geoffrey Canada, who runs a charter school in Harlem, insisted that "the people who produce the children are the teachers," Brown let that stand without batting either of her lovely green eyes. I remember scratching my head, trying to figure out how my teachers produced me or how they produced my four kids.

Well, good job, teachers! All my children turned out fine.

And so it came to pass.

The "heroes" of school reform sounded the charge, stood back, and let educators storm enemy lines. Tens of billions of dollars were spent to implement NCLB. Hundreds of millions of hours were devoted by teachers to preparing for, and by students to taking, standardized tests.

Standards didn't rise.

They fell.

President Obama rode into office in 2009, promising to fix flaws in how NCLB was implemented. A "race to the bottom," he said, had been touched off when states lowered standards to avoid punishment under complex provisions of the law.

Mr. Obama would task Arne Duncan, ninth Secretary of Education, with leading a "Race to the Top." Fresh billions would be offered to states if they created more charter schools and linked teacher pay to scores on standardized tests.

"It's all about the talent," Duncan assured any who would listen. It's all about teachers.

In 2010 Davis Guggenheim set out to discover what was wrong with U. S. public education. (His view may have been impaired because he sent his children to elite private institutions.) In a critically-acclaimed documentary, *Waiting for Superman,* Guggenheim put a finger on what he saw as the issue. Rhee featured prominently, sneering at the efforts of D. C. teachers. While viewers watched in disbelief the film seemed to strip away the last fig leaf of doubt, "revealing" teachers in all their sloth and shame. The message of the movie, focusing narrowly on five children trying to escape "awful" public schools and get into charters, boiled down to this: If families could pick their schools problems in education would fade away.

I remember watching with disgust as Guggenheim painted a simplistic picture.

Yet, Brent Staples, critiquing the film for *The New York Times,* could come away from a viewing stunned and impressed. Readers who planned to see the movie, he warned, should take along handkerchiefs. Staples left no doubt who filled the villain's role: "Public schools generally do a horrendous job of screening and evaluating teachers, which means that they typically end up hiring and granting tenure to any warm body that comes along."

(Hmm…maybe I should title my book: *98.6°.* Or: *I Was a Teacher! I Had a Pulse!*)

If assessments in the *Times* were harsh, educators had to take two steps back to avoid fire and brimstone from the right. Ann Coulter, in *Godless,* slammed teachers' unions, labeled public schools "the Left's madrassas," and compared the U. S. education system to Soviet era factories, staying open even though products were hopelessly defective.

At best public schools were:

…nothing but expensive babysitting arrangements, helpfully keeping hoodlums off the streets during daylight hours. At worst, they are criminal training labs, where teachers sexually abuse the children between drinking binges and acts of grand larceny.

Neil Boortz, in *Somebody's Gotta Say It*, argued that the danger went deeper. Teachers weren't just incompetent. They were a threat to the Republic.

"Our government schools are killing the spirit of our children and, in the process, our country," he groaned. "Our wonderful government educational system produces graduating classes of young Neanderthals with no sense of individuality, no sense of self-worth, and no understanding of what it means to live in a truly free society."

Somebody had to say it—even if what Boortz had to say was incredibly stupid. So he spewed. "Teachers' unions pose a graver long-term threat to freedom, prosperity and the future of this country than do Islamic terrorists."

If he was right it would indicate a need to scan teachers' baggage more carefully at airports.

***

What surprised me, what surprises almost every teacher I meet, was that no one challenged accepted wisdom. No one stopped to wonder. If we had a crisis, how did teachers cause it all by themselves? Scary lists, served up by TV news anchors and journalists interested in eye-catching story lines "proved" how far a nation had fallen.

In 2003 fifteen-year-olds around the world took the Program for International Student Assessment test (PISA) in reading. Scores for U. S. students appeared dismal. The rankings:

1. Finland
2. South Korea
3. Canada
4. Australia
5. Lichtenstein
6. New Zealand
7. Ireland
8. Sweden
9. Netherlands
10. Belgium
11. Norway

12. Switzerland
13. Japan
14. Poland
15. France

We limped in sixteenth out of 38 countries.

In 2006 a PISA test of math skills, again administered to fifteen-year-olds, produced, on surface, even bleaker results:

1. Taiwan
2. Finland
3. South Korea
4. Netherlands
5. Switzerland
6. Canada
7. Japan
8. New Zealand
9. Belgium
10. Australia

…and finally, way down there, two points below Azerbaijan:

33. United States

A third international comparison in 2009, this time covering three subject areas, and surveying 65 nations, caused renewed bouts of red, white and blue weeping. The United States was tied with Iceland and Poland for 12th in reading, finished 20th in science, and tied with Ireland and Portugal for 28th in math.

A fourth test in 2012…oh, hell…what was the use. The numbers looked totally depressing.

Panicked reaction obscured a number of salient points. One might start by asking: "Why is anyone concerned if U. S. students get beat in math by kids from Luxembourg and Lichtenstein?" New York City Public Schools have more *students* than those nations have population, combined.

In the same way, if a Harvard professor wanted to compare results in Finland (5.4 million people), a nation which always finishes near the top, with results on this side of the Atlantic, he might more accurately have compared with Minnesota (5.4 million), where high school graduation rates, for instance, are well above average for the U. S., as a whole.

And what factors, other than the relative intelligence of teachers, might explain differing PISA results? Finland has as many educators as New York City, but they work with half the students (600,000 vs. 1.1 million). Finnish kids do score higher in science. In Finland science classes are capped at sixteen students, allowing for more frequent experimentation.

Here's another idea from Finland. If we want to match their success, we could do away with interscholastic sports. Finnish schools have no sports teams at all.

Sure. We're ready for that.

What else is different? In Finland all schools are funded equally by the national government. So you don't have rich districts and poor districts as we have across the United States.

Finally, only 1 in 25 children grows up in poverty in Finland. *Here the figure is 1 in 5.*

***

If it seemed to a casual observer that the corpse of U. S. education had been found, and a teacher wielded the smoking gun, it might have calmed rattled nerves if critics had taken a breath and stopped trying to scare everyone. Complaining about American education is a time-honored tradition. Will Rogers, the humorist, put it in perspective long ago: "The schools ain't what they used to be and never was," he assured a Depression Era radio audience.

In 1940, to cite a second example, the U. S. high school graduation rate was only 50%. In other words, the "Greatest Generation" was tragically unschooled by modern standards. Yet we crushed Hitler and smashed the Japanese and dominated economically for the next twenty-five years.

In 1953 *Life* magazine ran a series of articles on U. S. public high schools. Secondary enrollment—not graduation rate—was 76.5%. Among other observations offered was this: "Of this year's graduating class 40% of the boys and 20% of the girls will go on to college."

Part of the problem for young women boiled down to that "modern" bugaboo: teen pregnancy. There was *more* teen pregnancy sixty years ago than there is now. It just happened within the confines of marriage. So schools adjusted even then to reflect a changing society. They always do.

"Within a year after they graduate," *Life* explained, "25% of the girls will marry and set up housekeeping. For them particularly there is purpose in home economics instruction that years back, before girls were so numerous in the schools, they got at home—courses in cooking, dressmaking and child care."

Ah, the "good old days," when girls went to school to learn how to bake cookies and darn socks!

Or: the even better "good old days," when most African Americans couldn't get in the front door of schools—unless accompanied by a few hundred U. S. soldiers.

Even then critics cited chilling evidence to show we faced an education crisis. The book *Why Johnny Can't Read* shocked the nation in 1955. The author was a proponent of phonics. Phonics became a fad, touted as the path to reading redemption. Yet, *USA Today* could publish a story in 2009 citing continued problems, noting "1 in 7 U. S. adults can't read this article." The headline:

WHY JOHNNY STILL CAN'T READ

Sadly, phonics had not proved to be the cure-all an earlier generation of experts predicted.

In 1957, when the Soviet Union launched Sputnik, pundits were apoplectic. According to experts, the "commies" were going to bury us all in red underwear. The *schools* were to blame. Russian third graders knew way more science than U. S. third graders. The Soviet system was producing two or three times as many scientists. One authority claimed the average boy or girl coming out of a Russian high school had "a better scientific education—particularly in math—than most American college graduates."

The Russians were going to dominate in space. Then they were going to dominate on earth. Yet they didn't.

The clouds over America's schools only darkened during the 60s and 70s. Hippies crowded the halls. No respect for authority! Drugs! Too much sex! Rock and Roll!

Did we mention: too much sex!!

In the 80s, with foreign competition slicing deep into the nation's industrial base, critics looked under the bed and discovered the Bad Teacher Boogie Man waiting to grab a kindergartner by the leg. This time, Japanese schools were racking up amazing results. Our educational system was second-rate.

In 1983 the report, *A Nation at Risk: The Imperative for Educational Reform*, commissioned by President Ronald Reagan, sounded a claxon of alarm. One memorable line evoked Armageddon: "If an unfriendly foreign power had attempted to impose on America the mediocre educational performance that exists today, we might well have viewed it as an act of war."

Average scores on the Scholastic Aptitude Test (SAT) had fallen steadily from 1963 to 1980. Reading scores plunged fifty points. Math scores slipped thirty-six. "For the first time in the history of our country," authors of the report concluded, "the educational skills of one generation will not surpass, will not equal, will not even approach, those of their parents."

Much of the drop was a result of demographics, but critics didn't see it or it didn't suit their agendas to admit it if they did. More minority and female students were taking the SAT. Their scores were traditionally lower. Averages declined as the testing pool deepened. Yet the door to college was swinging wide, which should have been recognized as the positive trend it was.

Then it happened again. Good schools and all, Japan fell on hard times in the 90s. The Japanese economy tumbled into recession and remains stagnant to this day.

By contrast—good job U. S. educators!—our economy boomed in the 90s, kept booming until 2008, then stumbled. For once no one blamed teachers. No one said we crashed the housing market.

***

"Will we ever learn?" Wasn't that the question the Harvard professor chose to ponder?

Perhaps we might speed the process if we keep the wisdom of Thales in view. It's easy to tell teachers what *they* should do. Unfortunately, following the "education experts" to victory is never as easy as they make it sound.

Michael Herr, the famed war correspondent, noted the same problem at the height of the Vietnam War. When Herr first began reporting from oversees he relied on rear echelon types for info. It wasn't long till he realized these men were prone to bold pronouncements, like, "Would you rather fight the communists here or in Pasadena?"

They weren't fighting anyone and Herr was tempted to point that out. But the clean-uniform types, or "Dial Soapers," as he called them, were sensitive about what they were doing, or not doing, which was dodging actual bullets.

Like leading school reformers today, such men assured Herr we could win the war if only the top brass would listen to them. One day a colonel buttonholed the reporter and insisted we could bring the fighting to an end "by dropping piranhas into the [rice] paddies of the North."[1]

Herr was too stunned to respond.

The colonel, he explained, "was talking fish but his dreamy eyes were full of mega-death."

Quickly, then, he came to see that if he was going to understand the war he would have to steer clear of men in clean uniforms:

> …you had to leave the Dial Soapers in Saigon and a hundred headquarters who spoke goodworks and killed nobody themselves, and go out to the grungy men in the jungle who talked bloody murder and killed people all the time…In Saigon it never mattered what they told you, even less when they actually

---

[1] Corporations are also pushing hard for "school reform" because they sniff profits in the form of children. The for-profit charter school chain, K-12, Inc., to cite one example, paid five top executives $35.4 million in salaries and bonuses in 2013 and 2014. To put that in perspective, you might have hired 354 teachers, for two years, at $50,000 each, to work *directly with students*.

seemed to believe it. Maps, charts, figures, projections, fly fantasies, names of places, of operations, of commanders, of weapons; memories, guesses, second guesses, experiences (new, old, real, imagined, stolen); histories, attitudes—you could let it go, let it all go.

Herr realized he would have to talk to the foot soldiers, the "grunts," to understand.

That's where I come in. I served in the Marine Corps during some of the bloodiest days of that conflict. That sounds impressive if you stop there. But I did my tour of duty behind a desk, in a supply unit, in Camp Pendleton, California. I was more likely to get sunburned at the beach on weekends than be hit by flying bullets or trigger any booby traps.

I don't know diddly about combat.

So I don't pretend I do.

Teaching is *all* I know. I came to the profession filled with idealism in October 1975 and left, idealism frayed but intact, in May 2008. What I learned, I learned by teaching. I learned ordinary kids—all of them—are filled with potential. I learned the primary battle in school is determining how best to bring that potential out. I learned I could have a positive impact every day, despite my imperfections and a healthy share of blunders and mistakes.

I also learned that defeat was part of the process, that neither I nor the best of my peers could save every teen.

(The "Dial Soapers" of school reform ignore this hard truth.)

I learned, finally, that you could always *improve* on what was happening in your classroom and in your school. That you could do in a myriad of ways and that forms the core message of my book. There are obvious clues if we want to follow this path. Still, it's a hard path, long and steep.

Fortunately, if our goal is to improve education, then we will find two legs suffice.

Author's Note

In cases where stories might embarrass former students and in most situations where I question actions of colleagues, I disguise identities in various ways. Some stories have been shifted from one year to another to help insure anonymity.

Names, family and professional details have been altered in the same cause.

There are times I would have liked to honor students by naming them but reveal details they might not want brought to light. I disguise identities then, too.

If I say colleagues were excellent or good, that was the consensus, as far as I knew. Students, parents and staff shared opinions and I was always interested in why some educators were more effective than others. Hundreds of former students came back from our high school to see me. I always asked which teachers they felt were good. Two names, of many, that came up regularly were Marge Henderson, a choir director I knew, and Bob Wagner, a physics instructor I never met. I feel safe, then, in saying they were very good at what they did.

Kids in my class also told me about teachers who taught them most in the lower grades. Virgil Clausen, Kathy Davis and Steve Federman, among others, were frequently mentioned.

Or students came to my room second or seventh bell, excited by what they had just done in Herb Partin's English class or in art with Barb Rockwood.

I wish I could mention dozens of other educators and three or four thousand more kids. I should note that I did write about others, but had to drop sections of chapters and entire chapters from this book. Mike Rich, a coach who taught teens to win with character in five or six sports, got cut, as did all kinds of students.

So, let me say: I'm sorry, Dwane. But you and Kelly and I can keep arguing politics on Facebook.

Sorry, Dan, John, Jerry and all you others who showed up to play basketball at school every Sunday afternoon over the course of two decades.

Sorry, Derrick, because I never could figure out how to describe the incredible job you did switching between roles, as a soldier in George Washington's army, and as the "lovely" Martha W., in a skit about the American Revolution.

Sorry Kyle, even though you convinced your entire class to trick me on homework.

Sorry, Mo and all your friends who gave me potato chips as a peace offering.

Sorry, Zac, although I'm glad I was able to help you with all the bullying.

Sorry, Sydney, Erica and Hannah, Dawn, Paul, Suzi and Heather. Sorry, Rip Van Kayla.

Sorry to all I failed to mention.

Finally, I should note: I made up no dialogue for this book. If I quote anyone that is what was said. (For narrative effect, I did change what was written in two cases, by students, to read as if statements were dialogue. But the context was in no way changed.)

In dozens of cases, however, I use tags like, "Lynzi replied," or "Nate agreed," when I can't remember which student said what was said. I inserted tags because I wanted to mention as many kids as possible. I wanted to show I remembered their contributions in class.

My intent throughout is to focus on what worked—and why it worked—in what I believe was a typical classroom. For that reason, I have devoted minimal space to various and sundry mistakes I made. I didn't want this book to be longer.

I didn't want it to look like War and Peace.

2.

The Quintessential Fact

*"...there are three powers simultaneously in action
—the will, the muscles, and the intellect."*
Oliver Wendell Holmes

I'm finishing up my bicycle ride for the day, but I've misjudged time and distance and I'm stuck pedaling in the dark. Trees arch close overhead. Here and there a street light glows in the branches. Periodically the lights of an oncoming car wipe out my night vision. My bicycle headlight has stopped working.

This is how riders get killed.

I'm staying close to the side of the road in case cars coming up behind fail to see me. Then—whack!—I run right into a low-hanging branch from some damn bush or damn tree. For a moment I think I'm going to get swept off my seat like a losing knight in a tilting match in an old Robin Hood movie. I recover my balance and consider the ironic possibilities of being wiped out during the last mile of a solo bicycle ride across the USA.

On this particular evening I'm weaving my way through Golden Gate Park in San Francisco. My goal is to get down to the beach and dip my front tire in the Pacific Ocean. After 58 days, I will have ridden 4,615 miles.

***

The first question, of course, is how did I get here? Ask my wife and she'll tell you I'm crazy.

I disagree. I think pedaling across the country is easy.

The second question is: "What does riding a bicycle across America have to do with teaching?"

Let's begin with first questions first. I got here by pedaling up Cadillac Mountain in Maine on June 17, 2011. I got here by adopting an idea I heard about in ninth grade when my classmates and I studied ancient Greek history. (Years later I would present the same idea, that true living means a "sound mind in a sound body," to students.) I got here by sloshing through torrential rains in New York State, by following U. S. 42 across Ohio to Cincinnati, where I live.

I got here because when I was nineteen I joined the Marines. I got here despite being handcuffed in Indiana. I pedaled across Illinois, crashed in Iowa, and zoomed across South Dakota. I rode into Yellowstone National Park—and out—and in again—and out again—during the course of a week. I crashed again. (Maybe my wife is right.) I kept cranking, south to Salt Lake City, across the Sevier Desert, across Nevada, along the "The Loneliest Highway in America." Finally, I churned up and over Tioga Pass into Yosemite National Park. A few days later I completed my journey in San Francisco.

That's how I got "here" to this park in the dark. I kept pedaling. That's also how I got where I wanted as a teacher. In the long run, understanding education is as plain and simple as that.

How do you ride a bicycle across America? How do you survive life in the classroom? You keep cranking.

***

To the basics then: September 7, I finish my ride across the USA, 58 days (with a two-week break in Cincinnati), almost eighty miles per day. I am 62 years old at the time.

Some days back, during a stop for lunch, in Cold Springs, Nevada, I talked with a waitress about my journey. She was probably the only attractive female within a hundred miles. I don't mean to imply that Nevada women are hideous but if you pick up a map you'll see Cold Springs shown as a white dot or "town." It's really nothing more than a bar/motel, with fifty miles of barren landscape to the east and fifty miles of sagebrush to the west. At that point, figuring on a napkin, I told her I'd burned 250,000 calories during my trip.

God knows how many I've consumed since.

This marks the second time I've pedaled across the country. I did it first in 2007, when students pitched in and helped raise money for the Juvenile Diabetes Research Foundation (JDRF). Now, whenever I tell people what I've done, I get odd looks. They say I remind them of Forrest Gump.

I'm not sure that's a compliment.

I've said this to all kinds of people too: I don't think what I do is difficult. I've got wheels and 27 gears.

And, no, I don't get lonely biking solo. People see me coming, loaded with gear, and they're happy to talk. I don't get scared either. Despite what you might think if you watch the nightly news, America is not overrun with psychopaths. The occasional car comes too close but the vast majority of drivers are considerate. Only once during my second trip did occupants of a vehicle shout profane encouragement as they passed. I suggested loudly that they go home and engage in intercourse with certain family members.

If Man, the most dangerous beast, didn't get me, neither did the woodland creatures. I did a lot of "stealth camping" during the ride. So they had their chances. Stealth camping means pulling off the road when no one is looking and setting up a tent along the edge of a cornfield or in sagebrush or deep woods. Then you sleep under the stars at God's premium price.

The ride from Rapid City, South Dakota, up into the Black Hills involves plentiful sweating and low gears. It was late evening by the time I approached Mt. Rushmore. So, rather than settle for a hasty tour before dark, I pulled off the main road and put up my tent in the forest. Two deer watched me inflate my sleeping pad at bedtime. Four watched me brush my teeth in the morning, before I headed off to pay respects to Abe and Teddy and George.

Stealth camping has its drawbacks, of course. In Maine, where my trip began, I put up my tent behind a pile of logs in one of those breaks utility companies create when they build towers. I passed a restful night but awoke to something unpleasant. Ticks. Two were crawling up my leg. A third was smashed to my stomach. Luckily, they weren't carrying Lyme disease.

This also brings to mind the growing moose threat to Americans—which I admit has nothing to do with my topic, teaching and schools. Bear with me, if you will, as I set the scene. I began my ride at Acadia National Park, in Maine. Unaware of impending danger, I pedaled 68 miles the first day, under beautiful skies, and felt great. The next day, June 18, with light rain falling, I fiddled over breakfast in a Belfast, Maine restaurant, where pancakes were the size of garbage can lids. I was reading the Bangor *Daily News* when I noticed an article about Trooper Thomas of the Maine Highway Patrol.

(All photos from author's collection.)

Thomas had been involved in a collision, on duty, with a Maine moose, and it was clear the moose (singular and plural) were out to get him. Thomas had been targeted for a hit before. In 2007 he was forced to take evasive action to miss three moose crossing the highway. He missed two, plowed into the third, and caused $10,000 worth of damage to his cruiser. Thomas barely survived that antlered assassination attempt.

I should add that New Hampshire addresses this issue with the seriousness it deserves. A large sign as you pedal across the border warns: "BRAKE FOR MOOSE. It could save your life."

I keep my eyes peeled.

***

If you're thinking about riding a bicycle across the United States—and who isn't—I assure you most roads in Maine are fine. Traffic is light, which has something to do with the fact the state is slightly smaller than Ohio, but with 1/8th the population.

Traffic is even lighter when you hit South Dakota—with nine people per square mile—and Wyoming—with five.

The roads in New Hampshire are mostly good, the scenery fantastic. Near Conway, you start up Kancamangus Pass and for ten miles you're pedaling along the Swift River, past some of the prettiest swimming holes in America. You have to chug uphill for another ten miles to crest at 2,855 feet, but then you enjoy a free-wheeling ride down the other side of the mountain.

At North Woodstock, you take Lost River Road, which on the map I'm using looks like a shortcut. This is only a mistake if you're not trying to kill yourself. If you talk to most riders who cross the U. S. they agree old roads in the eastern mountains are by far the worst. Lost River Road is typical. A nondescript state highway, it must have been laid out in colonial times to trace a path blazed by Billy goats. There are almost no cars for fifteen miles, though, because locals aren't stupid enough to use the road if they can avoid it.

Heading for Middlebury, Vermont, a beautiful college town, I ride up and over Middlebury Gap, at 2,144 feet. In places the grade is as much as 18%. If you're not a rider, trust me. That's a killer climb. It's not too terrible going up a pass at four mph. When you drop as low as 2.2, which is "stand-on-the-pedal" speed, it gets hard to be philosophical.

Then you mumble a curse.

I had been to Middlebury before and remembered riding over a bridge with a beautiful green river forty feet below. There was a large swimming hole under the span and I stopped to watch youngsters jump off the bridge into emerald waters. Before starting this ride, it was one of my goals to work up the courage and jump off that bridge on my way through. When I passed this time the issue was no longer water below but water from above. It started pouring right after I topped Middlebury Gap.

I like bicycling and raising money for JDRF, which is a large part of why I ride. But my bike is *not* amphibious.

Here's what I learn while getting soaked in Vermont. If you wear glasses and rely on a mirror attached to those glasses to provide rear visibility, this is what you cannot see once glasses and mirror fog:

1. Road signs
2. Potholes
3. Pedestrians
4. Large farm animals
5. Blimps
6. Ocean liners
7. Basically…anything.

Still, I meet nice people all along the way—the Middlebury couple that sees me come slopping into the public library and offers dinner and a dry place to stay—bar patrons in Diamond Point, New York, who get me a free room at the Super 8 motel, when they hear I'm riding for a cause.

But I get rained on all the way across New York. In a blog post on June 28, I report:

Okay, this is getting ridiculous. I'll be riding out of New York State this afternoon and I've hardly seen the sun peek out from behind the clouds. I've been on the road for eleven days and rained on seven. If you want to know what the weather has been like go put on a bicycle helmet, t-shirt, gym shorts and biking shoes. Put on a pair of glasses, too, even if you don't normally wear them.

Now go stand in the shower and turn it on full force. Be sure your glasses steam up so you can't see. That's what the riding has been like at times in this state.

It's causing a lot of soggy underwear.

Eventually, I zoom across the Pennsylvania panhandle and when I hit the sign that says, "Welcome to Ohio," the wide shoulders I've been enjoying vanish like Jimmy Hoffa. No joke. Ohio roads are the worst. I make it back home in one piece, go to a wedding my wife wants to attend, and two weeks later I'm off again.

The key, of course, is to keep pedaling. True on a bicycle. True in any classroom in the land.

True for everyone on a seat.

***

If the New Hampshire moose don't get me the Indiana coppers do. The first day out of Cincinnati, on the second leg of my ride, I have to contend with 100° temperatures and high humidity, tough cycling even for someone one-third my age. After pedaling 70 miles, I get caught in an early evening thunderstorm. Normally, I hate getting drenched but since I'm broiling, I'm glad to cool down.

Still, this was a deluge.

I pulled behind one of those electric transformer stations you see along highways and threw up my tent in tall weeds. I was thinking I'd do a little stealth camping. The rain poured through the opening in the top before I could attach the rain flap and poured through the door as I tossed in my gear. I scrambled inside, removed my shirt, and started mopping up water. Fifteen minutes and it was over.

Emerging like some bedraggled Punxsutawney Phil, I called my wife to let her know where I planned to spend the evening. Before I could tell her she was the hottest-looking lady in North America, a cop car, lights flashing, siren wailing, came flying up the road and skidded to a stop.

"Well, it looks like I'm going to get kicked out of my camping spot," I said. "I'll call you back later."

At almost the same instant, a Wayne County deputy jumped out of the cruiser, gun drawn, and shouted, "Hands up!"

"Seriously?" I responded.

"Hands up!" the officer repeated, and waved his pistol in menacing fashion, to clarify the point.

"Really?"

"GET THEM UP WHERE I CAN SEE THEM," he yelled, pointing his pistol, this time more carefully.

Cell phone in hand, I reached for the sky.

The deputy called me out from behind the fence, told me to turn around so he could see if I had a gun in my waistband, and then cuffed me. It seemed like an over-reaction to trespassing.

I'm in shorts and bicycling shoes, with no shirt, mind you, and the officer can't see my bike in the weeds. So I tell him I'm riding across America to raise money for the Juvenile Diabetes Research Foundation. "My daughter Emily has type-1 diabetes," I add. They won't arrest a do-gooder, will they?

I think not.

By now two more cruisers have arrived and four officers have me surrounded. The first deputy explains there has been an armed robbery, ten minutes before, in nearby Richmond. I want to point out that the scene of the crime is six miles south and I'm not riding a rocket-propelled bike.

I don't quibble, though, because police officers aren't always known for their sharp senses of humor. I start laughing, but quickly add: "I'm not laughing at you. You're just doing your job. But this will make a good story for my blog."

The first officer is pretty sure by now I'm not the guy, but says he has to keep me cuffed while he calls in a description. He checks my ID and I hear the dispatcher describe the suspect: "White male....

...in his 20s."

Oh, so close!

They let me go, but one of the deputies tells me I can't camp where I am and need to move. I want to ask: "Can you put the cuffs back on and take my picture." But they might not see the humor. So I take down my tent and pedal away. Five miles down the road, with dusk settling over the land, I see a likely spot along the edge of a cornfield and go to ground again. I'm Clyde Barrow—without Bonnie—on a bike.

The next day is boiling hot, over 100° again, and by late afternoon I'm wilting once more. I'm way out in farm country but hope to find a motel for the night. I log on to Google Maps and discover I'm 8.2 miles from the "Dog Patch Hotel." I call to see if they have rooms. The owner is a gravel-voiced woman named Marcia Clark and says she usually closes at six p.m., which seems odd, but my phone is dying, so our conversation is abbreviated. She says she'll wait a little longer and I pedal furiously to get there in time.

To my surprise, when I arrive, I find Ms. Clark runs a doggy day care. We broker a deal and I spend a night on the floor of her air-conditioned office. Some hotels you worry about bedbugs. Some you worry about fleas.

I get pretty much boiled every day for the next two weeks. I get boiled across Indiana, into Illinois. Or, as I describe it in my blog:

> Here's the short version of the first four days out of Cincinnati (20th to 23rd): hot, cornfields, hot, sweat, cornfields, holy s#@%, it's hot.

I hit Iowa. That means more cornfields. I have the pleasure, near Dubuque, of riding for a day with Joe Ossman, who made his own cross-country trip in 2010 at age 64. (Rich Fowler, his companion, was 67.) He's kind enough to take the lead, cutting wind resistance, which makes my pedaling easier. I let my attention wander, focus on an interesting mailbox, catch a pothole and crash to the pavement, landing square on my camera. What do I learn? I learn you cannot break your fall by landing on your camera. But you can break your camera.

By now the moose population has thinned; but I'm still meeting nice people. There's the lawyer in the pastry shop who hears what I'm doing and writes out a check to JDRF for $100. There's Kathy Frizoel, a type-1 diabetic for half a century, now confined to a wheel chair, and husband Mike, who has a tiger tattoo on his back, in honor of her indomitable spirit. Kathy doesn't pedal but rolls.

On August 1, I cross the Big Sioux River into South Dakota. The heat index for the day is 118. No psychopaths yet; but my brains are cooked.

I zoom along, over the Great Plains, until one day I pick up a ferocious headwind, twenty miles per hour and constant. On days like this, if you're human, you think about quitting. I pass an old 1970s Oldsmobile for sale. It's primer gray but looks like it might run. Or that used tractor for sale? Either might get me back to Ohio. I could commandeer a harvester. I could knock that old lady off her riding mower.

Luckily, the mood passes before the psychopath you hear about on the news turns out to be me.

I do want to quit though. Only you can't quit. Not pedaling. Not teaching. Not when learning, either.

You'll see.

***

I spend several days crossing South Dakota, with grasshoppers ricocheting off my helmet. That's better than Iowa where one evening two mosquitoes flew up my nose. I meet more nice people—a story in itself. I see the Badlands from the saddle of a bike and the landscape is inspiring. On to the Black Hills, passing through during the week of the Sturgis Motorcycle Rally, which brings 400,000 riders to the area. Twenty-five years ago the scene was "like Halloween on steroids," as one veteran of several rallies informs me. It's still not tame, but today the average person in attendance is fifty years old. At Mount Rushmore I notice a gray-haired Hells Angel wearing his colors, an oxygen tube stuck up his nose, a tank by his side.

Generally, the riders prove conservative but friendly. I see one RV with this slogan painted on the rear:

OBAMA KISS MY WHITE AMERICAN ASS.
YOU STUPID F*CK.

I suppose the painter was trying to be discreet, putting a star where the vowel was supposed to be.

You could get a chapter out of Wyoming alone. Yellowstone—on a bicycle—amazing! Then a trip north to Bozeman, Montana, to see the --- family (mom asked me to leave out the last name), and daughter Sidney, a seven-year-old type-1 diabetic I met during a Florida ride. Sidney's a darling and her brother, Sam (below), is a comic, with a pet pig he calls "Slugbutt."

Then I pedal south again, down the beautiful Gallatin River Valley. It's pure joy to be alive. My plan is to do 80 miles and get close to West Yellowstone and reenter the park the next day. A check of Google Maps shows a campground along the way, right about where I want to stop.

So I enjoy the sun and scenery and go flying along. At the 50-mile mark I pass the last town where I might take shelter. Bah! I'm riding 80! At 60, I see cabins for rent: "$50 for the night." Ha! I'm riding 80!

At the 75-mile mark I start looking for the campground. Nothing. At 80? Nope. I pass 82, 83, 84, 86, 88. Now it's getting on toward evening.

I pick up the pace and rip along, with darkness settling over the land. Soon I'm trying to keep my tire close to the white edge line.

Then I'm bent low trying to *see* the white line.[2]

When I crest a high hill, the lights of West Yellowstone shimmer faintly in the distance. By now, I'm stopping to dismount when cars pass, or switching sides to ride in the dark, with lights behind me. Finally, traffic coming out of West Yellowstone picks up and headlights keep blinding me. One more time, I aim for the side of the road to dismount, turn my wheel too sharply, and go crashing to the pavement, bloodying my elbow and whacking my helmet.

Finally, I spot a campground. When I start down the road, I see a warning sign: "Keep all food, drink and toiletries out of sight and locked in your vehicle. You are in grizzly bear country."

I am *definitely* not stealth camping tonight.

I walk the last two miles into town and find almost every motel sign flashing, NO VACANCY. I settle for a room at the Brandin' Iron Inn, where another sign warns: "Room price established at check-in time." I figure the clerk sees my bloody elbow and jacks up the price $25. Then he figures it's dark and sees I'm on a bicycle and jacks it another $50. I get branded, myself, and pay $154 for the night.

Back I go through Yellowstone the next day; more nice people; the Grand Tetons by bike; incredible. South to Salt Lake City, where a couple of nice Mormons try to convert me. Then it's out across the Sevier Desert, a ninety-two-mile moonscape, with no services. I go up and down a dozen Nevada passes and follow what's called "The Loneliest Highway in America" across the state.

Then I decide to cut south and follow what I'll call the "Bleakest Highway in America," toward Yosemite National Park. For the next 36 miles I don't see a single house or tree. I develop a tire hernia in Gabbs, Nevada (population 349) and have to do some serious tap dancing before I can hitch a ride to Reno.

Eventually, I get a new tire and it's up and over Tioga Pass, the highest point of the trip at 9,943 feet, and a week spent amid the marvels of Yosemite. I ride out of the valley, meet my older brother at the park

---

[2] My headlight died long before I reached San Francisco.

boundary, and he pedals with me for two days. I finish my trip at San Francisco where my younger brother resides.

I fly home on the tenth anniversary of 9/11, and when I get home, I sit down on a seat of a different sort and start on this book. Even writing is like bicycling (or teaching). It's nice to be talented; but the trick is to keep pedaling.

***

When this tale finally sees print I know people will ask: "What's the solution? How do we fix America's schools?"

I counter with this. What's the solution if we want one hundred people to pedal across the United States? Or one hundred teens to succeed in the classroom? What is the key?

What troubles me, when I read stories about U. S. education and what's wrong, is this. We act, so to speak, as if all we need to do to get *everyone across the country is* to build better bikes. No, someone will insist: What we need most are better bicycle mechanics. No, someone else will interject. We must have improved roads and bridges. Not true, another argues. What we need are GPS maps. Before long, ideas are flying in all directions like brickbats during a prison riot. Someone says we can make it happen if we construct rest stops every twenty-five miles. Another disagrees. We must have a tire that doesn't go flat.

"I have it!" another shouts. "What this country needs is an improved kind of energy bar."

In this analogy, I think someone argues next that supplying riders with Gatorade is the solution. Then the individual in favor of Gatorade hits the person in favor of energy bars over the head with—product placement alert—a bottle of Glacier Blue.

My favorite flavor when cycling.

Soon, an education expert happens along, raises a hand like a prophet, and stills the maddening crowd. "I have a dream," he begins. Then he realizes someone has already used that line in a great speech.

"I have a bold plan," he tries again. "I have a plan to fix this bicycle riding business! We develop a common road map and all riders follow the same route across the land. We standardize everything. All riders wear matching shirts, shorts and shoes. All riders carry the same kind of gear—same tent, sleeping bag, and tools. And all riders shift the same way.

"Then everyone will bicycle across America. I promise *my* plan will work!"

As for me, I don't buy for one fragment of a second the idea that one solution fits all. Each person carries a solution within—that is the "solution," I think. The individual must pedal, on a bike, or in the classroom.

In the end, only those who are willing to sweat reach their goals.

3.

Fantasy of the Fixed School

"Wrong from the start, to chase what cannot be."
Sophocles

What lessons did I learn, simply by teaching? I learned I *loved* teaching. I loved catching young people on the verge of adulthood, helping them step into the future with success.

I also learned that the challenges teachers face are more formidable than anyone imagines.

***

Of 5,000 students who passed my way, I could count on two hands those I didn't like and have both thumbs left over.

I'm Facebook friends with a thousand former pupils. Every time I'm "friended" I consider it an honor. Sam would be one. He had a tough home life and struggled in my class decades ago. Then in 2011, leading up to my second bicycle ride across America, he helped raise money for JDRF by organizing a huge yard sale. Dave stopped by my house to drop off a copy of his first book. Brian travels the world, raising money for his charity, Journey4Youth, and playing a hard-to-categorize, but enjoyable style of music. When he invited me to hear him play one Saturday night he explained he was leaving for Kenya the following week.

The young people I taught have gone on to become truck drivers, carpenters, models, members of jazz quartets and NFL cheerleaders. Betsy is a fitness trainer, a hard worker when I had her in class, a hard worker a quarter century later. Todd graduated from Harvard Law. Kellie served as a U. S. Army nurse during the War in Iraq. Lori, Terrie and Vicki are just as creative in their Facebook posts as they were when I had them in class. Jesse is proudly raising his daughter.

In old notes I describe Kelsey as a red-haired "fountain of energy, great in debates, skits and plays." Today she manages an Outback Steakhouse, where her sister Holly is also employed. I could have had a classroom full of students like them, and Jay, their younger brother, and my job would have been easy every day.

Dozens of former students have entered the field of education. Occasionally, one will say I inspired them to go in that direction. I hope I didn't lead them astray.

I'm "friends" with Lynn, too. She doesn't hold a grudge even though I swatted her in seventh grade. I won't be advocating a return to corporal punishment in pages to come. Still, Lynn believes I helped turn her life around when she was young. Today she runs her own landscaping business.

Do I remember everyone I taught? No, I don't. Halfway through my career I realized I was forgetting names and faces and created a database to help. I still have only 85% of pupils listed—but would gladly tell you about great individuals and groups of siblings covering every letter of the alphabet ten times over. The A. sisters were outstanding as were the Y. brothers. So were the D. siblings and the E. twins and their talented brothers. Christine N. was cool, as was Ben O., as was John P., and a thousand others.

Most of what I know about teaching I learned by working with all types of kids. I found something to like about almost every one. In my database the phrase "didn't like" appears five times. Four reference students who didn't like me.

(Surely, there had to be others.)

The fifth refers to an unhappy parent. Mom sent me an angry email after I accused her daughter of lying. I responded electronically, asking if she preferred I call the girl a "prevaricator."

For some reason that didn't help.

By contrast, I use the adjective "funny" to describe Chase and 386 others. The word "nice" appears 572 times. "Good worker" is applied 147 times, "worked hard," 96, "hard worker," 80, "hard-working," 28. Abby, Allie, Annie, Jessica and Patrick, Reed and Susan are listed as "favorites," as are 240 others. The longest description is a dozen words. So when Ted gets "great student, great attitude," you know he was a pleasure to work with in class. Samantha, Dave and Jim are labeled "artistic." When I go to Dave's Facebook page I see he still is. The adjective "bright" appears repeatedly. Dan is "bright but lazy." Tracy is "very bright and personable." Stephen receives a mixed mark: "lazy but still smart; nearly failed; funny; good participation." I liked them all.

Yet, because I taught as long as I did, I wince when experts insist: "We must fix the schools." I know it would make no sense to say you planned to fix families by "fixing homes."

Probably 90% of all teens who came to my class arrived needing no fixing, or minor tinkering at most, because their parents raised them well. As for others, you had to believe you could do your part to help them salvage their futures.

There's nothing wrong with "kids today." Not as a group and not, in most cases, individually.[3]

Still, let's not be naïve about the challenges educators face. Some teens I taught went on to become drug dealers, rapists and murderers. That's a reality the non-teaching, advice-giving types blissfully ignore.

A certain fraction of students, greater in some schools, lesser in others, present in all, have severe problems that have nothing to do with what goes on in schools.

***

One afternoon, I was sitting at my desk in study hall, trying to catch up on the tall stacks of paperwork that define the existence of all good teachers.

The room was quiet, kids hard at work, or pretending to be. I glanced up when I heard a stirring in a back corner of the room. Three boys were trying to suppress their laughter.

---

[3] Sour individuals have been complaining about "kids today" for centuries. As early as 55 A. D., the Roman writer Petronius grumbled, "I'm sure the reason such young nitwits are produced in our schools is because they have no contact with anything of use in everyday life."

I pushed back my chair and they blanched when they saw me coming. One hid a paper under his books. I loomed over him and commanded: "Let me have it!"

"What?"

"Let me have it!" I repeated. He shifted nervously and Rick, one of his friends, blushed.

The boy pulled a drawing from its hiding place and handed it over. I unfolded it carefully and found myself gazing at a crude pencil drawing of a penis and two hairy balls.

After brief discussion, it turned out Rick was the artist and I escorted him to the hall. "Rick," I said, "I'm not going to tell you why this is wrong." I waved the paper for emphasis. "I'm going to let your dad explain.

"I'll keep this for now but give it back later. I want you to bring me a note from your father, saying he saw it."

I wasn't mad. That's one reason this incident surprises me to this day. I had a reputation for coming down hard on students who needed it. I didn't come down hard on Rick at all.

When study hall ended I headed for the office to make a photocopy of his art. Before he went home I handed him a sealed envelope and told him to bring a note the next day. That was the day before Christmas vacation. When Rick reappeared twenty-four hours later no note was in sight.

"Please, Mr. Viall," he begged, "I'll be grounded if I show my dad. If you let me turn it in after vacation, I promise, I will."

I didn't want him to be miserable. I only wanted his father to sit down and address the inappropriate nature of his drawing. "Okay," I agreed, "but you better have it when we get back."

The Christmas tree went up. The Christmas tree came down. Vacation ended and Rick returned.

No note.

"I lost the picture," he cried when I led him to the hall once more.

I still didn't come down hard. I said I had a copy, made a copy of the copy, and told him the day of reckoning was at hand. He had to have a note the next day or I would call his dad.

Like any job, there are good days and bad in teaching. The one that followed was one of the worst—and might have been my last.

Just before lunch an argument erupted in the hall outside my room. I stepped out to investigate and a girl I didn't know, who seemed to be at the center of the trouble, ended up calling me a bastard and a motherfucker. I hauled her down to the office and listened as she cursed the principal too.

"Go ahead and suspend me," she wailed. "I don't care, I just don't care. I can't take it anymore."

Being told to fuck off (and more) is not a rare experience for educators. Still, it's no fun.

Could the day get worse?

It could.

In study hall, which followed lunch, Rick still didn't have his note. What he did have, we found later, was a loaded pistol in the book bag under his seat. His plan to stay out of trouble—hopelessly misguided as it was—was to pull the gun and shoot me. There was at least one other target, a teammate on the wrestling squad who had taunted poor Rick about his weight.

Luckily, this was before a wave of school shootings made the news in the late 80s and early 90s, before the bloodbath at Columbine High and the slaughter at Sandy Hook. Rick lacked, I believe, what someone called the "newsreel in the head." We all play out scenes in imagination, based on what we see in life, in movies and on the news. Rick did not yet have so many violent newsreels running in his head.

At heart, I also feel he was a decent kid, confused, but not evil or mean. So he never pulled the gun.

That afternoon, as he was gathering gear for wrestling practice, he told a friend he had the pistol. The other boy took it, stuffed it in his locker and locked it up tight.

That night Rick's friend worried about the trouble he'd be in if the weapon was discovered. He spilled the story to the principal the next morning. The rest of that day was filled with the comings and goings of law enforcement officers. Parents arrived ashen-faced and left in tears. Administrators huddled and I was kept abreast of developments. I felt sorry for Rick's father, who had to sit in on a meeting with police, administrators and me, for his wife, and for Rick, most of all.

I had the boy for history too, had seen nothing in his behavior to indicate he was troubled. He had a quiet sense of humor and had caused no problems before. Now, I was a walk-on character in a tragedy, read my lines, and departed from the stage. The family would be dealing with ramifications for years to come.

Rick had a loaded weapon in our school for an entire day. But we were fortunate and he never opened fire. As you might expect, he was expelled for the remainder of the year.

I never saw him again.

So I put the incident behind me and went on with my career. A decade later I heard he was already dead. Suicide, someone said. But I'm not sure.

***

We had a second incident the following year when an eighth grader, who had broken up with his girlfriend the night before, pulled a pistol in math, put it to his head, and threatened to fire. Again we were lucky. A substitute teacher talked the young man into laying the weapon down. By chance the regular teacher was out sick. Normally, this might have been a recipe for disaster; but the sub had experience working in a group home for troubled teens.

Since then there have been dozens of bloody school shootings. Depending on how you score, there were twenty-three in the 80s. There were thirty-three in the 90s, thirty-nine in ten years following. Since January 1, 2010 there have been more than a hundred new shootings in and around schools.

One week in October 2013 illustrates how reductive the term "fixing the schools" really is. On Monday morning, October 21, Nevada teacher Michael Lansberry, a former Marine, was gunned down while doing playground duty.

Lansberry had survived a tour of duty in Afghanistan; but a 12-year-old boy with a pistol was as deadly as any Taliban. The "assailant" also wounded two classmates then killed himself.

The following afternoon, Colleen Ritzer, a pretty 24-year-old Massachusetts high school teacher, was stabbed to death in a women's bathroom at her school. Her alleged attacker was a 14-year-old in one of her math classes. The details were chilling, for the boy was said to have planned the attack with care. He brought gloves and several changes of clothing to school that morning. Then he trailed Ritzer into the bathroom after classes ended for the day. There he robbed and raped her, finally slitting her throat with a box cutter.

He left a note too. "I hate you all," it read.

Terrible as the week was it could have been worse. Wednesday, October 23, an 11-year-old boy at a Vancouver, Washington middle school was stopped before he could do harm. He explained to police that "a voice in his head" told him to kill a classmate who had made fun of one of his friends. The boy was carrying several knives, a handgun and 400 rounds of ammunition when intercepted.

So let me emphasize again: The idea that we can "fix the schools" is a fantasy, an illusion, a chimera. Teachers don't fix families and don't fix society, either.

If we hope to *improve* what happens in America's schools we must be realistic from the start.

***

In pages to come I will often say, for example, that I do not believe in standardized testing as a measure of what teachers do, assuredly not as a measure of what students learn.

I don't believe in education plans. I believe in educating people.

So we might more correctly ask: What sound do you get when you flush $1.7 billion down a giant toilet?

By 2012 that was how much states were spending on annual high-stakes testing.

By conservative estimate, then, $10 billion had been wasted over a decade on tests tied to No Child Left Behind. That law is now essentially dead, all tests developed in response are obsolete, and we have almost nothing to show for that pile of cash squandered.

If someone had handed me those billions and told me to spend them to benefit kids, I'd have used the $10 billion to hire 20,000 additional counselors, at $50,000 annually, for ten years. We could have put them to work helping youngsters like Rick and the boy in Vancouver and countless others during a decade now lost.

4.

Liberal Yin, Marine Corps Yang

"Sharp wits can lurk in unpolished skulls."
H. L. Mencken

What else did I learn by teaching? I learned all kinds of individuals come to the profession for all kinds of reasons. Nearly half abandon the field within five years, which should tell us something about the challenges inherent to the profession.

As for me, at no time during my youth did I imagine myself as a teacher.

Starting in seventh grade, I didn't even like being a student. What I wanted to be was a hero. I wanted to be John Wayne.

***

From what I could tell there was never a recipe to follow to create good teachers. A liking for kids and a capacity for hard work seemed the sole absolutes.

When I was twelve, myself, I took an interest in the Civil War and got hooked on history. From that point forward I devoured war books and ignored most of the reading assigned at school. Oddly enough, being both an avid reader and a reluctant student in my youth helped once I entered the profession.

My own path to the front of a classroom began at 3 a.m., on December 29, 1968. Despite the concerns of my father and the entreaties of my mother, I had dropped out of college at the start of sophomore year. I had no idea what I wanted to do with my life. So I joined the Marines.

Like all new recruits, I completed the journey to Parris Island on a bus packed with nervous young men. In the dark of night, a stern-faced guard waved us through the main gate and moments later we pulled up in front of the Recruit Processing Center. The brakes hissed and grabbed. Before the vehicle stopped rocking, drill instructors were already storming down the aisle.

"Off this bus you maggots! Move IT! MOVE IT! MOVE IT!!" they shouted.

When one stunned traveler failed to react an instructor hauled him to his feet by his shirt and propelled him toward the exit with a boot in the butt. The rest of us took this as our cue and piled from our seats.

With instructors snapping round us like Dobermans endowed with speech, we were driven to the barber shop and sheared like sheep. Then we headed for a locker room and stripped off civilian garb amid a storm of insults. We were issued olive drab jackets, olive drab shirts, olive drab pants, socks and web belts, and white boxer shorts. We dressed in a mad rush, were driven back outside, and ordered to stand at attention on yellow footprints painted on the street.

Staff Sergeant (S/Sgt.) Jones, a truly intimidating black Marine, took position to our front and identified himself as our head drill instructor for the next ten weeks. We were ordered to shoulder our bulging sea bags. Then he barked: "Right face. *Forwarrrrrrrrd*, march."

That's where my journey to the front of a classroom begins, with those yellow footprints in the street.

In 1968 it was possible to enlist for two years in the Marines. This had something to do with the fact that sensible fellows had no desire to get shipped off to Southeast Asia and blown to bits. For my part, I never bought into the gung ho Marine mentality entirely. I'd be lying, though, if I said I wasn't impressed or that my time in the Corps didn't shape me in critical ways.

At Parris Island our instructors began by crushing out our old identities. Then they set about building us back up in the image of Marines. With our shaved heads and olive drab color scheme, we were no longer civilians. We were no longer individuals. A recruit, or "boot," was a cog in a mighty machine. He could not refer to himself as "I." Not: "I need...." He could only say: "Sir, the recruit requests permission to go to the head, sir." Or: "Sir, the recruit does not know, sir."

We said that a lot.

S/Sgt. Jones also made this clear from the start: Excuses would not be tolerated. "Excuses are like assholes," he growled. "Everyone has one." Produce and keep your mouth shut. Or pay a price.

(That idea—that you should not settle for excuses—would be a building block of my career.)

In boot camp, only the unit—the platoon—mattered. Jones warned us a hundred times that if one man screwed up in combat the entire unit might suffer. So, in training, if one boot screwed up we all paid. Reveille sounded one morning. Eighty-nine men were standing at attention when Jones noticed a lone recruit still fumbling with the laces on his boots.

"Oh, look, ladies!" he sneered. "Private Thaxton must be tired! Private Thaxton needs his beauty sleep!"

Jones barked command and ninety men hit the deck. He began counting off pushups and kept going until weaker recruits started giving out. A boot down the line from me collapsed. I heard him gasp that he could not continue.

"Yes, you can," an assistant drill instructor said. With that he seized the boot by the belt and began bouncing him up and down like a yo-yo, counting "pushups" as he went.

I summoned some reserve of strength I never knew I possessed and kept going—up, down, up, down, up, down—till arms vibrated with fatigue.

Sweat coursed down my face. I could see it dripping from my nose to form a puddle on the deck.

Since the unit was what mattered and since marching fostered unit cohesion, at Parris Island we marched everywhere we went. We did a "left face" every morning and marched ourselves to the head. We marched to the mess hall, at breakfast, lunch and dinner. We spent hours on the parade ground practicing platoon maneuvers, changing from column of fours to column of twos, reversing front, and advancing at right oblique.

Early on I made some impression on S/Sgt. Jones and he appointed me squad leader. A few days later we were marching across the parade ground when Jones called out some complex movement. I missed a cue and failed to give the required secondary command and my squad went careening away in highly creative fashion. Jones bellowed us to a halt.

I knew I was doomed.

Taking position squarely in my front, Jones exploded in a pyrotechnic rage. His mouth was so close to my face I felt like I was looking down a cannon. The day was sunny and I noticed spit bubbles floating in the light and landing on my nose.

I considered bringing up the matter of hygiene but decided this might not be the right time.

Suddenly, Jones shot out a powerful hand and grabbed me by the throat. Applying a vice-like grip, he began asking my opinion on various matters of military decorum.

"No, sir," I squawked in response to the first. "Yes sir," I croaked to a second, third and fourth.

I could hardly breathe.

Finally, he released his hold, gave me a withering look, and turned to resume his position beside the formation. Then some spasm of fury reanimated him. He wheeled, snatched the M-14 from my hands, and hurled it at my chest like a lethal exclamation point.

I was left, stunned and gasping, but that day and in weeks ahead I learned something vital to success in a classroom. I learned motivation was the most potent fuel in the world. And it was the fuel that *never* ran out. At Parris Island, I learned I could do more—that my comrades could do more—that we could do more by far. I learned more about motivation in ten weeks at boot camp than in all my life before and all my life since.

During a platoon meeting one afternoon, I had my epiphany. Jones was blasting us for some fresh incompetence. At last, he snarled, "How many of you even *finished* high school?"

I shot up a hand. Only ten others followed. I shook mine for emphasis. No use. My comrades weren't listening and a lapse like this could only mean another round of pushups or worse.

A moment passed before Jones and I realized what this show of hands meant. Seventy-nine boots in one platoon had dropped out of high school and enlisted, often because they had no other options. It struck me powerfully then—all that lost potential. It dawned on me I might someday want to teach. I thought to myself: I know what it was like to be unmotivated in school. I could motivate students.

I could.

After boot camp I was sent to Camp Lejeune, North Carolina, for basic infantry training. Then, to my sorrow, it was off to supply school.

From there it was on to Camp Pendleton, California, where I would defend my country with a loaded staple gun.

I still had hopes of following in the footsteps of John Wayne. So I volunteered to go to Vietnam.

Twice.

That's how dumb I was.

The first time, my sergeant informed me he was getting rid of one of the black Marines in our unit, though he did not refer to him as a "black Marine." I ignored his troglodyte mentality and said I'd like to go at the next opportunity.

How, then, did I avoid the trip to Southeast Asia most in my generation were avid to miss? It wasn't because I wised up and changed my mind. It was nothing more nor less than dumbbell luck. One evening a sergeant I had never seen before was passing through our barracks. He saw me doing pushups in a space between two racks (bunks) and stopped a moment to observe.

"If you like to stay in shape, Marine," he finally said, "we're getting up a battalion football team."

I jumped to my feet, asked when tryouts began, and promised I'd be there. I made the squad and the next time my sergeant asked if I wanted to go to Vietnam, I said, "No. I'm on the battalion football team."

I did my paper-shuffling duty for the next fourteen months. Then, in the summer of 1970, I applied for a 90-day early-release program to return to college. By the time my discharge came through, on September 30, fall classes at Ohio University had been in session a week.

Less than twenty hours after my papers were placed in my hand, on the morning of October 1, I was seated in a college classroom once again. The chairs around me were filled with long-haired young men in army-surplus jackets and bra-less hippie chicks. And those hippie chicks looked sweet.

***

During my time in the Marines a wave of liberalism had swept campuses across the land. Freshman year at Ohio University, in 1967, during my first attempt at higher learning, girls had a strict 11 p.m. weekday curfew and an only slightly-less-restrictive weekend curfew.

I wasn't known for social graces in those days; but if you had a girlfriend (I didn't), she could visit your dorm room only once per quarter. On that glorious day the door had to remain open and both host and hosted had to have at least one foot firmly planted on the floor. Now, three years later, there were coed dorms, the sexes divided by sections, but living on the same floors. Drugs were everywhere, too, and the smell of marijuana wafted across the college green on every breeze.

If I learned valuable lessons in the Marines, I learned equally valuable lessons on return to Ohio U. The idea that we should accept people of every creed and color, that we should expect both sexes to perform equally, that we should seek truth in all ways, those lessons eventually helped make me a better teacher. Academic life had also become easier. Now that I wanted to teach, I found this intriguing. By 1970 most professors had altered the way they worked. We had a philosophy instructor who started every class the same way. He entered the room, took a seat cross-legged atop his desk, and intoned, "Let's rap."

So "rap" we did. We "rapped" every time class met. In an entire quarter he assigned seven pages to read.

I don't think anyone learned shit.

Grading had also evolved. Grades were "symbols," man. (True.) Only "learning" mattered. (True.) Grades were "tools of oppression" to control students. (Okay: that one seemed a bit much.) College kids insisted they wanted to experience life, find truth, and "do their own thing." Rules were altered in accord with this philosophy. Attendance no longer counted when figuring grades. So I stopped wasting time going to boring classes if I knew I could learn the material on my own. Often I used the time saved to head for the library and study.

Other times I headed for the gym to find a pickup basketball game. There, too, I learned useful lessons, all of which applied perfectly to life in a classroom, as I later found.

HARDWOOD MAXIMS

1. On any basketball court, if you are not tall or gifted, ceaseless effort is a powerful equalizer.

2. Criticizing teammates, individually, has a corrosive effect, often leading to argument. Urging teammates, generally, to hustle can be motivating.
3. Maxim #2 is true only if you hustle the most.
4. There is one ball. So: involve *all* teammates. An involved player is motivated.
5. If a teammate makes a good pass and you score do not brag about scoring. Complement the passer. Sincere compliments are motivational.
6. A motivated player is always willing to expend greater effort. So motivation is a key.
7. The more you practice shooting, work on dribbling, and run full-tilt up and down the court to get in shape when no one is watching, the better you perform in games.
8. There is no one path to victory on the court. Many varied paths lead to success.

I can't claim I was ever more than a good pickup player, and three decades of practice to follow did nothing to improve a shooting touch better suited to blacksmithing. But I was willing to sweat and that always helped. Because I played five or six times a week, I improved steadily. Often I found myself the only white player on the court. I have a florid complexion and when I exercise it blooms. One day a friend came looking for me at the gym.

"All I saw," he laughed, "were nine black guys and one pink guy running up and down the court."

The pink guy was me.

When I did attend class I discovered new rules made it easier to protect your GPA. If you started a class badly you could drop it. If you stuck it out to the end and earned a low mark you could retake the course, earn a better grade, and replace the lower with the higher. One class per quarter could be taken pass/fail. School reformers in those days believed this would encourage students to tackle challenging courses they might otherwise avoid.

In other words, learning would be enhanced.

Sadly, education reforms based in theory produced strange fruit in reality. Flesh and blood students quickly discovered that many of these changes opened a smooth and easy path. If attendance didn't count, sleeping late was a wonderful why-go-to-class option. If you blew off English Lit 102 and failed, no problem. Ask mom and dad to pony up for another quarter. "Do your own thing," and try again. You could even do a little professor-shopping. Find out who graded easy and take the easy professor second time around. As for pass/fail, many an undergrad in 1970 learned that what pass/fail really meant was getting by on reduced effort. C work was as good as A work. So they turned in C work and slept in late.

For the first time in my life, now that I had returned from the Marines, I was serious about my studies. Even then I saw ample proof that attitude often trumped intelligence.

In my case, I "discovered" that if I reviewed four hours for a midterm or exam, I usually earned a high mark. If I studied six hours, or eight, I earned A's almost without exception.

It was the same for my peers. Junior year, I roomed with two friends in an off-campus apartment. Terry studied diligently. Dave preferred TV. Every Friday afternoon he returned from his last class, snapped on the set, and plunked down on a tattered couch in the living room. He watched all evening, late into the night, deep into Saturday morning. He slept through the day, watched TV Saturday evening, late into the night, deep into Sunday morning.

Dave would watch anything, including old Tarzan movies. One day I overheard him talking to the animals.

"Simba! Simba!" he shouted from his seat, repeating the signature Tarzan yell.

I stepped out of the kitchen, where I was frying up a little bologna for a healthy college breakfast. Dave was pumping his fist as Tarzan led a menagerie of jungle creatures in a charge which routed a set of cartoonish villains.

What did I learn? I learned if you studied, like Terry, you got good grades. If you binged on old Tarzan movies, like Dave, you ended up with a lot of C's. This might sound like a tautology, but I learned students had a powerful impact on how much knowledge they acquired.

(Every modern school reformer in America insists that more must be done by *teachers* to raise test scores. I believe the surest way to raise test scores is extraordinarily clear.)

Like every undergraduate in the College of Education, I was still formulating my philosophy of teaching. A. S. Neill's book: *Summerhill: A Radical Approach to Child Rearing* had profound effect, liberal Yin to balance Marine Corps Yang.

Neill ran an English boarding school for forty-five students. At his school no boy was forced to do anything. If a young man felt like coming to class he did. If he felt like napping in the shade he could. No one was going to stuff learning down his throat. He had to *want* to learn.

He would not be punished with poor grades if he came slowly to that realization. He would not be rewarded with high marks once he did. Knowledge was the only prize worth gaining.

True then.

True today.

True a thousand years hence.

I found Neill's ideas inspiring and marked numerous passages for study. One day Neill received a phone call in his office. The voice on the other end said one of his pupils was required at home and needed money for the trip, 28 shillings. Neill called the boy in and gave him the fare, only to discover later the call was a hoax. He and his wife discussed how to handle the situation and decided not to accost the boy. Neill went to his room and said his mother had called again. There had been a mistake. The fare was 38 shillings.

He threw a ten-shilling note on the bed and left.

The boy admitted the ruse soon after and the headmaster asked him how he felt. "You know," he told Neill, "I got the biggest shock of my life. I said to myself: 'Here is the first man in my life who has been on my side.'"

The story touched me and in typical undergraduate fashion I scrawled across the top of the page: "This is of key importance: to be truly on the child's side." I vowed when I had a classroom of my own I would be on my students' sides.

I would work my own kind of miracles.

***

Before I could put any lessons learned to use I needed a teaching position. By the time I graduated in 1973, I was dating my first wife, a Cincinnati native. My job hunt began there, but lasted longer than expected. First, there was an abundance of social studies candidates at the high school level, which is where I wanted to teach. Second, many of those candidates had a passion for coaching: baseball, basketball, football. Foosball if they could manage.

I had interviews.

They just didn't turn up any work.

One principal informed me that if I wanted to teach in his building I would need to cut my hair, which curled over my ears by the summer of 1973. He added, as if imparting some nugget of wisdom, "Of course, you know, we don't allow facial hair."

"I'd be happy to get a haircut if it would help," I responded. "I really want to teach."

I could have stopped there. I should have stopped there. No, I felt compelled to observe: "You realize if you had an opening teaching government you wouldn't hire Abraham Lincoln?"

A pinched expression came over the interviewer's face. I don't think he liked my potential for pot-smoking perversion.

I didn't get the job, of course, but took consolation knowing Abe wouldn't have either.

My next interview was promising. I talked for an hour with a principal in one of the area's finest districts. I told him I was confident I could handle discipline. My mother, who served on the school board back home, had tried to steer me away from social studies, I said. Too many candidates. This was my passion and I was certain I could make history interesting.

Clearly, the principal approved. I could sense the job was mine. I had my first imaginary check cashed and started counting out the bills.

The principal broke in on my reverie: "I'd love to hire you...."

Angels sang and cash register bells rang in heaven

"...but I need a soccer coach."

The song died as suddenly as it began. The angels were practicing. The imaginary check was lost in the imaginary mail. At point in my life I had never *seen* a soccer game.

45

The author in 1973.
Okay, the hippie look might not have been good.

In the summer of 1974 I had two more interviews. I missed out on the first job, because what the principal most wanted was a ninth grade basketball coach, and all I really wanted was to teach.

The second interview started well, when I met with the superintendent of a country district near Oxford, Ohio. My interviewer was a kindly gentleman and clearly liked my attitude. I told him I intended to get more out of students than teachers got out of me.

Finally, he turned serious. "I'm going to send you over to our high school," he said. "But to be honest that place is a cesspool. They don't have any good ideas and they'll resent you because you do."

If I could convince the principal, though, the job was mine.

The principal's disdain was clear from the start. He conducted the interview with fingers interlocked behind his head, feet atop his desk. He asked about discipline. Then content. I was safe when I said students should understand the ideals in the Declaration of Independence. I was safe again when I said students should grasp the import of the U. S. Constitution.

Then a fatal blunder: "I think history shows all people are alike. Take the Civil War. Students should know that black soldiers and sailors showed the same courage fighting for freedom as whites...."

With that the principal dropped his feet to the floor, jerked forward in his chair, and spit out: "Awwww, BULLSHIT!"

He recovered quickly and pretended what he wanted to know was how I would react to any parent who responded as he had.

For all real intents, I knew the interview was over. What I had to say now was no more pertinent than air rushing from a punctured tire.

5.

Dead Dogs and Milkshake Bets

"I didn't feel worthy of it, really. Adulthood felt like Halloween."
Allan Gurganus

The hunt for a position continued. My first year out of college, I dodged dogs and delivered mail for the U. S. Postal Service. I worked in a rundown section of Cincinnati, where vicious dogs were plentiful. One memorable day a young German shepherd sank its teeth in my buns. The following year I attended graduate school, earning a Master's in American history. The year after that—and still no whiff of employment in my chosen profession—I signed up for substitute teaching.

In October 1975, I took a call from the Loveland City Schools, then a poor country district outside Cincinnati. Could I fill in for two weeks at the junior high?

The regular teacher was out with ulcers. That should have been my first clue.

***

All through college and my years searching for a position I assumed I'd end up working at the high school level. This was something less and something more. At the junior high level I would need the skill sets of a football coach, parish priest and lion-tamer.

I also had to learn a number of humbling lessons. For starters, my discipline was far too rigid. My notes were too long and—even worse—boring.

The nuances of the job also escaped me. One day we were reading a section in the textbook. I asked Tony to take a turn. To say he began haltingly would be to show his performance grave disrespect. He stumbled over the simplest words and my sympathies were immediately aroused.

"T…T…The…….p…pre….si……dent c-c-c-can st….stop a…. bill….by…u…u…(he looked hopefully in my direction; I filled in: 'using')…using…his….vet…toe…"

I felt bad, exposing him to ridicule and began considering the best way to switch readers without embarrassing him further. If only he could make it to the end of the paragraph. I was getting ready to correct his pronunciation of "veto" when classmates began grumbling.

"Quit faking!" someone shouted.

Tony reacted as if stung by hornets. He plowed through the rest of the section in regulation fashion and looked up with a sheepish grin.

"So, we can read, after all?" I smiled. It was one of many subtle lessons I would learn, all by teaching.

My employment was supposed to last two weeks. At first, students enjoyed my fresh approach. I looked "cool" too, with thick reddish-brown sideburns, Ben Franklin glasses and green-and-cream checked polyester pants and matching green polyester shirt. The regular teacher's ulcers refused to heal. He was out four weeks, then six, then nine. Pupils began peeking behind the curtain and realized the polyester Wizard of Oz didn't know what he was doing.

I worked hard; but the secrets of the adolescent mind were only slowly revealed. What were those secrets? What could distract the hormone-addled teen from a daily dose of history? Episodes of *Happy Days* and a thousand imitations of the Fonz. Rumors of fights. Fights. Rumors of romance. Romance. The handsome boy moving in, the popular girl moving out, friends awash in tears, promising never to forget and then forgetting as teens would.

What else might distract my charges during another scintillating lecture? The first snowflakes of winter. The first snowflakes of any afternoon.

Problems with parents.

Problems with friends.

Problems with me.

Kids at this level can be fearlessly blunt and I had to learn to steel myself or weep. On one occasion I admonished a young lady named

Monica for incessant talking. She shot me a look and pinpointed the font of her disdain: "You're the most boring teacher I've ever met."

What does the rookie teacher learn? He learns teens can be brutally frank.[4]

Another distraction at this age is sex—the tiniest whiff of sex. Trouble erupted in third period one day, just as the bell was about to ring. Dana was furious and expected me to intercede. Matt had her hairbrush.

"Give it back, Matt," she shouted. "Mr. Viall, make him give it back!"

Matt was acting like a dunce because Dana was pretty. Matt lacked aptitude for mature conversation. So he pestered her till she ordered him to stop. Matt now knew Dana knew Matt *existed*. Descartes as a 13-year-old boy: "I act like a fool. Therefore, I am."

Dana and Matt might not know how to deal with the opposite sex but this was junior high and some knew way too much. After classes ended one afternoon an eighth grade girl named Callie stopped by my room to ask if we could talk. She was only fourteen, but tall, intelligent, and strikingly beautiful, with hair like Farah Fawcett.

"Mr. Viall," she began haltingly, "I have a problem." When she hesitated, I urged her to continue.

"I've been seeing an older guy and I've been lying about my age."

"Oh, no," I responded. I thought to myself: You could pass for a high school girl, easy.

I could see how she might be pulling it off but was not prepared when she added: "I've been telling him I'm twenty."

"That's not good...."

"It's even worse," she said. "He's been lying, too. He told me he was 28. He's really 36."

"*Oh no*," I said, "Callie, you *have* to tell him how old you are. You can't go out with a guy like that!"

---

[4] Many years later, I bent down to assist a young man with some problem. I was intent on helping him learn.

He, for his part, felt compelled to observe, "Do you know you have a lot of nose hair?"

I did. And I did.

I told her she had to talk to her mother, see the school counselor, do whatever it took, but had to break it off, and fortunately, she soon did.

How mature, then, are junior high kids? It depends. All too often, in years ahead, I would counsel pregnant teens. Others had the same level of understanding in matters of sex you might expect of second graders. In the hallway outside my room I picked up a note one day, dropped by some Lothario. He was writing an apology to his girlfriend: "I'm so sorry if I hurt you at the assembly," he began sweetly. He insisted he didn't like Kim at all.

"I love you," he wrote. "Why don't you believe me?"

Then the telling detail, revealing his maturity: "I was just kidding when I said I'd eat the cicada. Richard and I were joking around."

He recovered from his faux pas and finished strong. "If I could change you, I'd change nothing. I love you. I'm gonna describe you in one word. Perfect. See I'm good. I love you."

***

I also learned that first year that there were ten thousand basics a teacher might choose to address. Ask kids, in 1975, to name the bloodiest war in United States history, and responses were unanimous and wrong. "Vietnam," all agreed. Mike, a polite, blonde-haired boy, couldn't spell "if" and doubled down on "f." Asked to find Hawaii on a blank map one day, five kids in first bell stuck a finger on Cuba. I was stunned until I realized they were accustomed to seeing maps of the U. S. with the fiftieth state crammed in a box in the corner next to Florida. So that's where they thought Hawaii was.

When I asked what kids knew about George Washington all they could say was he was our first president and chopped down a cherry tree. I felt bad telling them the cherry tree story was a myth.

The need to identify true basics was made crystal clear my third or fourth year during discussion of the Mexican War. I admitted most adults remembered very little about the war. Students wouldn't need to know much either.

Nevertheless, our victory had profound consequence. First, I said, we stole the Mexicans' girlfriend (Texas) which touched off the fight. Then we beat them up and gave them two black eyes (pick any two battles;

51

we pretty much won them all). While they lay unconscious we took their wallet (California, New Mexico, Arizona, etc.) by treaty. Tucked inside was the winning lottery ticket (discovery of gold in California in 1849). So we cashed it ourselves.

I could tell my analogy was working and remember thinking, "Hey, look at me, I can teach!"

Trust me, in the life of every young teacher there are plenty of times when you think you can't.

Danny, sitting in the back of the room, raised a hand and brought me crashing back to earth. He was only an average student but his comments were usually good. "Mr. Viall, whatever *happened* to Mexico?" he inquired.

I wasn't sure what he meant but the look on his face hinted at the truth. He wasn't asking what happened to Mexico after the war. He was curious. Did Mexico still *exist*?

I stammered: "Uh.........it's still there."

"Oh!" he exclaimed, like an elderly gentleman realizing he held his "lost" keys in his hand.

Like any new teacher, my first few years, I had to feel my way. Teaching writing seemed like a basic. So every year I asked students to complete a personal history, 500 words in length. Initially, they were aghast, especially when cautioned to be neat, check spelling, and keep sentence and paragraph structure in view. I even warned against use of "mutant letters." That is: a wrong letter written out, say "a," and then plastered over with a correct choice, "b" or "g," or both, or the whole alphabet, forcing the poor educator to crack a code.

Personal essays were good writing practice and highly revealing. The American family had taken a beating and divorce was a common theme. Terry explained that her mom had been through four divorces, the first when Terry was two. Danielle lived with mom and rarely heard from dad. Her sadness was palpable. "When we do not see him we miss him very much." Royce admitted his father was an alcoholic. "If he asks me to clean up the garage I just say, 'I did it yesterday.' And he doesn't know." At the opposite extreme Dave started his story from inside the womb, a personal history brilliantly conceived.

Loveland wasn't a bad district in those days but wasn't the elite district it would later become. We were chronically short on funding. I remember once a secretary coming to me and saying, "John, here are some of the supplies you ordered." She handed over six Flair pens and ten strips of staples. Not even a full box! Textbooks were old. Paper for copies was scarce. There was little money for supplemental materials. Teachers ended up subsidizing the district for basics like paper clips and scotch tape.

There was one slide projector for the building and to get it you had to sign up far in advance. I bought my own and used it until it burned up one day during class. The fan stopped working. Before anyone noticed the plastic top melted like peanut butter, fell in on the hot bulb, and began smoking in ominous fashion.

I solved that problem by buying another projector.

A typical Loveland class in the mid and late 70's was filled with kids who grew up in modest homes and on farms that dotted the countryside. They walked to friends' houses on weekends, cutting through fields and woods. Often they spent time playing in grandpa's barn or swimming in the nearby Little Miami River.

They were hard-nosed kids, too. Fights were common. One day I watched John Baumgart, a fine veteran teacher, clamber over a line of tables in the lunchroom to separate two teens before they could knock out each other's brains.

Another day, I broke up a wild slugging match involving two big eighth grade boys. I grabbed the first one I could reach and tossed him left. I turned right, saw the second winding up—hoping to punch his opponent—or possibly punch me. I've been punched in fights before when I wasn't an active participant. It's no fun. So I shot out my right hand, wacked him in the chest with my palm, and sent him tumbling over a cluster of plastic chairs with a crash.

Loveland City Schools had plenty of poor kids in those days but few minorities. The year I was hired, Loveland hired Chuck Battle, the only black educator in the district at that time. In years to come he would prove to be a man of unflinching integrity. In those days a school board member labeled him a "nigger."

On a different occasion I gave a young man detention for telling this joke during class: "What's long, black and smells?"

Answer: "The unemployment line."

Classmates clamored for reprieve, saying this was the same joke a teacher told earlier that day. I wasn't about to tolerate racist comments, regardless of sourcing, and gave the comedian detention anyway.

Fortunately, attitudes were changing. In fact, you can make a case that "kids today" are better than we were. They're less likely to be racist, sexist or homophobic, much less likely than their grandparents.

I remember when the Loveland Junior High girl's track coach had to threaten to sue the district. This was 1982, when much of the country was still waking up to the fact females were actually interested in sports. One day Coach Jo Puls was looking over a district salary schedule when she noticed the boys' track coach received double the pay she did to coach girls.

Puls went to the principal. "We have the same number of meets and the same number of practices. Why does he receive twice the money?"

The principal replied with what in those days passed for unassailable logic: "Boys' track is more important."

Threat of a Title IX lawsuit, however, soon convinced the district to change policies.

***

At the junior high level (and later the middle school level when we switched configurations in the 90s) a teacher may be dealing with a 175 personalities every day. For that reason, teaching is never dull and learning to deal with all kinds of people is central to the job.

Consider Perry, a likeable young man, but an inveterate liar. We were talking about the Battle of Iwo Jima one day. Perry informed the class his grandfather fought there and won a bunch of medals. He wasn't sure which ones or how.

Still, his claim sounded plausible.

As the weeks passed, Perry's comments strained all credibility. Mention slavery and Perry's ancestors owned slaves. Talk about the Alamo and his great, great, great grandfather was at Davy Crockett's side, matching shot for shot before both died.

I feared to mention Pilgrims, because I knew Perry would insist his ancestors steered the boat.

Eventually, I learned to ignore him if his hand was up and he had that *look*. By mid-year, peers were scoffing at his Bunyanesque tales. He wasn't fazed and kept right on inventing.

I recorded these comments in a single period:

* Perry says he has read the fifteen-page assignment in ten minutes.
* Perry says he needs to make a trip to the bathroom.
* Perry says he needs a drink.
* Perry says he saw a guy cleaning the St. Louis Arch on television, changing light bulbs on the outside, without safety belt or equipment, just ropes.

I said gently, I didn't think there were any lights on the Arch. He insisted he saw them on TV.

Perry eventually moved on to high school and his trail went cold. A decade later, I was standing at the counter in the main office. Classes were over for the day and I was getting ready to head home. A young man entered and addressed me by name. He was lean, with a crisp military haircut.

"Remember me?" he asked with a smile. I recognized the face....

"Perry Jones," he said, before I could reply.

He was happy to see me. I was happy to see him. I asked what he was up to. He said he was in the army.

"Are you still playing basketball?" Perry asked politely.

"Yes," I said. I was.

"I'm on our base team," he volunteered. "I averaged 26 points a game last season." Then he told me he could dunk. I looked him over. He was rangy enough and probably 6' 3." It might be true. It might be a new Perry. "Yeah, I dunked once from the foul line."

Nope: same old Perry.

Naturally, all types of talented kids stepped into my classroom too. Virginia was smarter than me and ten times more serious about learning than I was at the same age. I had her my first year. Judging from her expression, I think there were times when she wondered how anyone so inept received a teaching license.

In later years we always did a unit on the U. S. government and I handed out a diagram of the three branches in the form of a tree. To help students remember the parts and duties I asked them to do their own renderings. Kids turned in three-ice-cream-cone designs, and three-clusters-of-colorful-balloon designs. One year Pat created a Ronald-Reagan-as-beaver-gnawing-at-the-tree design. Ruth turned in a gorgeous three-ring circus with the voters as applauding audience.

She was a brilliant young lady and conversing with her was like talking with an adult. One day Ruth raised her hand to question my use of "affect" and "effect" in some piece of writing I'd provided. I was foolish enough to disagree. "I don't know, Ruth, I've been using 'effect' the same way for years and no one, even in college, ever corrected me."

"I still think you're wrong," she insisted politely.

"I'll tell you what," I said, "I'll bet you a milkshake and we'll send you down to Mr. Partin to see who's correct."

I made out a pass and off she went to seek a ruling from our senior English teacher. When she returned she gently broke the news. Mr. Partin supported her interpretation. I was so shocked I sent her off to seek a second opinion. The appellate court upheld the lower court's grammatical decision.

So: I learned by teaching, how to use "affect" and "effect" properly.

Not everyone was as smart as Ruth. On another occasion we were working on an important assignment, a timeline worth a hundred points. Each inch on the line equaled ten years. Jeff was confused. When I checked progress he told me he couldn't decide where to place the end of the Civil War. I reminded him each inch equaled ten years. Where would "1865" go?

Jeff scanned the line like a bettor looking for a fast horse. I pointed to the inch marked 1860 at one end, 1870 at the other. He stared at the line like it was covered in hieroglyphics.

"How many times will five go into ten?" I hinted.

"I don't know," he replied.

I disguised my astonishment, tapped the middle of the line, and moved on to help another pupil.

I was also meeting the walking wounded of teen society. One young lady ingested a toxic mix of illegal substances on her way to school.

During first bell Language Arts she lost control of bodily functions, tumbled from her seat, and exited school on a stretcher.

Then there was Jen.

She was a heavy-set girl, piling up terrible marks. She came to school in filthy clothes and it was obvious there were problems at home. Loveland wasn't yet a rich community and Jen didn't draw the scrutiny she might have twenty years later, when farmland filled and we had become an affluent suburban district. When she came near, though, I had to pretend not to notice the odor that followed like a sour shadow. If I talked to Jen she listened, promised to do better, and shrank as if in hiding.

All attempts to contact parents failed. (This might surprise school critics, but teachers learn quickly that while most parents are good, some are not, and kids with bad parents are far more likely to struggle in school.) The math teacher tried calling. No answer.

The English teacher tried too. The number was out of service.

The science teacher sent a note.

No response.

Eventually, Jen's family was evicted from the house they were renting and she and her academic problems vanished from our sight. The home, we heard from health authorities later, was filthy beyond belief. Rooms were choked with trash, piles of old magazines, unwashed dishes, and cast-off clothing in malodorous heaps. The water had been shut off long before the family moved. Toilets overflowed with waste.

One final detail clinched the horror of Jen's home situation.

Under a layer of newspaper in the bathtub police found the corpse of the long-dead family dog.

6.

Luke and His Pompoms

"Somewhere between the ages of eleven and fifteen, the average child begins to suffer atrophy, the paralysis of curiosity and the suspension of the power to observe. The trouble I should judge to lie with the schools."
Thomas Edison

My career with Loveland, which began with two weeks as a substitute, might well have ended when the regular teacher made a saltines-and-milk-for-lunch recovery and returned to work. Luckily, another gentleman decided to lay down the grade book and leave the profession at the end of first semester. I was tapped to fill his post. I left for Christmas vacation as a humble substitute and returned in January 1976 as a real live teacher.

In those days Loveland Junior High "tracked," or grouped kids, by ability. Second semester I had the top 110 seventh graders in four American history classes, a plum assignment if ever there was one. Given a chance to "start," as they say in sports, I began finding a footing. I cut down on notes and came up with several creative strategies to use the rest of my career.

I was still a rookie, though, and when the school year sputtered to an end in June I knew I had done only an adequate job. I learned by teaching that I wasn't particularly good at teaching.

Not yet.

***

That Bicentennial Summer, I set out to do whatever I had to in order to improve. During a trip out West I took slides of Indian reservations, sequoia trees and Yosemite waterfalls, and used them the rest of my career to illustrate important points. I read voraciously, too, searching for interesting material to bolster key historical points.

I was finishing *Bury My Heart at Wounded Knee* when an idea began rattling around in my skull. It was hard to see how anyone could fail to sympathize with the natives who lost their lands and saw their culture destroyed. Yet it was clear they were guilty of crimes of their own. If I sat down and searched my books it would be easy to create two readings for students. One would lay out a legal brief damning to settlers. The other, relying on *identical sources*, would list sins that made the natives sound like savages.

By September the two handouts were ready. With four new classes to work with I sprung the trap early in the year. I handed out materials at the start of every bell, told kids to read, and said we'd discuss when they finished. The two versions looked the same and ran four pages. Once kids were ready we opened for business.

Depending on which one they received, comments sounded like they were coming from different planets. "The settlers were worse," said one young man. "They destroyed the forests and wiped out the buffalo."

Students thought this was a big tree. It's part of a sequoia branch.

"The settlers were greedy and took the natives' land," a second agreed. "If the Indians went on their property and killed a single cow they slaughtered them, even women and children."

"Well, how many Indians were there?" I asked, without revealing my motives. I called on one of those who had the other version.

"There were only a million in what is now the United States," a young lady replied. "They didn't *use* all the land."

"They owned it. They were *here* first!" retorted a classmate who had read about the crimes of the settlers.

"Okay. Wait a minute." I pulled down a map of the United States. "Only one million people lived in this huge area." I swept my hand across the continent. "Couldn't the Indians share?"

"They were here first. It was *theirs*," insisted the same student.

"What if only 100,000 Indians lived here? Would that make a difference?" He seemed confused. "What about ten thousand," I pressed. "That's the population of Loveland. What about one? If there was *one* Indian could he claim North America because he was here first?"

Shelly raised a hand in disgust. "The Indians tried to share but the settlers murdered them. Look at Chief Logan. He tried to be friendly and they wiped out his family."

I nodded to show agreement no matter which side speakers favored and called on the next volunteer. I didn't want gaps in discussion and only tried to keep a fire burning under the stew.

"The Indians were worse," a classmate countered. "Look what they did to William Crawford. The Shawnee burned him at the stake. They cut off his ears and scalped him while he was alive."

I let the argument continue until the time seemed right, and then inquired again: What happened to Chief Logan? Someone said, as before, his family was murdered.

I asked another boy to tell us about Lewis Wetzell. His family was wiped out by Indians, the boy explained.

For Joanna, the smartest girl in the room, that was the final straw. She snatched her friend's paper from her desk, flipped the pages to confirm her suspicions, and exclaimed indignantly, "These two stories aren't even the *same*!"

The class was hooked, trying to grasp what was happening. We turned our focus to the import, in reading history, *and in life*, of being sure you had all sides of a story.

I drew two stick figures on the board. One was Lewis Wetzell, the other, Chief Logan. "I am a great artist, as you can see," I added for comic relief.

"Suppose they met in the forest. Both have seen loved ones murdered. You know how you'd feel. What would happen?"

They'd try to kill each other, students agreed.

"Say they shot at the exact same time," inquired. "Who would be to blame?"

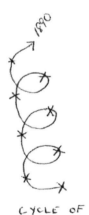

CYCLE OF
VIOLENCE

One boy said Wetzell, adding that the settlers stole Indian lands. Many said neither. Others said both. I left the decision to them and drew the "cycle of violence" on the board.

I said the first "x" represented the trouble which began when settlers arrived at Jamestown in 1607. "Let's say, for our purposes, the settlers started the problem.

"Once the Indians—actually some Indians—took revenge—usually killing the wrong settlers—the cycle began. The settlers killed Indians, the Indians killed settlers," I explained, adding x's as I went. "Round and round it went for 300 years.

"How do you stop the cycle?" I asked. No one was sure, including me. "Anyone know how we brought the cycle to an end?"

"We learned to get along?" Claire replied hopefully.

"I wish you were right, but, no. We basically ran out of Indians to kill. We never got one bit smarter."

We used this lesson for decades (until I tired of repetition and replaced it with two readings on slavery, diverging in the same way). One of my favorite moments came during my fourth year, courtesy of a young lady named Carolyn. She was a tiny thing, probably four-and-a-half feet tall, and looked like she was nine or ten, not twelve or thirteen like peers.

I followed the usual practice, gave time for the reading, and then asked, "Whose fault was all the bloodshed?"

Carolyn had a handout blaming the Indians. She was horrorstruck. She set herself and gave examples. As debate heated up kids began shaking their heads. Were classmates crazy? The Indian side put forward an argument. The settler side demolished it with one of their own.

As always, kids came slowly to the realization that something was amiss. "I guess, when you see both sides, they're each partly to blame," Scott admitted.

More and more members of the class settled on this middle ground. Finally, Carolyn stood alone. The Indians were to blame. She had her mind made up and kept digging into her handout for evidence.

"The Aztec religion was based on human sacrifice," she exclaimed. "They cut out people's *hearts*!"

A young man countered with an example of his own. Another insisted, "You only have one side, Carolyn."

A third groaned with exasperation, "Come on!" I felt bad for her but decided to let them go.

"The Cherokee owned slaves," Carolyn continued, "and the Apaches stole little kids and sold them."

The period was about to end. This was the point at which we normally wrapped the lesson; but I let Carolyn make a stand. She was hit from all sides by competing arguments. Regal, the loudest boy, was against her and the three strongest intellects and the biggest jock and the most popular girl and the most popular girl's friend. Carolyn was outnumbered 22-1, with two or three uncommitted classmates waiting to see how the wind blew.

It wasn't Carolyn's reasoning that impressed me. In a teen world, where kids sway like tall prairie grass in accord with peer pressure, it was how she stood up to everyone else. It was the kind of stand you take to stop a bully, or an adult takes to halt a mob.

I let the contest continue despite the odds. Finally, the bell rang, signaling the period's end.

As students rose from their chairs and discussion spilled into the hall, I watched Carolyn gather her books and rise with dignity from her seat. As she passed my desk, I stopped her a moment. "I'm proud of you, young lady," I said. "You stood up against the crowd."

"Thanks, Mr. Viall," she answered with a bright smile. "See you tomorrow."

And off she went to boldly face the world.

***

One of the joys of teaching is to get students excited and lead them in directions neither you nor they expected to go. When time came every year to look at Native American cultures we began with a quick discussion of what I called the "TV Indian" stereotype. We took time to list features of the "TV Indian" lifestyle on the chalkboard. Answers always looked like this:

Teepees
Feathers
Skin clothes
Painted faces
Bow and arrows
Ride horses
Hunt buffalo
Talk stupid, "how," "ugh," grunt a lot

I explained that Native American civilizations varied. Some relied on corn, beans and squash as dietary staples. "How come no one ever does movies about farming Indians?" I asked.

"Because it would be boring," kids agreed.

I broke into a soulful rendition of "Old McDonald Had a Farm" and asked everyone to sing along. No one ever did.

When the last note died away we turned to a brief look at Native Americans who lived along the Pacific coast, a group which hunted whales and lived mainly on salmon. They didn't fit the stereotype at all. In their culture, power and prestige depended on wealth.

TV Indian stereotype (drawn by Emily, a star student, for extra credit).

To my surprise the word "prestige" baffled the class. I chalked a definition on the board: "Your rank or standing in the eyes of others." My audience seemed perplexed. I tried an example.

"Whitney," I said, picking the liveliest girl in the room, "imagine you're at a party. You see the handsomest guy ever, standing off to the side alone. He is so hot! He spots you and walks your way. Your head is spinning.

"You start talking and he tells you he drives a porta-potty truck." The class gets a laugh. "He's still hot," I remind Whitney. "Do you rank this guy high or low because of his job?"

"Low," she admits.

"What if he was a doctor?"

"High," Whitney says emphatically.

Students now volunteered to list factors that determined prestige in modern society: Clothing. Money. Job. Cool car.

I was ready to wrap the discussion when Jessie, one of my favorites, put forth the idea that the way "popularity" was determined in school was just as shallow. This swept the rest of the class into the mix. A consensus formed that cheerleaders and athletes, like the star quarterback, rated high in teen society.

"If cheerleaders are cool and cheerleader costumes make you cooler, what about a guy cheerleader?" I inquired. "Wouldn't that be cool?"

I singled out one of the natural leaders in class and winked, "Luke! You would be *sooo* popular! You would be so cool with your pompoms!"

The class shouted down the idea that a cheerleader uniform would make Luke cool.

"Then how can the uniform make a girl cool?"

Amy, one of the popular girls, admitted teens judged each other based on clothing of all sorts. What brands, I wondered, were "best" and won the greatest prestige among peers?

Answers changed over the years but students always agreed on what was popular at the time. The last few years I taught, prestige lines included Abercrombie and Fitch, Aeropostale and Old Navy. Sports teams were big. Kobe Bryant and the Lakers. Ohio State. Florida Gators.

"If I buy a blank white t-shirt and write Kobe's name on the back and Florida Gators on the front," I asked, "won't I be double cool? I have *two* magic names on my shirt."

Students said that was stupid, but they were being forced to examine their values.

"Mr. Viall," quipped one class wit, "you could give away money and you wouldn't be cool."

I gave the comedian the death stare—and then started laughing, like everyone else.

"Okay. So let's say I tell you, hey, I went to Goodwill yesterday and picked up an Abercrombie and Fitch shirt for $2. That makes me popular, right?"

"No, you can't *say* you shop at Goodwill," Amy responded.

"Then the magic word is only good on the shirt if people think I spent a lot of money for the magic?"

Amy wasn't sure how to respond.

The last time I ever used this lesson we turned it into performance art. Students earned extra credit by putting names of popular styles on regular t-shirts and wearing them to school. Adam had a piece of brown shopping bag inscribed "Old Navy" taped to a dress shirt. Meredith used magic marker to list all kinds of sports heroes and teams on a plain white tee. Everyone agreed that in the realm of prestige/popularity this made her "cool."

If I kept class interesting for students, and after my first year, I usually could, I know they kept it interesting for me. As part of this unit on Native Americans, I showed a slide made from an old photo. It depicted a woman of the Pacific Coast culture with a strange elongated skull.

I explained that standards of beauty varied from culture to culture and how board-like devices were used on babies to reshape their heads. For years I asked kids to make comparisons to our culture, how we were willing to go to extremes to look good. Girls brought up high heels and plucked eyebrows. Brett mentioned weight lifters who sucked up steroids.

One day, Stephanie raised her hand, thought it over, and lowered it again. I always encouraged kids to speak their mind. I called on her, insisting she give her answer. She hesitated. Then she looked down from the high dive and took the plunge.

"Mr. Viall," she said, "their customs seem dumb, but it's no dumber than women who pay for boob jobs."

The class exploded, and after I stopped laughing myself, I replied, "That's why I like having you in class, Stephanie. You always know how to think."

When you come up with a lesson that works you don't mess around. When I switched to teaching Ancient World History in 2004, I adapted points from the discussion about prestige for a look at castes in the Hindu religion. Now I asked students to write essays about how people in the United States were divided into "castes" according to factors like wealth or appearance.

Again, kids came through. "Adults are almost the same as us 7th graders," Valerie responded. "Folks are rated on their monthly income, size of their house and even what schools their kids attend…People are usually not rated on their hearts and minds, but on their wallets and cars."

Rob's essay was filled with angst: "People still make caste systems out of certain kids, especially at schools. Like me, I'm probably at the bottom with the untouchables or if someone made a lower caste for fat kids."

I gave him an A. At the bottom of his paper I wrote, "I rank your ideas high. I rated as a skinny loser in seventh grade myself."

I only hoped a touch of empathy from a "survivor" might take a bit of sting out of adolescence.

7.

Frankenstein Gets a Brain

"It is only the ignorant who despise education."
Publilius Syrus

Like the "N" word in respectable circles, the "L" word (lazy) has vanished from current school reform debate (except when applied to teachers). Students "struggle." They need "help."

Schools must put them on "a plan."

Unlike unicorns, my experience, personally and professionally, proves lazy students do exist.

When I was a young man I had a "plan." That plan was to do as little as possible for as long as I could.

***

I attended public school during a mythic age known as the "Good Old Days." Even then we had the same age-old mix of teachers—good, bad and ugly—and I was content to bump along, reading a book a week on my own, tuning out most of what the professionals had to offer. I dreamed of becoming a hero. Until I could win a chest full of medals, however, I would have to settle for the attention I could garner as class clown.

Like all students, at least in the upper grades, I knew what I was doing and charted my own course.

Student choices and the attitudes they reflect are critical variables in every secondary classroom in the land. It's a fact the non-teaching types ignore.

As a teen with a questionable attitude, I took pleasure at the start of senior year in high school, knowing I ranked 129th in my class (out of 197). My actions in Senior Social Studies are especially relevant to my thesis. First semester we were assigned a research paper. I chose "The Reality of

War" for a topic. Since the subject interested me, I worked hard for a change. Either my subject was unacceptable or my footnotes were fatally flawed. When Mrs. Bond, our instructor, returned my paper an F showed at the top like a raw red wound.

She offered no explanation.

I asked for none.

Another day, Mrs. Bond was passing my desk when she halted and turned, horror in her look. I was reading *Hitler: A Study in Tyranny* at the time. The paperback sat atop my stack of unused textbooks. A photo of the dictator had once graced the cover. Now senior pictures were out. I thought it might amuse my peers to cut out my face and glue it atop Hitler's body.

So there I was: a subtle smile adding charm to my air-brushed-senior-picture-good-looks, a swastika armband on one sleeve. As often happened, my comic talents went unappreciated. Bond delivered a stinging lecture at my expense.

By spring of 1967, I'm sure she was fed up with my approach to academics, as well she should have been. I had already made it clear I had no intention of doing a second semester research paper. She asked why. I told her I worked hard on the first paper, felt an F was undeserved, and said I was determined not to bother second time around. She countered with some defense of grading policies, now long forgotten, and warned my year-end average would suffer.

I countered politely: "I already have figured it out. No matter what I get last grading period (we had six six-week periods and two exams), I can't get more than a B for the year. If I flunk the last grading period and get an A on the exam I'll still have a B."

"How do you know you'll get an A?" she frowned.

"I will," I promised. And I did. I was an ass in those days, but a smart one, at least.

***

What I discovered years later, in my own classroom, was that theories of education laid out in textbooks had all the tidy certainty of chess. So we sent young teachers into schools and they expected to play by clear and timeless rules. What they encountered was messy and confusing and the canons of chess were warped out of all recognition.

On the chessboard of any classroom all 32 pieces are animated. Schools function as they do in large part because the pawns make choices of their own. In this scenario they may refuse to sacrifice themselves to save the queen. The white rook insists on jumping around like a knight and says you "don't like him" when you tell him he can't. The black bishop has an awful home life and doesn't show up at all. You start the match with an empty square. When the bishop does arrive, in time for his ninth turn, he says he doesn't feel like moving because he was up all night listening to drunken parents fight. He lays down on his square and is soon fast asleep.

What I learned was that the white knight studies the board and plans his own moves. Often he takes positions that seem solid from his point of view, yet prove inimical to learning in the end.

This "bad-rational thinking," as I call it, is at the root of a host of problems in any school. I tried to meet this challenge head on, always encouraging the rook, the knight and the bishop to move in the proper direction. If that failed I had no qualms about dragging the white knight up two spaces and over one, even if he dug in his spurs.

I quickly discovered, if I was demanding, no matter whatever else I might do, I could have a class where four students out of 19 did homework over a weekend. Or I might give a test on Thursday, even provide a study guide, and have seven D's and six F's in a class of 27.

Some experts would say this proves "homework doesn't work" or blame teachers for "uninspired methods." I think this proves *students* don't always work unless pushed. And only real teachers understand this Sisyphean challenge. That is: it's hard to move every student up the hill.

Since I graded hard and set high standards, I had to be sure I wasn't overly demanding. One day, I asked a boy named Chris if he was ready to take a test. Had he studied?

"A little," he responded. "I was going to study more but there was a program on TV I wanted to see."

What, I asked?

"Superman II," he admitted with a sheepish grin.

On another occasion, Glen explained how he came to miss his third homework in a row. "I don't know what's wrong with me. I watch one movie and then plan to do my work, but then I see there's another good movie on cable. So I watch it, or go eat, and never get my work done."

Early every school year, before students realized how I operated, the problem was most acute. One day I assigned four pages of reading in the textbook and four questions on Viking settlements in America for homework. What I got the next day were a whole lot of dumb answers. I don't believe the fault was in the book, or in the way I taught, or in the school.

I was lazy once myself. Goofing off was fun.

These weren't answers you got because something was wrong with U. S. education. These were answers you got when the chess pieces decided it was too much trouble to move:

1. By what route did the Norse [Vikings] reach America?

Kelly said the Vikings "went through China, Mongolia, India and Venice." Mike had different ideas. He explained: "They came across it by the Pacific Ocean." That's a reasonable guess; but when we checked the section in the book, the words "Pacific Ocean" did not appear, not even on maps. Another young man took Dr. Seuss for a model: "The shores of the places they went to."

Lisa got directions wrong and did questions on another page. I could live with honest mistakes, but she didn't read that section either. Asked to describe the Inca Empire she tap-danced furiously: "The Inca Indians builded their empire with tree branches, great big leaves."

It dawned on me, then, that sympathy for "struggling" students was often misplaced. I realized many weren't struggling at all. They were refusing to move or kicking over the board and scattering pieces across the floor. One day I received a fresh bundle of poorly-done work and began lambasting my class (always in a general, not a personal way) for weak effort.[5]

If I was chewing out a group, I would say to those who had done the work, "Mary, Chas, Cam, you can tune this out."

---

[5] I tried not to criticize students, individually, but only in a broad sense, to demand greater effort. My thinking relates to my experience in basketball. (See page 41: Hardwood Maxim #2.)

"This is pitiful effort," I'd say to others, waving a stack of papers in the general direction of offenders. "I expect better out of every one of you. Do you think I won't *notice* all these mistakes?"

Rebecca offered valid defense: "Last year, Mrs. Lumpkin never checked anything. So we just made answers up."

"Mr. Dennis was the same," Tim interjected. This comment elicited a chorus of agreement.

Dennis was a good-hearted fellow but his classroom management skills were weak. When time came to check homework he asked students to hold papers high. Then he walked up and down rows to see who had their work. He was in a hurry because he didn't want the class to start acting up. One boy told me he used the same science paper all year, waving it like a patriot waves the flag. Another admitted he held up his history paper in science and earned credit. He repeated the experiment the next day and the magic continued.

So I learned if a teacher was going to assign homework and not check it, if a teacher was going to accept careless work, if a teacher was going to grade easy all the time, then the white and black pawns might adjust their effort to the detriment of learning.

One day, I gave a map test on the Thirteen Colonies. To my amazement, thirty-six students failed. Some might say I needed to question my methods. Not me. I had a fit.

(See map, facing page.)

"You mean to tell me," I stormed at offenders, again, in a general way, the next day, "you can't remember where the Atlantic Ocean is? You can't recognize this hook?" I jabbed Cape Cod on a roll-down U. S. map.

"Virginia has a pointy neck!" I stabbed the map again. "How can you miss that?"

I told everyone who failed they'd have to stay after school and study the next day.

The reluctant chess ladies and gentlemen made appearance the following afternoon and took their spots in rows. I tried to make the hour as enjoyable as possible and assured everyone I knew they could do better. Then we hammered away at basic study tips. The most basic of all: *Try studying!*

The hour ended and I sent everyone home.

The map that made the author flip!

The kids were barely out the door when my principal called over the PA system and asked for a word. I trooped down to the office and to my surprise found my judgment under question. Had I given a day's notice so kids could find rides home? Did I realize students might be getting worn out and might not benefit from staying late? I considered asking the boss if he felt I was benefitting from staying later, standing there, listening to him. I bit my tongue.

It turned out a mother had complained. She was angry because she had to wait in the parking lot while her daughter finished reviewing. And since the boss got stuck listening to her, I got stuck listening to him. All I did was try to get students to use their talents.

I gave notice, I assured the principal. (The girl told me later she didn't tell her mom where she was because she didn't want to be grounded for earning an F.) But for twenty minutes I had to justify my approach. I stood my ground and told the principal I wasn't about to accept lousy effort.

I would stand on that spot the rest of my career if I could.

The next day the "failures" stayed again to retake the test. Did they benefit? They did. The map was the same. Only the numbering and order of matching choices had been changed. After putting in time to study, twenty-four earned A's. Eight had B's. Two had C's, one had a D, and one failed to show.

I knew when I totaled results that this was a pivotal moment in my career. Checking Rusty's answers first, I was electrified to find he had twenty-five in a row correct. Dwight's paper was next. He scored 96. The next day I made a point to tell both young men, and many others, this time individually, and in front of peers, how thrilled I was with such results.

I knew, like S/Sgt. Jones, but without the high-decibel profanity, that I had managed to squeeze more out of these kids than they had been willing or perhaps known they could give. My experience then and in all the years to follow—and this example could be multiplied a thousand times—was that once students knew they *had* it to give they often started to give it without being pressed.

From this point forward, I decided I would always give those who needed a push a push. I would insist they try again. If they failed again, I would insist they try again, again.

Two Legs Suffice

***

Although I soon shed some of the ideas I picked up reading A. S. Neill in college, I held on to many of his principles my entire career. If I had trouble with a student, I felt the first place to look was in a mirror. Discipline was rarely an issue after my first couple of years. Grades always were. Most years, I failed more students than anyone in our building.

I had to be sure I was fulfilling my end of the bargain. Was class boring? Was I killing enthusiasm? Grading too hard? Did a child think I was unfair? Had I done something to upset a student and had he or she tossed in the towel and the history book too? If I was having trouble motivating anyone I checked with other teachers to see how they viewed the student's attitude. If they all said, "good kid," then chances were high the problem was *me*.

I also compared grades. If I was giving an individual a C and he or she had A's in other classes, again chances were the problem was me. If they had a D or F in history I asked, "How are you doing in math? Science? English?"

Although I graded hard the spread was rarely dramatic. A boy might have an F for me, a D in math, a D+ in science and a D- in English. In such cases I was less sympathetic.

I focused heavily on motivation and was quick to praise, alert to catch students who didn't normally do well when they did. But I had no problem coming down hard on those who were lazy. As a reformed lazy person, I knew the pleasures of doing nothing in school.

Above all, I talked with students and gave them an opportunity to present a case. The first question I wanted them to answer was whether or not they felt I was giving them a chance.

Almost all agreed I was. If they didn't, I was quick to offer a deal. I had no trouble throwing out a grade if a student said it was unfair. But my bargain had to be matched by a promise to work harder in the future. I was happy to give two chances to take a test three to make up missed work— more if need be. It made no difference to me.

The grade didn't matter. The learning did.

I gave everyone who needed one, extra opportunities to catch up, until even they were usually forced to admit—well—it *was* their fault for not getting work done. Once a boy or girl admitted it was a problem of their making, I felt we could make progress with anyone.

If I could convince a student to work, it was hard for them to fail. I offered to stay and help after school, to miss my lunch and help, to come in early, to give extra credit so kids could fill in zeroes in the grade book. If you had a D or F and weren't interested in taking me up on these chances, I phoned your parents and encouraged them to require you to stay.

Not everyone was thrilled with my system. On one occasion I called a young man to my desk and whispered warning. He was failing history. He returned to his seat without a word but by the time he sat down he was crying.

I asked him to step to the hall and tell me what the trouble was. As soon as the door closed he began blubbering.

"I hate you," he explained.

I asked why he was crying.

"Now I'm ineligible for basketball," he sobbed.

I reminded him he had missed multiple chances to make up work. I wanted to know how it was my fault, since he had to be failing at least two classes to become ineligible.

"I hate you," he repeated. It was hard not to notice a snot bubble forming on his lip.

I patted him on the shoulder and said, "Come in for makeup work tomorrow at lunch and let's see what we can do." Then I told him to take a moment to gather his wits and went back to work.

I used the same approach, offering a hundred chances to any kid who needed them, over decades to come. Each year I asked students to memorize a crucial section of the Declaration of Independence, 84 words in length. To my thinking, the ideas in that document are critical to understanding what makes this nation great. Every year, like swallows returning to Capistrano, you could count on a significant minority of students failing the quiz.

Failing, not "struggling."

I remember Henry showing up for class, taking out a blank sheet of paper, and writing...nothing. He didn't know the first words, not even, "We hold these truths." I told him to come in at lunch and try again. The next day Henry missed half his lunch. I missed half of mine. Henry still

76

didn't know the Declaration but smiled when I told him he could leave, as if his ordeal was ended.

"See you again tomorrow, Henry," I told him, flashing the peace sign.

The Declaration of Independence

We hold these truths
to be SELF-EVIDENT,
that all men are created equal;
that they are ENDOWED
by their Creator
with certain UNALIENABLE RIGHTS;

that among these
are life, liberty and the pursuit of happiness;
that, to SECURE these rights,
governments are INSTITUTED
among men,
DERIVING their just powers
from the CONSENT of the GOVERNED;

that, whenever
any form of government
becomes destructive
of these ends,
it is the right of the people
to ALTER OR ABOLISH it,
and to INSTITUTE
a new government.

Thomas Jefferson, July 4, 1776

WHAT IT MEANS:

1. Government gets its power from _____.

2. If government does not work we have the right to _____.

3. Governments are set up to _____.

4. If government works as it should everyone will be treated _____.

5. Certain basic rights cannot be taken away from you by _____.

6. Government should leave you alone to enjoy _____.

I expected students to recite the section above. They had to answer the six questions on a test over the American Revolution.

The next day Henry was absent. The day after, he didn't show for lunch. I hustled down to the cafeteria, interrupted him between bites of cheeseburger and marched him to my room.

Henry missed half his lunch.

I missed all of mine.

Henry still didn't know the Declaration. He did know something nearly as good.

"See you again tomorrow," I called as he was leaving. He knew I wasn't willing to watch him let his talent go to waste.

The next day Henry stopped by my room before school. "Can I recite the Declaration now and not miss lunch again?" he wondered.

"Certainly," I replied. "I don't like to miss my lunch either."

Henry delivered the section with two words missing and earned an A. Most teachers in this situation average grades, one high and one low. Not my style. I wanted to catch kids at their best. I inked an A in the grade book and told Henry he was free at last.

***

If you had two eyes in your head and either one focused, it was hard not to see "struggling" students often had the least work to do even in study hall. "Got it done in class," they'd claim.

Or: "I'll do it when I get home."

You almost expected someone to insist: "I'm a conscientious objector."

Saul would be a perfect example, a young man who never had any work in study hall. I didn't have him for class, but his history teacher told me, at the end of first quarter, that Saul had turned in zero homework assignments.

Saul eventually failed for the year. I had him second time around in eighth grade. When I pushed him, calling his house if he failed to complete work, he turned out to be extremely bright and starred repeatedly in skits and debates. Of course, what I did or didn't do wasn't always the issue. On one occasion, when I called home, his father admitted, "We don't know what to do with Saul. He may be spending Christmas in jail." Smart or not, the young man had pulled a knife and threatened a neighborhood boy.

Eventually, I instituted a system of my own. I sent out scouts to study halls around the building and *collected* kids who owed work.

Sometimes, I liked to watch students at the end of the day, as they packed up and headed for the busses and home. There goes Molly, a top student, arms loaded with books.

"Hi, Henry," I smile as he passes. He's carefree as a chipmunk, carrying nothing more than a light coat.

In the early 80s, Ed Lenney, my second principal, and a fine one, let me take my system to another level. All I did was look for "struggling" students and house them under one roof.

The rules on Devil's Island were simple. Each individual had to keep a homework log, record assignments, and gather signatures from teachers. They had to take the log home nightly. A parent or guardian had to sign it, showing they knew what work was due. Then the student had to carry it back and show it to me. During study hall they had to be working on an assignment or reading. No idle sitting, doodling, or Zen meditation. I offered to help anyone with any subject any time I could.

At the end of every day I stood in the hall and watched my prisoners pass by, clanking their chains. They had to *show* me the books they were carrying home. I had no mercy.

No work in study hall? Lunch detention!

No assignment sheet? Lunch detention!

No books at the end of the day? Get back to that locker, missy!

Here were typical results, comparing first and second quarter history grades (not all for my classes):

	Before	After
Mark	D	B-
Caleb	D-	C
Karl	D-	B
Gina	D+	A-
Steve	C-	B-
Julie	D-	A
Dawn	D-	D
Chris	F	D

John	D	B
Amanda	D	F
Marcus	D+	C
Josh	C-	A-
Walter	F	C
Danny	C+	B+
Bryan	D+	C
Barry	C-	B
Jeremy	C-	B-
Jason	B	A (volunteered for group)

The following year, Nancy Greenwald (later, McCoy), one of the best teachers I ever met, and I took 31 students who piled up 71 F's in all subjects first quarter under our wings. Using the same system we cut failing marks to 23 in second grading period, not Lazarus rising, but real progress.

Third quarter we started with a fresh crop of kids. Failing marks fell again, from 44 to 24. At the end of that quarter a colleague sent us a note, listing improved grades for six pupils in his class: Mary rose from a D to a B-. Agnes and Brad went from F's to C's, Doug and Jill from F's to C-'s, Howard from an F to a B.

In the Hollywood version of this story all these kids go on to college. In real life I can't claim all the teens we tried to help lived happily ever after. We couldn't say for sure we worked any permanent change in attitude. All Nancy and I could say was we did what we could.

Like Sisyphus we rolled the boulders up the hill and prayed a few remained in place.

***

In years to come, I tried to help students every way possible, to prove to them they *could* do more. I tinkered with grading until failed tests always meant a call home and a retake after school. I offered a wide variety of extra credit to appeal to kids with differing talents, and tried all kinds of tactics to give weak pupils a chance.

One gimmick involved giving essay quizzes over reading, where kids had to "write what you know," rather than focus on specifics and be tripped up by detail. I liked to start class by plucking some interesting incident from a reading and ask if anyone remembered what happened. If they did, chances were they read the entire story. I gave that person a "free A" and let them skip the quiz.

I loved catching two or three of the poorest readers in this fashion, rewarding them for effort above all.

Other times, I told classes they could read an assignment and take any notes they wanted and use them on the quiz the next day. This backfired when some of the hardest workers copied entire readings, and it seemed to me they were wasting their time. I switched to saying they could have any notes they could fit on an index card. Naturally, hard-working kids wanted to know: "Both sides?"

Sure.

On one occasion a young lady typed out lengthy notes on her computer, reduced them to size-6 font, glued them to an index card, and brought them to history the next day.

I took one look, burst out laughing, passed the card around as an example of excellent effort and gave her a "free A," plus a candy bar from a stash I kept in my desk. As always, a few "struggling" students with rock-bottom averages showed up with nothing in the way of preparation except clean underwear and socks.

Some kids *do* struggle, but others loaf and it's a fundamental error to conflate the groups. To ensure every child had a chance, I offered daily redemption and used to tell kids, "Your grade is never dead in history."

"Unless you are, Mr. Viall," some wit once replied.

Naturally, some pawns figured out how to game the system and took advantage of all the breaks. I was willing to deal with a little recidivism because knowledge *is* all that matters. If most students got it on the first try, it didn't bother me if others got it on the second, third, or forty-fourth.

8.

Water Buffalo and Rumble Seats

"History...should be, as all her most accomplished narrators have promised, not just instruction but pleasure."
Simon Schama

If you teach as long as I did, you learn there are always fresh plans afoot to fix the schools. These plans focus not on students but on new technology, new processes, new structures, or, recently, on improving the quality of teachers, as if they worked in rooms by themselves.

One problem with most plans to fix the schools is that when carried out they patch a hole at the bow of the boat and blow another in the stern. In the early 80s one idea was to fix schools by fixing textbooks. Texts would be made "accessible" to the slowest readers. That made perfect sense—for the slowest readers. In 1981 our social studies department selected *The Free and the Brave,* the best of all mediocre American history textbooks available.

In an effort to help slow readers we ended up with a book written at the fifth grade level, when some of our students were reading like ninth or twelfth graders. Sentences were chopped and shortened, descriptive words heavily excised. What remained was a "Look! George is crossing the Delaware! Go, George, go!" kind of narrative.

Here is the story of trench warfare in World War I: "Row after row of men dug themselves into the ground and fired guns at the enemy." That was pretty much the entire description of fighting.

One day Rosemary, one of the best students I ever had, approached my desk with a question. Her book was open and resting on her arm. I have long since forgotten what she wanted to ask, but not her follow-up comment: "Mr. Viall, this book is *never* interesting."

"I'm sorry Rosemary," I agreed, "but I didn't write it."

Two Legs Suffice

***

The way I looked at it, it seemed almost impossible to make history as dull as the textbook companies did.

Here we have *The Free and the Brave* on guerrilla warfare:

> In 1957 [the North Vietnamese] began sending small bands of trained soldiers into the South. They also urged South Vietnamese Communists to revolt. These rebels called themselves the Vietcong. Both groups fought hit-and-run battles with South Vietnamese government troops. This kind of fighting is called guerrilla warfare.
>
> [Our enemies] were experts at planting bombs and land mines. They struck quickly in small bands and then disappeared into the countryside.

This was adequate description, but in no way compelling, like saying nothing more evocative than: "Marilyn Monroe was attractive."

To kick off a unit on Vietnam, I turned from the text to my personal library for details. In class we focused on booby traps of all types. There were punji sticks buried in holes, points smeared with excrement, land mines to take off a foot or leg or end a life, and grenades strung head or belt high with trip wires hidden in thick undergrowth.

I'd ask students: "Which of those last two ways of getting it would be worse?"

The question made boys cringe.

There aren't a lot of "tricks" in teaching. Make presentations interesting and you always have a chance. In this case, it meant using a story from *Dear America: Letters Home from Vietnam*.

Enemy forces, I told my classes, planted an unexploded 250-pound bomb, an American dud, under a trail. Then they waited. A U. S. patrol came along and they touched off the blast. One G.I., who had passed, took hundreds of pieces of shrapnel in his buttocks, back and legs. A soldier coming down the trail lost both legs at the knees. The man directly over the blast ceased to exist.

I reached in my back pocket and said, "All they found was a piece of his wallet," waving mine for emphasis.

It was easy to keep teens engaged if I worked hard enough. One day a girl named Lorie volunteered that she had a neighbor who might be willing to come to class and talk about the war.

When I called Phil Ward that evening, it was clear he had a compelling story to share. He said he'd be happy to visit—and would later return, several years in succession, like Batman when summoned. The kids helped line up a second veteran too. Ray Bailey, a former lieutenant and local scout master, also made multiple appearances in years to follow. Phil or Ray usually brought a third veteran, a friend of Phil's or someone Ray knew, or we invited the father of one of the kids.

Phil and Ray and the others were willing to take an entire day and speak to my classes, one by one, which gave their talks an intimate, living room feel. They took questions, too, and kids had plenty. The first year, a girl asked Mr. Ward what it was like to fight in the jungle. He said he once went sixty-three days without changing his filthy uniform. This brought groans from the audience but Ward assured us after a week you hardly noticed.

Asked about his scariest moments, Mr. Bailey explained that his unit did duty as tunnel rats, searching underground enemy complexes. He said it would have been poor leadership to ask his men to go in if he wasn't willing. He crawled into the first tunnel alone, flashlight in left hand, pistol in right. After fifty feet the tunnel turned up and he had to stick his head into an underground room where the Vietcong might be waiting. No enemy soldiers were present but he admitted being rattled. Everyone in the room, including this old supply clerk, could understand.

Phil talked about his own worst moments. One night his company's firebase on a high hill came under attack. With mortars and artillery pounding their position, the men hunkered down in bunkers, until the phone to Outpost 3 went dead. Ward's commander told him to "get down there quick and find out what happened." If there was a hole in the line the enemy might be pouring through and the hill could be overrun. Phil said he wasn't going outside under such killing fire.

His captain exploded: "I'm giving you a direct order."

"I would have been court-martialed if I disobeyed," Phil explained. "So, when fire slowed a little, I flew out the door and sprinted down to where Outpost 3 should have been.

"All that remained," he continued, "was a smoking hole in the ground.

"The position and the men in it had suffered a direct hit."

Most years we asked if visitors had any funny stories. One veteran told about a pitch black night, mounting guard. He was in a sand-bagged bunker with wire strung out in front and felt relatively safe. Then—he wasn't positive—he thought he nodded off for a moment. A noise overhead brought him back to reality. He heard it again, right on *top* of his position. At any moment he expected a grenade to land in his lap. He was sure he was going to die. Fear paralyzed him. Moments later, he heard a monkey chattering atop the bunker and realized he had nothing to fear except maybe a bite.

Another visitor described riding down a dirt highway in the back of an open army truck. Rice paddies stretched out on both sides and a grenade launcher rested across his lap. "My buddy spotted a water buffalo in a rice paddy fifty yards away," he explained, "and bet me five dollars I couldn't get it with one shot. I loaded and fired and registered a direct hit.

"I blew that buffalo to bits," he admitted with an apologetic laugh. "It seemed funny at the time but I felt bad afterwards. The Vietnamese use water buffalo to plow their fields.

"It was like I blew up some farmer's tractor."

The most touching moment involved a friend of Phil's who was up visiting from Tennessee one year. We had asked the usual questions about "worst moments" and you could tell memories were flooding back he might not wish to revisit.

Finally, one boy asked, "Did you ever see anyone killed?" It was a question posed in all innocence; but I had a sinking feeling.

The veteran looked stunned. "Well, I was…in…a jeep…."

That was as far as he got. His lips trembled and tears started down his cheeks. Phil and Ray tried to console him. The boy looked at me across the room and mouthed "sorry." I raised my palms, as if to say, "It's not your fault." The veteran struggled to continue, while I tried to think of some way to extricate him from his spot.

He began crying openly, but kept trying to force out the story: "I was…in the back…manning a machine gun…."

"You don't have to talk about it," I said.

"That's alright," he sniffed, "it's a fair question."

The emotion in the room was unmistakable. The Tennessee vet kept struggling until he choked out the details. He was riding in the back of the jeep, assigned to provide cover. Suddenly, a Vietcong popped out of a ditch and fired, hitting the driver in the head before our guest could react.

When the bell rang the class filed out somberly, students stopping to thank the visitors for coming. One girl patted the red-faced Tennessean on the shoulder. Another stopped a moment to thank him for his service. I told him how sorry I was and said if he didn't think he could continue with the last class, Phil and Ray would understand. He brushed the offer aside and, voice thick, replied, "No...I needed to get it off my chest."

At the end of the day he told us he felt better after talking.

"Let us know if you want and we'll be back again next year," Ray and Phil both agreed.

***

After that, I was hooked on using guest speakers. When we talked about the Quakers and the settlement of Pennsylvania, I invited Nancy Neumann, a retired Loveland High School teacher, and a Quaker, to visit for the day. Mrs. Neumann wore the plain dress of her sect and spoke of her aversion to violence. She never struck any of her children save once. "I was asleep on the sofa one day," she told us, "and my son hit me with a toy and I reacted instinctively."

Mrs. Neumann started teaching in 1934 and spoke of changes over the years. She was no fan of "social promotion" (promotion due to age rather than attainment of skill) and said they used to hold an eighth grade graduation ceremony because "that was an accomplishment and as far as many kids progressed."

She explained that the attrition rate in high school in those days was "fearful." The problem students "simply disappeared."

Another one of my earliest attempts to bring in guests involved lining up three older women to talk about growing up in Loveland in the 1920s and 30s. Martha Wells, 81, was a lifelong Loveland resident. Ruth Hill, 66, worked in the school cafeteria. Grace Frisby, 71, was a friend of the others. Mr. and Mrs. Malott, an elderly couple, tagged along for moral support.

Martha, an African American, talked about when she was nine and saw a cross burning on a hill above her home. "I was terrorized," she admitted. But we could sense her pride when she explained how her father and his friends got shotguns and prepared to defend their families if the Ku Klux Klan came knocking.

On a lighter note, she told us about the day in 1920 when she "bobbed" her hair, or cut it short.

"My husband," she laughed, "wouldn't speak to me for a week."

Mr. Malott was drawn into discussion and carried us back to 1918 when he was about the age his audience was the day he visited. He explained how his father took him along to purchase the first car the family ever owned, a Model T, for $300.

"The salesmen drove it round the block to show us how it worked," he explained. "Then my father let me drive it home. You kids might not realize, but in those days most roads around here were dirt."

What Mr. Malott and the ladies did was bring history alive in a way textbooks rarely do. Ruth talked about growing up during the Depression. She laughed when asked about high school romance and admitted, "My friends and I liked to cram into rumble seats to get close to cute boys."

Grace remembered a time in high school when a girl who smoked was considered "fast." A woman's dean "waited in the halls to catch girls wearing makeup and order them to scrub it off."

Another time I saw a story about Henry Schaengold in the Cincinnati papers. Henry, a Polish Jew, spent ten years in a Siberian prison camp before coming to this country. We were studying government. So I called him up and invited him to speak. Mr. Schaengold had a thick accent and we had to listen closely, but he spun a gripping tale. During World War II he was accused of spying and the Russians sentenced him to twenty-five years at hard labor.

They just didn't bother with a trial.

"Life in Siberia, it came down to animal essentials," he said. "You lost track of days and veeks and came to feel almost not human." "Stinking fish 'vas za best part of za diet."

Mr. Schaengold talked about losing the tip of a finger in bone-chilling cold. He was chopping wood, with a hole in a glove he hadn't noticed. Frostbite numbed his fingers and his flesh froze to the head of the axe. When he tried to pull his hand away the top of an index finger came off. To illustrate his point he wiggled a stubby digit at his audience.

When he finished his talk he apologized in a heavy accent, "I hope zis has not been boring."

Not at all, I told him, and students applauded warmly.

One year, Kristen, one of my star students, said she could line up a Holocaust survivor, but the woman could only speak after school. Sixty students and staff stayed to listen.

Our guest told of the day she watched her family and hundreds of Jews lined up by soldiers and marched away to be shot. She saw baby carriages saved because carriages had value, and watched the Germans take babies away to slaughter.

She herself was spared for slave labor but looked on as her parents and younger sister were led to their doom.

"The last thing I remember," she told us, "was my mother turning to wave goodbye."

That simple statement, so freighted with human implication, left many of us in tears.

Often, when I turned up a good speaker, I asked them to keep coming back. Five, six, seven years running, Melvin Gilbert was happy to spend a day talking to all my kids.

Gilbert was a soft-spoken World War II veteran and all he did when young was shoot at, and be shot at by, a few Germans. The first year he visited he told me about the horrors of war when students weren't around but seemed reluctant to share in class.

I started asking him to tell the kids how he survived the Battle of the Bulge. After German forces shattered the American line he and a G.I. from another unit ended up in an isolated foxhole.

"The ground was shrouded in fog," Gilbert explained, "and enemy troops were closing in. The other fellow stuck up his head to see where the Germans might be. 'Crack,' went a rifle. The bullet hit him right in the forehead, spraying blood and brains."

Melvin hesitated. I urged him to continue. He told spellbound teens he used the man's helmet to scrape up the gore and flung the mess as far from the foxhole as he could.

Another time he mentioned how he and his buddies used a bazooka to blast open a bank vault in a town they had liberated. He laughed as he explained how he and his comrades threw German money around and "used hundred-mark bills to light victory cigars."

Then he turned serious. "In March 1945, I was badly wounded when a rocket exploded nearby. At first, I thought I was going to die. I had shrapnel wounds in seventeen places, including my head and chest, and a hole in one thigh so big you could put an arm through it."

Melvin shrugged off the long weeks he spent at a hospital down in Texas. But we could sense how much he suffered. Then he brought up that bank again. At some point an officer came through the ward where he was laid up and asked if anyone had German money.

"The soldier in the next bed said he did and the officer told him he could trade it in for U. S. dollars. It turns out my friends and I had allowed a fortune in good German marks to burn up or blow away."

9.

Case of the Egg McMuffin

*"When nothing is done to discourage wrongdoing
there is of course no limit to its growth."*
Procopius

After a soccer game one evening, I took my youngest daughter to the ice cream parlor to celebrate a win. She was nine. I summarized our conversation in a diary I keep the next day:

Emily and I had a nice talk...At one point, as we were talking in our usual, friendly fashion, she said, "You know I always wonder why my friends say they're afraid of their dads." Then she smiled and said, "Of course, when you're mad...I am." We are good friends.

That was the balance I aimed for with my children and the balance I aimed for with other people's children in school. I felt it was possible to love a person, still hold them accountable, and come down hard on occasion if that was necessary. [6]

I felt behavior was largely a function of attitude and tried to bend attitudes in positive ways.

***

When it came to classroom discipline, my approach was shaped in part by my experience in the Marines, as well as by my unproductive years

---

[6] One of the best descriptions of a good father I ever heard came from a student who described his dad as "stern, selfless and supportive."

sitting like a lump in a student desk. As a teen, I needed a metaphorical kick in the pants. But none of my teachers delivered it.

Up until the end of sixth grade, I was one of the "smart kids" in any class. Then, in seventh grade, at Eastview Junior High in 1961, puberty struck like lightning and interest in academics died. Classes were tracked according to ability. I kicked off junior high in a top group.

What I discovered in the No Man's Land between childhood and adulthood was that I wasn't going to be noticed for brains, and as a skinny 12-year-old, not for brawn, either. I had no known talents in music, art or sports, but glimpsed an opportunity to win fame with a budding comedy act. So: I chose to play the clown.

It probably goes without saying that today doctors would prescribe Ritalin.

A penchant for humor, combined with a disdain for study, soon landed me in hot soup. At the end of first grading period, my mother was called in for conference with the principal, an older woman with blue hair and scant sympathy for young wits. A few days later I had a new schedule and found myself demoted to the middle track. I never asked what happened. I never cared. Charting safe passage through adolescence was all that mattered.

Switching classes did no good. Fresh distractions compounded my confusion. My new classmates included Mary Ann, the "finest" girl in the seventh grade, impressive for two reasons. God had already graced her with breasts.

Kay was equally mesmerizing, a graceful blonde, always stylishly dressed, possessor of a musical voice. To a 12-year-old like me, Kay was frightening *because* she was beautiful. Teachers rarely deviated from seating in alphabetical order. So she sat in front of me in almost every class. At times she laughed at my jokes and turned to strike up conversation.

I tried to respond but my tongue was paralyzed by hormones. "Glaaag, glaaag, glaaag," I managed to reply.

I was twelve. No one ever warned me what questions related to sex might do to addle the brain.

If part of my trouble boiled down to a deep interest and an even deeper perplexity in regard to girls, I had other worries too. Even then I saw proof of a phenomenon every teacher comes to know. That is: *students* greatly color the atmosphere in any class.

If attractive young ladies made me nervous, Jake and the "hoods" in seats around me had me scared. I can still picture Jake in all his menacing glory, hair slicked back in "ducktail" style, shirt sleeves rolled up to accentuate taut forearms, a sneer pasted upon his lips.

Arnold, who did a stint behind bars for chopping cars after high school, wasn't as dumb as an ox, as James Thurber once said of a classmate, but wasn't much smarter. So Jake did the plotting and Arnold flexed the biceps.

Carlton was first mate of their pirate crew, the most jovial of the lot, surprisingly mature for a seventh grade boy. This had something to do with the fact he was taking time advancing up the academic ladder, often using two years where most of us preferred one.

Looking back, I can't see where teachers and students have changed much in the last fifty years. There were good teachers in 1961, and bad, and a young, blonde French instructor my friends and I considered a knockout. I don't remember her name, and don't know how to say "great legs," or anything else, in French today.

But she had them.

"Glaaag, glaaag, glaaaaaaaaaaaaaaag," I replied in class any time she asked me to translate.

Miss Hurliss, who taught English, stands out in a different way. Compactly built, with tight brown curls and horn-rim glasses, she looked like a nun in the Witness Protection program. The woman had a passion for sentence diagramming, even though most of us loathed the process. We diagrammed till minds reeled, subject here, verb there, adjectives sticking out like arrows from a grammar corpse. Thanks to her I learned a great deal about how to write.

(Hopefully, it shows.)

Another educator who left a lasting impression—and a few temporary bruises—was Mr. Rice, who ineptly taught math. A big fellow, he wore a crew cut that gave him a military air. Where Hurliss could freeze a class with her steely glare, however, Rice was clueless when it came to keeping order. If he turned to place problems on the board Jake or Arnold made rude remarks, falling silent when Rice whirled to catch them.

One day someone placed a thumbtack on his seat. When Rice sat on it he leaped up red-faced and lectured the class about respect. We respected him less for his feckless response.

Another afternoon, a classmate hid in the supply closet before math. Rice entered the room, set down his briefcase, and tried to begin a lesson. Each time he turned to chalk a problem on the board Steve was watching through a crack between two doors.

"Mr. Rice!" he'd peep. Rice would spin to face us and scan the room for signs of guilt.

Seeing nothing, he would turn to write. Steve would peep again.

Finally, the stowaway made a loud farting sound and his hiding place stood revealed. Rice yanked him out by an arm and sent him off to face the blue-haired principal's wrath.

I remember spending part of a class building a giant airplane out of art paper. Like a young Orville Wright, I launched it across the room. It sailed over the heads of admiring peers, hit a pegboard on the far wall, and hung there, nose stuck in one of the little holes. The class exploded with admiration; but when Rice looked up from his desk, where he was helping a more serious student, he had no idea what had happened or how to restore calm.

Eventually, the poor man lost all control. There were days when math ended and the floor, covered in paper wads and spit balls, looked like it snowed. On the way to school one day Carlton picked up a pocketful of cinders along the railroad track behind his house. Now, when Rice turned to place a problem on the board, Carlton let fly, a cinder cracking against the board inches from his head.

Rice whirled in fury but the class sat mute, as if flying cinders were as much a part of math as irrational numbers.[7]

On another memorable occasion I rose from my seat without permission and headed for the pencil sharpener. As I passed by where Rice was standing something in his makeup snapped. Without warning, for on this occasion I was innocent, he grabbed me by the shoulders. Then he started kicking, brown wingtips thudding into boney shins. Finally, he

---

[7] When I had a classroom of my own, I chose never to "whirl." I turned deliberately, as if I absolutely expected to catch any malefactors. It was a question of style.

twirled me round and propelled me toward my seat. My classmates were stunned.

I fought to hold back tears and failed.

Luckily, Christmas vacation was soon upon us and when we left for break that was the last we saw of Mr. Rice. I only hope he lived long enough to forgive us all.

***

Years later, in a classroom of my own, I discovered that keeping order required real art and skill. My discipline wasn't terrible my first year, but certainly could not be called "effective." My second year my methods were better. I still had a good way to go. The summer before the start of my third year I gave thought to what I was like in junior high and how I chose to act the clown. It dawned on me that the pawns *always* compute the odds.

This lesson was driven home repeatedly in times to come. One of the best examples is from my sixth or seventh year in teaching. In those days our school sat across a wide parking lot from a McDonald's.

One morning I snuck off during my conference period to pick up coffee. (Caffeine is the equalizer when dealing with teens.) The clock showed 8:16 when I stepped to the counter to place an order.

Two former students, by then tenth graders, were sitting in a booth and called out cheery welcome. I paid for my beverage and stopped to say hello. I couldn't help but ask if they weren't going to be tardy to the high school.

They admitted they were. If they showed up now they'd be tardy. If they showed up at 8:33 they'd be tardy. If they showed up at any time before 8:45, they explained, they'd be counted tardy.

It made perfect sense—to them—to relax and enjoy an Egg McMuffin and juice. This meant an additional half hour of learning lost but in their eyes that made no difference. A tardy was a tardy. And the decision to digest at leisure was a bad one only if you cared the white king was undefended.

I had little leverage when it came to herding high school kids off to class. But by that time in my career I had made it a priority to alter this kind of calculus in my own room. First, I tried to identify and eliminate "bad-rational" choices wherever I could. If students were allowed to come to class thirty seconds late on Monday, it made sense to hang in the hall and talk for forty-five seconds Tuesday. I eliminated any grace period. You had to be in your seat ready to work and I had to be at the front of class ready to go the moment the bell rang. Anything less, even if you were diving headfirst, like Pete Rose, for your seat, meant brief lunch detention.

To my thinking, instructional time was gold dust. I could not afford to spill it between my hands.

My policy was the same when it came to bathroom breaks. If students could leave history any time they claimed a need, there was no reason to hurry to the bathroom between classes. I made it a rule to take away part of lunch if anyone insisted they must go. Naturally, students complained, as did the occasional parent. Yet, when we discussed the rule, kids admitted when teachers allowed free exit they left in clusters and clumps and droves. The punishment was light. But even carving out three minutes from student lunchtimes cut the exodus by 95%.

The big change came during my third year, when I made improved discipline a priority. I got off to a good start in every class save one. My fifth period was a rowdy crew, right after lunch. Every day we wasted precious minutes settling down to work. Two or three girls were out of their seats when the bell rang, talking to friends. (This was before I implemented my in-your-seat-or-else rule.) The class clown was up sharpening his pencil, grinding away like a man possessed. When I told him to take a chair he moved slowly, almost defiantly, to his seat.

Two fellows stood out, Tom and Keith, sitting in seats close to the bulletin board. Clearly, they were potential leaders, possibly in a negative sense, if I allowed. Keith had a quip for every occasion and once or twice daily made classmates, and me, laugh. Almost as often he proved a disruptive influence. Tom was a big farm boy, bright, but not sure what he wanted to do in life or what he wanted to do in class. Like Keith, he pushed the limits when he felt he could. I went home frustrated the first week, frustrated the second.

Monday, Week Three, I came to class primed to act. Fifth bell began. The battle to bring order renewed. Time was trickling away, lost irrevocably to learning. I took attendance, passed out papers, and began our lesson.

The good students settled. They always do.

Tom and Keith were in no hurry to settle. They were calculating the odds. I called for attention. They ignored me. "Quiet DOWN," I said sharply. This silenced them momentarily.

I asked everyone to copy an assignment off the board and turned to put up notes. Laughter erupted behind me. When I turned, Tom and Keith were deep in conversation, oblivious to command.

"KNOCK IT OFF," I barked.

Again I held their attention briefly. When I turned to the board to write I lost them again. A fresh burst of laughter erupted and I turned to see the two pawns conversing happily, nonchalant as shoppers at the mall.

This marked the first time in my career I ever copied S/Sgt. Jones with absolute intent. I took three strides to the door and slammed it with a boom. That much was planned, but the glass in the middle frame exploded and slid across the floor at the front of the room. When fragments came to rest there was stunned silence. A janitor came running, broom and dustpan in hand.

(Luckily, no one was hurt, or my dumb ass could have been fired, turning this book into a short story.)

"I'll take those," I told the janitor in a quick, calculated move, trying to make the best of my mistake. "I broke it. I'll clean it up."

I started sweeping.

"Do *not* screw around in here. Do you understand?" I said in an affectless tone. Dead silence. A few brave souls nodded. Everyone went to work immediately on my next command.

I turned to notes. Founding of Pennsylvania. *Sweep.* Quaker religion. *Sweep.* No war. *Sweep.*

"You know," I assured the class, "those of you who come to history ready to work have *nothing* to fear." Tom and Keith, who knew they didn't, knew they did, and took notes the rest of the bell.

The next day—the next week—the next month—when class started, fifth bell was always ready. I assured them, gently, gently, gently, every day, that they had nothing to fear if they behaved. Keith recovered gradually, joking occasionally, but always with a wary eye. Tom was careful too. Both now proved leaders in discussion and I learned another valuable lesson. If I could control the behavior of troublemakers, many would quickly prove their talents.

One day the question of race came up for consideration. Tom's comments were interesting, but there was something dark in what he had to say. He disagreed when I told the class slaves were sometimes treated badly.

"My dad says slaves were better off here than in Africa. If they stayed there they would have been cannibals living in grass huts."

That line took my breath away. So I tried to make him think. "Tom, let's agree most owners were decent. Do you *like* taking orders in school?"

No, he admitted. He did not.

"How many of you," I asked his classmates, "would like to be living at home, in the same bedroom you're in now, taking orders from parents, when you're 30? 40? 50?"

"That," Keith groaned in mock horror, "would be *awful!*"

I smiled in his direction. "Well, then, Tom, why would anyone want to be a slave?" He shrugged, but it was clear he was mulling it over. "Good master, or not, a slave could not control his *life*."

Another day, Tom informed us his father hated "coloreds." He had not yet bought into this thinking but offered to bring in the Ku Klux Klan book of American history his dad preferred.

Taken aback, I responded: "I'd be interested to see that."

The next day he placed a large red softcover book with white titles on my desk and took a seat. I carried it home that evening, gave it a long look, and returned it the next afternoon. "I can't say I agree with what the authors have to say," I explained. But I felt I had to respect Tom was searching for truth and all I could do was help him form a more nuanced view.

Eventually, I lost track of him when he left junior high.

I heard later Keith was in a bit of trouble. Occasionally, I ran into him around town. He always grinned and asked had I broken any more windows? Keith told me he was living with an aunt who helped straighten him out. When his younger sisters came through my class he would drop by to see how they were doing. Then he too disappeared from view.

A quarter century passed before I heard from him again. One day there was a knock on my classroom door. As always, I was determined to keep everyone on task, and grumbled at interruption.

To my surprise it was Keith, an older, thicker version, but smiling broadly as before. "I just wanted to see if you were still teaching," he said by way of introduction. We talked briefly about old times.

"Remember when you broke the window?" he asked. Hard to forget. Did I remember Tom?

I did.

Keith turned serious. "Yeah, he's serving life in prison." I could feel my face fall. "Hard to believe, I know," Keith continued. "He killed his ex-girlfriend's new boyfriend with a baseball bat."

It was sobering news but I had work to do. Every teacher worth their paycheck always has work to do.

Keith asked if he might sit in and watch. I introduced him and directed him to a seat at my desk in back of the room. We were reviewing for a test and damned if he didn't raise a hand and answer four or five questions.

***

I don't recommend breaking windows, of course, but from my third year on, I made a point to be tough on kids if I felt it was needed. Because I tried hard to be fair and liked almost every student I ever met, they usually responded.

Andrew's case is a good example. I had him near the end of my career. From what I heard he could be a torment to other members of the staff. He was suspended once for pissing all over mirrors in the boys' bathroom.

By then a generation of teens had passed my way. Those coming to class knew my reputation. Even troublemakers tended to be cautious.

One day, however, Andrew was out of control. When I told him to tone it down he returned fire, like we were equals and would shoot it out. I was not dainty in my response. I did not consider his self-esteem. I did not stop to wonder about his home life or check records to see if he had A.D.H.D.

I had one purpose and one purpose only: to make clear to him a "bad-rational choice" in history was a *bad choice* indeed.

I closed the distance between us, leaned in above his seat, and snarled: "Don't *ever* talk back to me like that again." He looked stunned. I leaned closer and glared, like S/Sgt. Jones.

"DO YOU UNDERSTAND?" I roared, and he nodded, sensing debate had ended.

You can be tough, I found. You can't be mean. And you have to be tough with a purpose. You have to want to turn kids around. When Andrew settled down and answered a hard question that day, I made a point to stop him when the bell rang and tell him that was what I hoped to see.

The next day, when he answered several questions, I told him in front of the entire class this was what I *knew* he was capable of doing. I could tell he was smart, I added. I said I hoped he'd end up in college. "Lots of cute girls in college," I continued like a sage. After that Andrew never caused problems for me again.

Later he wrote a brief assignment for Language Arts. His teacher brought me a copy:

SCHOOL
By ANDREW GARRISON

My favorite teacher is Mr. Viall. I like him because he is creative. No matter WHAT the subject he finds a creative way to teach it. I also like that he will joke around with us (THE KIDS). Mr. Viall also has a strict side. He is a very unique teacher. He will be the coolest teacher sometimes (no exaggeration THE COOLEST) and other times he will be the strictest teacher ever (that's no exaggeration either THE STRICTEST).

So that's it. I tried to treat Andrew and all my students the same way I treated my four kids. If I could set proper limits I could keep those who usually caused trouble from disrupting the process of education. I tried to make sure kids like Andrew never went too far, which would have meant they got into more serious trouble and ended up suspended.

If I could work a change in attitude I could devote attention to letting their talents shine.

10.

Nothing Human is Alien

"Though the outside of human life changes much, the inside changes little, and the lesson we cannot graduate from is human experience."
Edith Hamilton

Sometimes, in the middle of one of my brilliant lessons, students would grumble, "Why do we need to know this stuff?"

Or shout encouragement: "This is *so* boring!"

I remembered what it was like to be bored in school, to wonder why we had to know this "stuff."

The question I faced as a young teacher, and the question we face across the spectrum of education today, is the same. What basics and *much, much more* should we be covering?

***

A textbook my social studies department once reviewed came with ready-made tests. All teachers had to do was run off copies and hand them out at the end of every unit. One question included on the Civil War test required students to identify the losing generals at the battles of Fredericksburg and Chancellorsville. I used to cite that example at Open House Night every fall and ask parents if anyone could supply the answer. No one ever could.

It seemed to me, then, students would be fine if we focused on more useful material. History—education, really—must have true purpose. Or we need to ask ourselves a question Henry David Thoreau once posed. "It is not enough to be busy…The question is: What are we busy about?"

A typical junior high or middle school class meets for 8,000 minutes per year. Time in school is finite. You have ten times as much valuable material to cover as you can. So a teacher should never throw minutes away.

Not one.

I always believed attitude was the driving force for every man, woman and child in every classroom in the land. For that reason, starting my fourth year, with a reputation for discipline established, that was where I put emphasis the first week. I skipped the traditional "first day reading of the rules" and went to work, trying to shape attitudes in a positive way. I had a fresh crop of students and 8,000 minutes to go. It hardly seemed necessary to spend the first forty-five trying to scare everyone. I handed out rules but told students to read them at home.

"If you have good manners, and I'm sure most of you do, you pretty much know the rules," I explained.

Really, 80% of these kids were going to be *no* trouble. Why start by scaring them? For the other 20%, many of whom would cause only minor disturbance, I added subtle warning: "Besides, I was in the Marine Corps. I don't have much trouble with discipline."

Most teachers assign seats the first day. I felt kids should have an opportunity to sit where they liked. "You pick your spot and stay there as long as you behave," I said. (See seating chart: end of chapter.) "Or until you start pummeling your neighbor."

Curious looks. That's good. Make kids think.

"Pummeling. It means 'hitting repeatedly,'" I added helpfully.

This "rules" process took five minutes. Now, on our first day, we had time to address the question students want answered and teachers must consider: "Why *do* we need to know this stuff?"

For thirty years I started my opening day lesson the same way, asking: "How many of you think social studies are boring?" Most kids sniffed a trap. With gentle urging nearly all raised their hands.

The problem, I explained, was that they had no idea why they were studying history.

"History is the study of *blank*?" I continued.

"The past," was always the first answer.

"Dates and events" was second.

"Dead people" was third.

When I replied in the negative to each, someone always tried: "Dead people in the past?"

No one ever got it right, till we suffered a series of false starts. At last, some teen would venture: "History is the study of…people?"

Good. Get it down in notes.

"This year, we will be studying people," I explained. "Today I'm going to show you people never change. If you want to make a lot of money when you grow up you should pay attention in science and math. If you want to understand people you should study history.

"Does anyone know who Balboa was?" I inquired. Almost no one ever did. I said he was the first European to "discover" the Pacific.

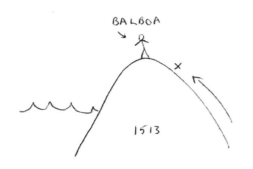

I drew a simple diagram, putting up the date, 1513, adding that we would not be focusing on useless names and dates in my class. This was merely a reference point.

I told the story of how Balboa led an army across Panama, cutting a path through the jungle, until Indian guides told him the "great sea" was over the next mountain. I added an "x" to show where Balboa stopped his army before going to the top alone. Now I asked why he would do so. I always waited for a girl to raise a hand and then called on her.

"He probably wanted to be famous," the young lady responded correctly.

"How can you know?" I wondered. "You don't speak Spanish do you?" She shook her head. "You aren't the same sex. Balboa has been dead 500 years. How could you know what he was thinking?"

I asked if anyone played soccer or basketball and if they'd ever been on a team with a ball hog. A flurry of response. Balboa, then, was no different than any ball hog. He wanted to hog the glory.

Lindsay, who had answered my previous query, turned out to be a basketball player and instantly grasped the point. That's what I wanted, for students to relate to the people we studied, to understand history was the story of humanity and for that reason had great import.

I shifted to a second example and called for volunteers to come forward and give a short speech. This was the first day of school and for kids new to junior high or middle school looked like a suicide mission. No one volunteered. I told them they could pick their topic.

No takers.

I chose two sacrificial lambs and they trudged to the front of the room, like Marie Antoinette approaching the guillotine. I kept them standing long enough to make their discomfit clear, then let them go, blending back into the crowd.

I didn't really want anyone to give a speech. I simply wanted to show that people never change.

I asked if anyone had heard of Harry Truman. Usually only one or two kids had. I said historians rated Truman as one of our best presidents but, like my nervous pupils, when he first ran for office he dreaded public speaking. The first time he tried he froze. I gripped the sides of my lectern, looked at the class, looked down and made loud gulping sounds. I looked up again, gulped once more, shifted from one foot to the other and shuffled my notes.

Finally, I mouthed a silent phrase and bolted for the door.

Moments later I returned, said sorry, had to come back, need the money. One bold soul interjected, "Awwwwwwwww, too bad."

"Truman never got a word out," I added, "and fled the scene."

Next, I asked: "How many of you could draw a Pilgrim if you had to?" Almost everyone agreed they could.

"Yeah, remember drawing around your hand to make a turkey in first grade?" Brandi said.

"Well here's a story your first grade teacher never mentioned," I continued. "The Pilgrims and natives didn't always get along. There was a fight the first week they landed. Another time, the Pilgrims saw natives standing on a nearby hill. According to eyewitnesses, they were touching the points of their arrows and making 'gestures plainly obscene.'"

Now we needed someone who knew what "obscene" meant. Then: could anyone guess what the Indians were doing? Several kids looked like they knew. It was the first day of class. They weren't sure they should say.

"It's okay. Just be careful how you put it."

"They...mooned...the Pilgrims?" Tyler finally offered.

"Yes, they did," I admitted. "Yes they did.

"History," I continued, "is the study of people. The people in the past are like us. They hog the glory, freeze up trying to speak and moon people they don't like."

I put the word "empathy" on the board. Could anyone provide a definition? The kids had plenty of ideas, all related to "sympathy."

I told them "empathy" was better. I added a definition to the board: "You can feel what another person feels."

A young lady in the front left corner of the room responded, "So sympathy is like you feel sorry for someone when their mom dies and empathy, you know how they feel, because your mom died?"

"Exactly," I smiled.

I used several more examples to make the point—that through history we can feel what others feel. This included a quote from Virgil, twenty centuries ago: "Love conquers all."

"What did he mean?" I asked.

No one was sure.

"Look, most of you have been in love. Jake, I know you've been in love!" I singled out a young man who had shown hints of a sense of humor. "Don't deny it. What does 'conquers' mean?"

"Defeats," he offered.

"Right, love defeats all. All what?"

Here Jake and his peers were stuck. "How many of you have heard the song that goes, 'Ain't no mountain high enough?'" I asked. "What comes next?"

One student gave the answer straight. Several sang: "Ain't no valley low enough, ain't no river wide enough, to keep me away from you...."

"So, Jake, what did Virgil mean?"

"It means love overcomes all obstacles!" a girl in the back shouted before Jake could respond.

I smiled and told everyone to get that down in notes. "The people Virgil knew—and the people we know—are the same."

Time was growing short and we were rushing now, rushing to cram in every scrap of learning we could. We had 7,960 minutes left. So we finished with another quote, from Terrence, a Roman playwright: "Nothing human is alien." This was the touchstone of what we would do the rest of the year.

"What did Terrence mean?" I asked, as we brought the lesson to a close. Again, we followed several false leads. Finally, I hinted: how can we tell Jake is human and not alien?

"I'm not sure we can," his friend Brad joked.

Natalie replied, more seriously: "Aliens look different."

"Nothing human is different? That's not right," I told her. "You're young and I'm old. You're a girl. I'm a guy. I'm pretty. Jake isn't." Even Jake laughed. "We need at least one more word."

"Nothing human is…totally…different," Natalie tried again. I wrote it on the board: "Nothing human is totally different."

Now students had some idea why they were marooned in history class and we had used our first forty-five minutes to good purpose.

***

That first week we dived into material and didn't stop swimming until June. That's how any dedicated teacher addresses basics and how every dedicated teacher now and for all eternity will.

In 1976 I saw a brief newspaper article about Bruce Jennings, a long-distance bicycle rider, and used it till I retired. Jennings lost a leg in a motorcycle accident but that didn't stop him. Using a bicycle with stirrups and sporting a prosthesis he set out to pedal across the United States. He was in Indiana, heading east, when Cincinnati papers filed a report.

Now I started my second day's lesson by asking students how many thought they could bike across the country.

Few did.

"Then how could Jennings do it?"

I poked at kids until someone admitted, "Well, I guess I could if I wanted," and others nodded.

We read the article, took time for comment, and I planted a seed I would water as often as possible in months (and years) ahead. How *do* people like Jennings do it? I've been intrigued by that question most of my life and wanted students to consider the matter.

I assured them almost everyone could ride across the country if motivated. The secret to success in my classroom would be the same. Which of them would be willing to pedal hard enough to earn it? I wanted teens to understand: Two legs suffice. One leg will do if you're determined.

We moved to a second example to bolster the first: the 1948 presidential election, Truman vs. Thomas Dewey. We covered details briefly. How unpopular Truman then was, only one president ever sinking lower in opinion polls. (Kids guessed who, until finally someone said: "Nixon.") We talked about how fifty reporters rode with Truman on his campaign train. One night they took a vote to see how many believed Harry could win.

The kids guessed again: "Half." "Ten." "Five." "Two."

Finally, someone got it right: "None."

I talked about why I admired Truman. Even though he knew he was going to lose he refused to quit. He decided to crisscross the country by rail, the famous "Whistle Stop Campaign." He gave speeches anywhere a crowd would gather, 275 times in six weeks. I reminded my audience this was the same man who couldn't get a word out the first time he tried to speak in public.

Truman lit into Dewey at every stop. Finally, someone in the crowd shouted, "Give 'em hell, Harry!"

Truman replied, "That's what I'm doing! I'm giving Dewey hell."

Students had funny looks. "It's okay. I'm quoting. Go ahead and put that in your notes.

"The polls showed Truman hopelessly behind but he never gave up. The night of the election it was obvious who was going to win. The people who conduct opinion polls hadn't bothered to check for weeks." I used a tone of resignation to show my hero was doomed.

Now, I held up the famous picture of the man holding the *Chicago Tribune* with the headline:

DEWEY DEFEATS TRUMAN

"Does anyone know why this picture is famous?"

If any student raised a hand and appeared to know, I ignored them and called on someone else. I wanted students to get this wrong.

"Because, that's President Dewey and he's happy," Ashley said.

"I didn't even know we had a President Dewey," Kia admitted.

"Well, you never heard of President Fillmore, either," I replied, deflecting the class from the truth.

"Dewey is smiling because he didn't like Truman," someone else offered. It made sense, I agreed.

I took a few more answers, none correct, then asked again, "Does anyone *know* who this is in the picture?"

I called on a boy who seemed to understand from the start. "I think that's Truman. I don't think Dewey won."

"Very good, sir. After all the reporters gave up and the polls stopped asking, Truman kept fighting. He kept giving Dewey hell. Over the last few weeks of the campaign Truman made a huge comeback. Dewey didn't win. The *Tribune* was so sure he'd be president they printed the story in advance, to get the paper out early and sell more copies.

"Truman defeated Dewey when everyone said it couldn't be done. He won because he wouldn't give up."

I asked everyone to take down the word "perseverance" in their notes and added a definition: "continued effort in the face of difficulty."

For decades I did my best to help young men and women see the point. We can *always* do more than we think—if we are determined—if we refuse to quit—if we have perseverance.

Seating Chart for My Class

My third or fourth year I happened to read about a teacher who did away with traditional rows. He arranged desks in horseshoe formation. There were two rows on each wing, seats facing inward, two more at the base of the shoe. His position was at the open end. From there he was free to roam the center of the room.

This arrangement proved a huge improvement over ordinary rows. First, it was popular with students, almost always a virtue. It allowed them to see each other, instead of backs of heads, and fostered a friendly atmosphere, especially during discussion.

The setup also allowed for improved discipline. Suppose, with old-fashioned rows, a child in back was thinking about poking his neighbor. Or he was penning a love note. Under the old arrangement you found yourself far away, at the front of the room, while the young man studied the distance.

To him it looked safe. He knew you wouldn't see him poke the cute girl in the back. Or he knew by the time you came down the row he'd have his note tucked away.

The horseshoe altered the calculation. If you roamed the center randomly, it was hard for anyone in "back" to zone out. If you thought the young man in Seat A was doodling, you strolled in his direction, since no rows impeded, and stood next to his seat. You just "happened" to stop nearby and ask Sara, to his right, to answer a question.

If a girl in Seat C was talking too much you walked over and without a word gave her your "teacher look" or tapped her desk.

Seat B (or its twin across the room) was a good place to locate any loquacious youth. Then you surrounded them with quiet or studious types. It was easy to stand close by during discussions or lectures and tamp down disruptive impulses. Proximity sufficed.

Cutting down minor problems helped avoid festering sores that lead to serious discipline trouble.

- Megan

Swimming

"You must do the thing you think you cannot do."
Eleanor Roosevelt

Standing in front of a roomful of teens you never know how students will respond to what you're offering. They may not respond at all, or only with grumbling. Megan contacted me via Facebook in the summer of 2013 and spilled out a powerful tale.

"Don't know if you remember me, Megan the writer kid," she began with trepidation.

I did. Nice young lady.

Still, I had no idea when she was seated in my class, fifteen years before, that she had so much trouble at home. She needed glasses for starters, she said, but her family was too poor to afford them.

She remembers squinting as I chalked P-E-R-S-E-V-E-R-A-N-C-E on the board. She said she remembers me telling the class, "In your own lifetime you will have moments you are stuck, or faced with conflict. You cannot walk away from it. You have to overcome it. Each and every one of you can overcome anything through perseverance. You have the power to do anything."

At the time, she had already tried to end her life. Now my words had a "great healing power."

"I knew what the word meant," she explained in another Facebook message. "I just didn't know there was a word for what I was doing…I had perseverance and I never knew it. A teacher broke the mold on giving me hope in such a tattered world."

How tattered? Megan's mother spent hours on the computer, visiting internet chat sites.

"She quit her job," Megan wrote, "stayed up all hours of the night online. I can recall nights, hearing her fingers tap the keys of the keyboard, hearing, 'You've Got Mail,' over and over again.

"The house we lived in began to fall apart, no food, no laundry being done, nothing to clean with. The bills stopped getting paid...All my mother did was smoke, eat, sleep and play on the internet."

Problems snowballed. Megan's parents had long since separated. Dad had suffered a heart attack, his second. He could no longer work or help Megan and her younger sister out. The bank took mom's car. By the time Megan was in high school:

I was...living in a house with no heat, no water and no electricity, and forget about food. Let me tell you, Best Senior Year ever! Nothing like taking a cold shower and going to bed freezing! Or once the water was shut off, riding your bike to shower at your grandparents.

By then...the roof was falling in on our house and I had a constant leak in the kitchen, a skylight, I kid you not.

Finally, mom ran away with a man she met through a chat site. Megan was close to giving up.

And who could have blamed her?

One day her science teacher called her "a loser" in front of the class. He said Megan would "never amount to anything." That might have been the final insult that tipped a young lady into disaster; but Megan's English teacher overheard from across the hall, walked into the science room, "wrapped her arms around me, and took me out of that class."[8]

The damage one teacher might have done was canceled out by the good done by another.

"But with hope from my wonderful English teacher and the power of one word," Megan explained, "it occurred to me I was going to make it through...I was SO CLOSE to getting out of high school, so close to

---

[8] Professional details changed, as per Author's Note. The English teacher, however, was the English teacher.

having my diploma. PERSEVERANCE. Why give up when I had already come so far?"

Megan continued:

I think perseverance is a good word…Never give up. Fight. I have been fighting my entire life to stay afloat. I am tired of swimming, but even if I give up, my mind is trained to swim, so I keep going. That is exactly what perseverance is.

In a message I sent next, I told Megan I couldn't have explained it better myself. If I was still teaching, I'd steal her story. I'd share it with a new generation of teens.

I'm glad her English teacher gave her reason to hope. I'm glad I did my little part to help.

I'm really glad Megan kept swimming and she has good reason to be proud of herself.

11.

Two "N" Words and a "D" Word

"Folks never understand the folks they hate."
James Russell Lowell

I was working out at the gym one afternoon, trying to burn off a few bag-of-chips-for-lunch calories, when I ran into an old high school friend. Ray Spicher spent a career in education, serving as a highly-regarded principal for the Cincinnati, Princeton and Madeira City Schools.

Naturally, we talked shop. I asked what he thought of standardized testing. I'm like an idiot savant when it comes to the topic and ask the same question of every educator I meet.

His answer captured perfectly what I believe is a central dilemma of school reform. He said he thought testing helped kids at the low end in school, forcing teachers to devote attention to their needs. Overall, he thought testing was a disaster.

Then he added (this is not a perfect quote, because both of us were huffing and puffing and pedaling stationary bikes), "I used to tell my staff whatever you measure you'll get more of. If you test for 'more cars in the parking lot,' you'll get more cars in the parking lot."

My fear exactly: We'll have more *cars* in the parking lot. Some will be old Ford Pintos, a model famous for its propensity to explode in a ball of flames when rear-ended. Others will lack tires and sit atop four concrete blocks. The engines of two or three won't turn over. Several that run will have the kind of air bags that explode. They'll be more cars, true, but the young drivers, if they can get them running, will have no better idea than before where they want to go.

I'm a history teacher. I know, when it comes to standardized testing, what history shows.

***

I taught long enough to see what happened in the late 80s and 90s when various states began using standardized tests. When state-level tests didn't help, I was around a decade later to witness what federal pressure might achieve. As for me, when I was teaching American history, and free to do what I thought best, I used to ask kids to take a map test and identify the fifty states.

Let's say, in a typical year, I had 140 students. By the time we were done all but two or three knew at least 35 states, the minimum required. (I'm sure former pupils will fondly recall how—if they failed—I called parents, "ratted them out," and required them to stay after school and retake the test.). Probably 138 ended up knowing where California was; 137 could identify Florida; 120 knew Wisconsin was next to Michigan. Maybe Carrie and Joel and two dozen others knew all fifty states.

I'm not going to deny there were those who mixed up Kansas and Nebraska. I'm not going to say that one boy didn't mark Tennessee as "Hawaii." I'm only saying if you're a good teacher you do what you can.

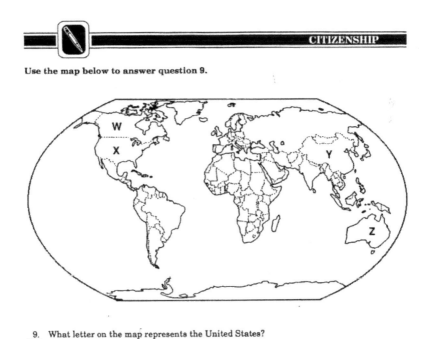

CITIZENSHIP

Use the map below to answer question 9.

9. What letter on the map represents the United States?

So: what happened in the late 80s, when the State of Ohio created a battery of Ninth Grade Proficiency Tests? This battery included a subtest in social studies. What cars were parked in the lot? The emphasis on government was heavy. That at least made sense. (We'll see in later chapters, when it comes to selecting "standards," this is not always the case.)

When it came to geography, the lot was essentially empty. All students had to do to prove "proficiency" was locate the United States on a world map and find Ohio and Washington, D. C. on a second map.

My 26 students who could find all fifty states—suddenly that knowledge meant *nothing*. It wasn't tested.

If my average student could find 44 states, which was roughly true, that too meant nothing. I needed to focus on that *one kid* who thought Hawaii was south of Kentucky and make sure he knew where *Ohio* was found. It didn't matter if he still thought Hawaii was south of Kentucky.

Ohio was the only car in the lot.

I know the Big Fixers, as I like to call school reformers who never teach, believe the fundamental problem in U. S. education is that the teachers we do have are dumb.

I know they tout standardized testing and talk about "holding teachers accountable" at every turn. I swear on my sacred grade book I have scratched my head almost bald and cannot fathom how such narrow testing represents progress.

***

By comparison, one lesson I'm proud of, created long before teachers were ordered to standardize everything, and maybe wear matching khaki slacks, went to the heart of human decency.

It began with a boy on the bus.

"Back when I was in ninth grade," I explained to classes, "we used to see kids we called 'hair lips.' I don't mean to be cruel. They were born with a birth defect involving a hole in the palate (here I showed what I meant) or lip. Doctors closed the hole. But this left scars and most 'hair lips' sounded funny when they talked.

"We had a boy like that, who had other handicaps, who rode our bus. The only person he talked to was the driver. Every morning he'd climb aboard and call out, 'Eyyyy, Brrnee.' Bernie. That was the driver's name. He'd walk down the aisle and two big high school guys would go: 'Eyyyy, Brrnee.' They mocked him every day. It made me sick then. It makes me sick now.

"If I had been bigger, I would have told them to stop," I added, "but I was skinny and couldn't do much to help."

Every student in the room could see the point. The cruelty of the two older boys. The evil of picking on one so defenseless. This held their attention and we went from there.

For homework students had read a handout based on *A Brief History of the Indies*, published in 1552, written by Bartolome Las Casas, a Spanish priest. Las Casas admitted when he first came to the New World that all he cared about was gold. He purchased Indian slaves and ignored the teachings of Christ. When he saw cruelties all around he began to feel a weight upon his soul. He freed his slaves and took holy orders, devoting his life to saving as many natives as he could.

Students read scenes like this:

The Christians, with their horses and swords and lances, began to slaughter and practice strange cruelty among them [the natives]...and spared neither children, nor the aged, nor pregnant women, nor those in child labor. They not only stabbed them but dismembered them [cut them up] like lambs in a slaughterhouse.

They made bets as to who could split a man in two or cut off his head with one sword blow...They took babes from their mothers...and dashed their heads against the rocks...Others they seized by the shoulders and threw them into the rivers, laughing and joking...and saying as the babies fell into the water, "Boil there, you offspring of the devil!"

Before classes began, I taped pictures of the Holocaust on the board and pulled down maps and a movie screen to hide them. Students entered and took their seats. I told them the story of the boy on the bus and asked simply, "How can people be so cruel?"

That was our question for the day.

"What was the worst example from last night's reading?" I inquired.

Almost every student raised a hand. "When the Spanish cut off the hands of the slaves," Maggie responded.

"When soldiers burned the building with 300 Indian leaders inside," said Marco.

"Throwing babies into the river," Deedee added.

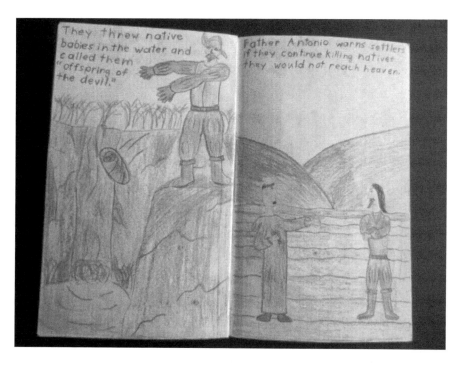

Ian's art project: to illustrate the story of Las Casas.

"How could they do it?" I asked again. "How could so many be so cruel? And what made Las Casas and others who tried to save the natives different?"

I didn't expect anyone to bite yet. I continued: "How long did Las Casas spend trying to save the Indians?"

Ken responded: "Fifty years."

I asked: "How many of you ever walk down the street and see a bug and step on it?"

All kinds of hands went up.

"Didn't you feel guilty?" I asked one boy. "Gary! You murderer! That bug had a family, and they're all like, 'Hey, when's Dad coming home, maybe he'll bring us a toy,' and you're like, 'No big deal. I'll just scrape dad off the bottom of my shoe and keep walking.'"

The bug idea always got a laugh—the last of the day. I asked how the Spanish (some of them) could do what they did. No one was ready to answer. "It's the same as the two boys on the bus. Or stepping on a bug. What did the soldiers say when they threw babies in the river?"

"Boil there, you offspring of the devil," Deedee offered.

Correct. "Now, if the devil walked in this room right now and Gary jumped up and killed the devil, wouldn't he be *good?*"

Deedee admitted Gary would be good.

"You admit you've stepped on bugs," I reminded her. "No one thinks killing bugs is wrong?"

They're just bugs classmates interjected.

Unfortunately, I explained, Hitler and his followers believed killing Jews was acceptable. One Nazi official said the world would build a monument in their honor because they had the courage to do what no one else did. Getting rid of Jews was "like killing vermin," he insisted, "a matter of cleanliness."

Did anyone know what vermin were?

"Bugs, fleas. Rats, I think," Jacob offered. I told the class he was right.

"It's a question of dehumanization," I continued. The definition goes on the board: "to see others as less than human; lower than yourself."

"I hate to tell you this," I said, "but most of you dehumanize others. You put labels on groups or individuals you don't like and you're on your way!"

"We don't kill people, though," Greg objected. True. I turned and added to our notes: "Labeling: to see all members of a group as the same, without individual difference."

In our school, students admitted peers were labeled "preps," as in preppy, well-dressed, college-prep types. Poor kids, at least when I started, were labeled "grits," dirty, lowly, unclean. Labels, we noted, allowed us to ignore the fact our enemies are human.

I threw this out: "Next time you see someone you don't like, say: 'I hate that *human being.*' It doesn't work."

I said I despised labels. But who could think of one? Every year I worried some parent would see this day's notes and flip. The examples poured out: nigger, fag, gook, bitch, jock, nerd.

"Yeah," I continued, "let's pick on him. He's a *nerd*!" I asked someone to tell me what made a nerd a nerd.

Oliver and Kayla both agreed nerds were weak. That's two "N-words" now.

"Oh! Even better! Let's pick on the weak!" I added scornfully. We were back to the boy on the bus. Students who knew they were guilty of such behavior were already shifting in their seats.

Then we moved to the final steps of the lesson. We raised the maps and movie screen. The kids came forward and looked at pictures of the Holocaust. There were young children being rounded up, Stars of David upon their sleeves. There was a grandmotherly-type looking straight into the camera. "Look: she seems like the type who'd bake cookies for the grandkids.

"Dangerous," I scoffed.

Another picture showed a house painted with the word: "Jude." "Notice," I told my class, "you can walk down the street and say, 'I hate those *Jews*!' You don't even have to see them to hate them."

"We do the same," Antoinette replied. "We label people according to skin color and don't think."

I nodded agreement.

Antoinette was staring at a photo of a long trench filled with emaciated corpses. Tears started. Her friend tugged her arm and led her to her seat. Students were subdued when I sent them back to their places. The bell was about to ring and we would pick up on the subject the next day.

I used this lesson plan for twenty-five years and it *never* failed. Then, one day, I heard something completely unexpected. Susie spoke up, one of my favorite students, but still gawky at thirteen. The lesson was finished. The bell was about to ring. Classmates were thinking about labeling and the cruelty that inevitably follows. Susie had her hand up. Clearly, she wanted a final say.

I called on her and she explained in an anguished voice, "You know, Mr. Viall, the other kids label me. They call me a 'dog.'"

For once I was speechless.

We all know teens can be cruel. No one had ever exposed this so perfectly, in such timely fashion, in its starkest forms. The word "dog" hung in the air like a Nazi victim on a scaffold.

We had just devoted an entire period to a discussion of human cruelty. Now those who had inflicted pain on Susie saw themselves, as it were, in a mirror. The image reflected wasn't flattering.

"That is *absolutely wrong*," I spluttered, my voice shaking with emotion. I looked to her peers for explanation. Chastened by a victim's revelation, no one dared utter a word.

The bell rang and I stood and stared as Susie's tormentors snuck out the door and made their escape to lunch.

***

If you're a dedicated teacher, and in my experience most are, you always try to improve. In the summer of 1996, I spent two weeks gathering material and writing a new handout on the Holocaust. The plan was to couple it with the story of Las Casas in the fall.

The first lesson remained the same. Now, on the second day, we addressed dehumanization in more modern forms. We began by listing basic terms: Holocaust; Gestapo, Nazi, swastika; genocide, dictator, and more. The last page of the reading, which we began in class, was nothing more than a large photo of Hitler's face in black and white. I had scrawled "a cesspool in the head" across his forehead before running off copies. As expected, few students knew what a cesspool was.

I had Rob, a young man we nicknamed Mr. Dictionary for his prowess with words, explain.

I did not expect to find there were those who did not *recognize* Hitler. We started every class after that by turning to the page where the dictator was shown. I wanted to ensure everyone knew who it was, with the drooping hair and toothbrush mustache. That's one of many basics a teacher discovers must be taught *only* by teaching. That's a car you need in the parking lot.

119

The story was filled with hard-to-pronounce names. So we read the opening section aloud. I told students not to worry about names and dates once I turned them loose. They should try to imagine a world gone mad. The story was titled HITLER'S BLACK HARVEST.

Angie, a hard-working young lady and one of my favorites, volunteered to be first to read:

> Most students today know a little about the Holocaust. They usually know gas chambers were disguised as showers. They realize Jews had to wear yellow stars. Some know six million Jews died. Only a few know non-Jewish victims totaled another ten million.
>
> Still, it seems impossible to come to grips with the horror. To understand the truth we must focus on the broken heart. We must go beneath the surface of the printed page.
>
> We must dive into an ocean of blood.

I asked Angie to stop a moment and allowed the words "ocean of blood" to sink in. Then she kept going:

> We must watch as German troops arrest Israel Lewi. Then we must see his tearful daughter rush up to say goodbye to her father. We must see a soldier's anger as he orders the poor girl to open her mouth. Then gasp as he fires his pistol down Liebe Lewi's throat.

"How many of you would want to say goodbye to your father in this situation?" I asked. You personalize history and every kid can grasp how terrible this was.

Caitlyn volunteered to read next:

> We must see Icek Bekerman steal a piece of leather to make into a pair of shoelaces, from the shop where he works as a Nazi slave. See him caught. Then see him hanged.
>
> We must see Sophie Scholl and brother Hans, not Jews but "good Germans," protest Nazi rule. See them paint: "Freedom!"

and "Down with Hitler!" on building walls. We must shudder as they are arrested, placed on trial, sentenced to death, and beheaded.

It is not easy to watch what we must watch. And sometimes we must listen. Hear the cries of a nameless Polish prisoner. His head has been caved in and both legs broken when police torture him to make him talk. His battered body makes a thump when he is thrown into a wood coffin and sent to the ovens to be burned. Listen now. Listen as he regains consciousness at the last second, screaming: "Open up! Open up! I am still alive!"

Listen. Let his terrified shouts enter your soul. Then you are ready to understand.

We stopped again to let the horror sink in. Silence filled the room. I warned that the reading would be hard to take and told everyone to go ahead and pick up where we left off. They would be looking evil in the eye and I asked them to see what they might discover.

I took a seat and settled down to paperwork. At first, the hush was broken only by rustling pages.

Then I heard quiet crying. I glanced up and saw that Nicole had tears running down her cheeks. I thought: I hope I haven't gone too far, but I want students to *feel* the evil.

I focused again on grading. The sound of crying grew. Melissa, normally a most enthusiastic young lady, was weeping.

Now I was worried. Had I delved too deeply into horror? Frankly, I feared some parent might complain. "Are you okay?" I asked Melissa. She sniffed, said yes, wiped her face, and turned a page. "Are you guys okay?" I asked the class. Nods. Tears. Most kept reading.

I started watching. Some were turning red, stifling their horror. Finally, I said, "Look, if this is too hard, you don't have to finish." One or two folded their handouts back to the first page and wiped their faces.

Melissa choked out a few words and kept going. "No....we.... need....to....know this," she sobbed. Classmates nodded and most kept reading till the bell rang, signaling an end to the period.

I asked everyone who could to finish the handout for homework.

The next day we focused on "empathy" once more, what I always called the "antidote for hate."

The definition again: "You can feel what another person feels."

In my experience, most teens grasped this concept quickly, that we are all human, that we are all the same.

The dilemma, if I were still teaching today would be plain. You can't "measure" empathy by bubbling in A, B, C or D on a fifty-question standardized test.

You can't measure most of the important lessons teachers try to impart. The parking lot is too puny, fifty spaces.

Max.

12.

Eat What I Serve or Starve

"For all your ills I give you laughter."
Rabelais

Humor turned out to be one of my greatest strengths and the book I read in college that most helped with classroom management had nothing to do with teaching. *Trout Fishing in America* by Richard Brautigan had almost nothing to do with fishing, either. What the author revealed was a unique way to employ language.

Eventually, I read everything he published. A story from *Revenge of the Lawn* that stuck with me was about a "witch" who lived across the street when Brautigan was growing up in Tacoma, Washington. He was eight when a friend dared him to sneak into the old woman's home after she left on errands.

Like a "midget Don Quixote," Richard set off on his quest. After tiptoeing up the steps and into the house he waved from a front window. Then taut nerves snapped. "All my fears collapsed on me," he remembered, "and I ran screaming at the top of my lungs outside and down the steps. I sounded as if I had stepped in a wheelbarrow-sized pile of steaming dragon shit."

***

I couldn't bring up dragon shit in class, steaming or otherwise, but Brautigan alerted me to the possibility that creative phrasing and off-beat comments might make it hard for teens to zone out. So, when a child got lost while we were reading and asked, "Where are we?" I never grumbled.

"Earth, third planet from the sun," I replied helpfully.

This brought moans from a captive audience but perked the class up.

I wanted to make it difficult for pupils to sit back in chairs, pay half-hearted attention, jot down desultory notes, and watch the second hand sweep round the clock. That's how I spent seventh through twelfth grades in school. I used to practice holding my breath for something interesting to do.

Got good at it, too.

So: if two kids were arguing in class I might inquire, "You're not being misanthropic, are you?"

Huh?

"Yeah, misanthropic: a person who can't get along with other human beings."

If we were talking about the rights of accused persons in court and Derek was winking at Emily, seated across the room, no need to bark at Derek.

I might say instead: "Imagine that Derek was arrested and charged with murder. He went berserk and beat Josh with a frozen loaf of zucchini bread. Now he badly needs an attorney...."

By including his name, I could refocus Derek's attention and do it gently.

If I wanted kids to get busy and they were slow to act I might single out a star student or someone I knew had a sharp sense of humor and add: "Nicki, Queen of the Dolts! Let's put pen to paper purposefully."

I had to explain at the start of every year that a "dolt" was "an extremely stupid person." Then I had to promise to use the term only in joking fashion. Once everyone was familiar with the meaning, the word became a signature of my class. One day, I made some harmless mistake.

Nicki piped up, "Well, Mr. Viall, who's the dolt now?"

"You are, I retorted," like a five-year-old with a teaching license.

"No, *you* are," Nicki insisted, happy at thirteen to play the kindergartner.

"Oh yeah? Well so's your mamma," I countered.

"Ooooooooooooooooooo," went the class.

"Well, your daddy was a dolt, Mr. Viall, and your grandpa and your great grandpa too," Nicki replied.

"OOOOOOOOOOOOOOOOOOOOOOOOOOOOOOOOO," said the class.

I pretended to weep, rubbed my eyes, and finished by blubbering, "Oh, it's all so tragic! My children are all little dolts...."

What I feared most was boredom, the cutting off of blood to the adolescent brain. If I thought I could keep kids engaged I'd try almost anything. One day, Susan, a lively young lady, made the mistake of telling me class was boring. She was an exceptional student. If she said class was boring it probably was.

I said we needed to liven up. Susan agreed. I picked up her history book and threw it out the window onto the lawn. That woke *everyone* up.

Susan was clearly miffed, even when the class exploded in laughter. She insisted I go outside and pick up her book. She wasn't going to. I told her I couldn't leave the room, because if anyone got hurt while I was fetching the flying text, I'd be in trouble.

She crossed her arms and said, "Well, I'm not going."

I was going to agree, and dash outside, when I decided to bargain. "What if I let you off the next quiz?"

She was a great student. She'd get an A anyway. Susan wavered. "What else?" she demanded.

"I'll throw in a candy bar," I added. I kept a stash in my desk and handed out Twix bars and Snickers for all kinds of reasons.

Susan smiled at last and the bargain was made.

The way I saw it, the element of surprise made it difficult to clock out mentally. Once the homework paper of a top student floated off her desk and landed in the center of the room. I walked over to pick it up and had an inspiration. Saying, "Here, let me get that," I placed one foot on the paper, grabbed to pick it up, and ripped it in two. I stood staring at half a paper in disbelief.

"That was my HOMEWORK," the owner of the dismembered assignment exclaimed. "What am I going to do now?"

"I'll give you an automatic A," I replied, and the class roared and that's just what I did.

***

Humor could also be used to make historical points. One day we were discussing French help during the American Revolution. "Look," I

125

said, "the United States probably wouldn't exist without French aid during the war."

"We should send them a 'thank you,'" Kevin suggested.

His peers and I immediately saw the possibilities. The next day we posed the class at the front of the room, with "WE ♥ FRANCE" chalked on the board. Then we took a photo and Denise agreed to write the French embassy in D. C. a nice note and we all signed.

But we never heard back.

I always teased students, especially ones I liked and those who could give it right back. I hate discrimination of any kind and we often talked about the fight for women's rights.

Sometimes, I prodded the young ladies to fire them up. Few knew, for example, why ships were referred to as "she" in the English language and were disgusted to find out.

"You would say 'the *Titanic* hit an iceberg and she went to the bottom two hours later.' Ships and other inanimate objects are referred to as 'feminine' because they're controlled by men," I explained.

This left the ladies fuming. So I tried to help. "Did you know some feminists want to spell women with a 'y'?" I wrote "womyn" on the board. "They want their own word, not one formed out of 'men.'"

I liked to throw up my arms in theatrical fashion and say, "Let's hear it! Womyn with a Y! Come on girls!"

It was stupid, but it worked, and Shannon, Midori and most of the other girls joined in, and some of the boys. I liked to compliment these astute young fellows and tell the ladies in the class, "Now look at Taylor and Kevin there. Those are the guys you want to marry."

The rest of the year, I would see Shannon or Midori in the hall, or they would see me, and I would throw up my arms or they would throw up theirs to make a Y. Womyn's rights all the way!

I also told the ladies to break the mold—to become plumbers, not secretaries—when they graduated. I don't know if Erica did; but Kerstin promised she would, only to end up playing guitar in a rock band.

Another time, I wanted to be sure the definition for "tyrant" stuck. I asked if anyone argued with mom or dad. Almost everyone said they did. "Next time they start telling you what to do," I suggested, "call them a 'tyrant' and run to your room and lock the door. They'll be so impressed with your vocabulary you'll only be grounded for a week."

I added a promise: "Make sure mom or dad has a sense of humor and if you call them 'tyrants' and they write a note I'll give you three bonus points on the next test." Colleen went home and hung a sign on her bedroom door that read: NO TYRANTS! REBEL CAMP!

Mom responded by posting her own sign: TYRANT'S KITCHEN. EAT WHAT I SERVE OR STARVE.

Mom wrote the note. Colleen got the points. We all enjoyed a laugh.

***

In the early 80s school reformers began insisting all written punishments be "meaningful." Suddenly teachers were not supposed to have students write sentences:

I WILL NOT DISRUPT MATH CLASS WITH SENSELESS CHATTER.
I WILL NOT DISRUPT MATH CLASS....

Instead, they should write "meaningful" essays about what they learned from their mistakes. Teens wrote hypocritically about how they would never disrupt math again, cure cancer and establish world peace, a "Miss America" approach to classroom management.

In a moment of reforming zeal, Kentucky lawmakers banned written punishment altogether. If teachers used writing as punishment, legislators reasoned, teachers were sending the wrong message. If writing was punishment students would learn to hate writing.

Fortunately, I was north of the Ohio River and never had to choose between conscience and the Fugitive Slave Law. One November afternoon clouds filled the sky above Loveland Junior High. Sixth period was restless, sensing a storm brewing. Wisps of snow began swirling outside our windows. I tried to focus attention away from the weather. It was a top track class and students settled. Then a gust of wind and whirl of white convinced them a blizzard was nigh. Stay calm. Stick to history. The group settled a second time.

Moments later, an even stronger blast sent snow skidding sideways and Jenny let out a shriek.

Okay, now we were wasting time.

I told Jenny she had to write. The look on her face told me she felt she was being singled out unfairly. With humble apologies to the legislators of the Commonwealth of Kentucky, it dawned on me what I needed to do. Jenny was the best writer I had ever had up to that point in my career. Why not make use of her talents?

I didn't need to punish her. All I needed to do was fire a warning shot over the heads of the mob.

"Okay, Jenny," I explained, "since you're so interested in snowflakes, why don't you write an essay about Frosty the Snowman."

Jenny grimaced to think she was being taught by a madman.

"Yeah, write 'My Date with Frosty the Snowman.'" I cracked up and so did the class.

The next day Jenny plunked her paper on my desk and said, "That was stupid, Mr. Viall." But her response was in the form of a poem and it was funny and creative and I started laughing and told her what a fine writer she was. I no longer have a copy but the relationship ended tragically when she melted Frosty's heart.

For the next thirty years I used "stupid essays" as a form of comic relief where minor breaches of decorum were involved. One day I brought a heated argument to a halt by ordering two boys to do an essay on the topic: "My Life as a Professional Pillow Fighter."

Some topics achieved cult status: "What Do People Say about Me when I Walk My Pet Banana Down the Street?" And: "My Life as a Marshmallow." One girl wrote about her pet banana, how she brought it home and "fixed it a little bed in a fruit basket...Next came the hard part: how to housebreak it." Dave described his marshmallow self: "2 ½ inches tall and barrel-chested...hobbies include tanning and making s'mores." A third student, writing about his depressing marshmallow existence, ended it all by leaping into a cup of hot chocolate. It was a ghastly death, punctuated by marshmallow screams.[9]

If ever I wondered whether such tactics were effective, the first great letter I received from a former student helped resolve the question. It came in the mail one day after I had been teaching nine or ten years.

I can still see Joey—the author of the missive—a seventh grader with unkempt brown hair, a perpetual smile spread across his face. He was bright and quick-witted and funny. Yet, his grades were abominable. He

---

[9] No scheme devised by teachers ever works to perfection. I still have a copy of Brian's stupid essay, "My Life as a Marshmallow"—written not by Brian—but in the hand of Brian's doting mother.

I had to call her at home and tell her I couldn't accept her efforts and Brian would have to perform his own penance. Mom wasn't happy. She would have been unhappier still, had I been honest, and told her that her essay was sadly lacking in creativity.

missed homework diligently, five assignments in a row. We talked. He missed seven more. We talked. He ran his string to twenty—thirty—headed towards forty, like Joe DiMaggio in reverse. We would talk again and Joey would look befuddled again and promise to do better and miss the next assignment.

Around that time, I hit upon the idea of fishing in my pocket occasionally and saying to a class in a game show announcer's voice: "You can win *all the money* in this pocket (jingling sound) if you answer the next question!" Sometimes I would pull out the coins and show them for effect.

"This *entire thirteen cents*, one dime and three shiny pennies, can be *yours* if you tell me who wrote the Declaration of Independence!"

In morning classes one day I gave a dime to anyone who could name the first man to walk on the moon. In every class someone could. So it took a few dimes to generate a bit of enthusiasm. I started offering fifty cents, *a huge prize*, if anyone could name the three astronauts who took part in the first moon landing mission.

The letter I received explains what happened next and shows how much teaching can matter:

> If you will, try and think back 5 or 6 years…In your history class I received the honor of having the most consecutive zeroes in your teaching career, I believe it was 32 or 37. In class I also received 50¢ for naming the two other astronauts that were with Neil Armstrong. And I will never forget your ability to throw erasers at pupils who were talking while you were conducting class, namely myself. I was one of the worst students in the junior high that year. Can you remember.
>
> The reason I am writing you is…to say thanks. You made me realize that if I didn't straighten my life out I would end up being a bum.
>
> It took me 2 years after having you for history to realize you were right. After my freshman year at Loveland Hurst, which was a joke, I moved to Grant County, Kentucky. I figured I would start out with a clean slate and settle down. I started doing my homework, a first, right? Believe it or not I was well respected there. I found enjoyment in excelling in my school work. I almost majored in mathematics in high school. I received

an award in my poetry class. Get this I Joey Caldwell was the only student to keep an "A" average in poetry class. I also got a couple of awards in Band. I have graduated high school this year and I am now attending the University of Kentucky. You will never believe what I plan to study, I am a pre-medicine student. You didn't faint did you? I am doing fine in college and I want to repeat a humble thank you. It seemed that you knew I had the potential and tried to bring it out of me but I would not allow you. Thank you.

Your friend forever,
Joey Caldwell

- Learning

Evaluations

"Would you like a truthful answer, my Lord, or a comforting one?"
Demaratus to Xerxes

There may be teachers who reach every student. But I wasn't one. I know I failed with a handful of kids every year. If I was too tough on some boy or girl, though I never intended to be, passive aggression might result. Occasionally, I hurt the feelings of some teen and they shut down in disgust. If I noticed signs, I apologized at once. In a few cases I heard about such mistakes only after students filled out anonymous, year-end surveys.

One of the best decisions I made, as a young teacher, was to have students rate my class. (I didn't think of providing a survey my first year, which is probably good—since I wasn't—and didn't my last, because I retired early.) It was easy enough to put together a questionnaire to get an idea what teens thought. There were fourteen questions, later expanded to sixteen.

You do *want to know the truth.* So I tried to ensure students knew they could respond honestly, no matter what they wanted to say. First, I waited till the last day possible to ask for ratings. That way, kids could be fairly confident there would be no retribution. The survey was meant to be anonymous anyway. I made a point not to look over shoulders or collect responses. I had a volunteer gather them up and shuffle them after surveys were complete. We even took time to talk about how to disguise handwriting if anyone felt the need.

On the last question a pupil could mark as many choices out of twenty (later expanded to twenty-five) as they felt applied. In June 1977, the first time I handed out the survey, 21% marked "can goof off in class." Not good. Not good at all.

Four out of five (78%) chose "teacher is friendly," while 4% disagreed, marking "teacher is unfriendly."

That last was a number I felt any educator should keep as close to zero as possible. In the next thirty years, I managed to get the "friendly" ratings up above 90% and kept the "unfriendly" ratings at 0% or 1% nine different times.

In any case, what I cared about most was whether or not students were *learning*. The first survey question was:

1. Consider all your classes together. When you take a sort of average, how do you answer: "I have learned ___ in history class than in my other classes."
A) much more
B) more
C) about the same
D) less
E) much less

I wasn't interested in finding out if I was "better" than peers. That was never the point. In fact, an answer "C" sometimes meant a young person believed all of us were mediocre.

Maybe worse.

Responses on that first survey gave me a shot of confidence I needed as a new teacher:

A) 21%
B) 34%
C) 32%
D) 1%
E) 2%.

The following year I added choices to the last question. Again, I asked students to mark phrases they felt described the class. I graded hard. So new options included: "you can pass if you're willing to work," "even if you try, you'll fail" and "teacher gave us many chances."

Over the course of my career, I flunked nine or ten kids every year. Yet, on surveys, only one or two marked, "even if you try, you'll fail." In 1991, when 149 teens filled out the survey, 100% marked "you can pass if you're willing to work."

Of course, no survey perfectly reveals what teens think, and 3% also marked "even if you try, you'll fail."

Eventually, I added a new question because I couldn't understand some of the feedback students were providing. This was simply another way to gauge what they thought of the job I was doing:

> 6. On your paper list any teachers you feel did an excellent job this year, Mr. Viall or anyone else. List as many as you like or none.

Inserting my name may have had a "leading effect" but since no one ever saw the results, except me and my wife, it hardly mattered. [10]

Was I really doing a good job? It helped me understand students' thinking to know what *other* teachers they felt did excellent work. Every year, kids were happy to express opinions. It was not unusual to get back a survey with no names listed, a vote of "no confidence," in our staff. Most listed two or three or four. Many listed more.

In 2006 here's how one student responded. On question #6 he or she cited Mr. Ball, a math teacher, Mrs. Weisbrod, a Language Arts teacher, and me.

Then this comment to explain:

> I liked these three teachers more because they did an effort to help us learn. They pushed us to our limits but at the same time made the time we had fun. They made learning easy by games that were educational. I didn't list ----- because for his first year

---

[10] I did like to share one bit of information with peers. Every year I went to colleagues who had received numerous "excellent" votes and told them so: Chuck Battle, Stephanie Beiersdorfer, Karen Clary, Bethany Federman, Carolyn Jauch, Trish Kemen, Cheri King, Kristen Williams and many others.

he gave to many notes, tried to trip us up on tests and was boring sometimes, he didn't have very much control over his students. But next year I think he'll do a little better.

I always felt a teacher who didn't consider learning sacred had no business in a classroom—and if students had said they weren't learning in my class, I would never have written this book. The high point for me may have come in June 1988, at the end of my thirteenth year. As always, I handed out the survey and asked for response. Again, answers to the first question were paramount:

1. Consider all your classes together. When you take a sort of average, how do you answer: "I have learned _____ in history class than in my other classes."
A) much more
B) more
C) about the same
D) less
E) much less

I was thrilled with results:

A) 53%
B) 34%
C) 11%
D) 2%
E) --

I apologize if that sounds like bragging. And I point these numbers out only because I believe if we're going to improve on what happens in schools we have to listen to those who *actually work* with kids. We need to hear what people who do all the fighting have to say in today's education debates. Sadly, Secretary of Education Duncan and the other Big Fixers have no clue.

As for me, five thousand students passed my way. On year-end surveys only 53 ever said they learned "less." Only 20 felt they learned "much less" while seated in my class. I would apologize to each and every one, if I could, even to he or she who summarized my efforts in one pithy phrase:

"You suck 4 real!"

Otherwise, with numbers running strongly every year, I never wavered in my basic approach.

I should also note that the "much more" numbers were never so high again. I used the same kind of tactics the rest of my career, but starting in 1989, cut back on time devoted to schoolwork. I stopped working students as hard. I still worked hard. I was still demanding. I just wasn't *fanatical* about what we did. I decided to put more time and effort into raising my four kids.

Most students still enjoyed my class. Based on survey responses, they actually enjoyed it more.

They just didn't have to work as hard and didn't learn quite as much, by their own estimation.

***

In 2011, the Bill and Melinda Gates Foundation spent good money, and plenty of it, to ask experts to discover what factors played the biggest role in student learning. According to Amanda Ripley, author of *The Smartest Kids in the World and How They Got that Way*, researchers "found that kids' answers were *surprisingly predictive* [emphasis added] of student test-score growth and more reliable over time than classroom observations by trained observers."

Student answers to these questions were the most "surprisingly predictive" of all:

1. In this class, do you learn every day?
2. Do students in this class usually behave the way your teacher wants them to?
3. Does this class stay busy and not waste time?

If anything surprised me, it was that it took a Harvard professor to design the survey and a bunch of researchers to tabulate responses from tens of thousands of kids, when any good frontline teacher could have saved them that time and effort.

I have a theory that if you asked enough kids in any secondary school in the United States to name their best and worst teachers—not the nicest—not the coolest—not the best looking—you would quickly know which educators were doing their jobs and which were not.

I noticed once that both my son and oldest daughter liked the same junior high history teacher. Abby was a top student. Seth bumped along, much as I did during my youth. At first, I assumed the gentleman must be good.

One day I asked: "Did you learn a lot in his class?"

"No, not really," they agreed. "If we were good four days a week, he let us have Fridays to talk with friends."

That's why student answers to #3, above, should be no surprise to anyone in education. You have those 8,000 minutes I'll mention again. You don't want to waste *any* if you can avoid it. And if you work at it, you can.

13.

Sisyphus Never Quits

*"Idealism increases in direct proportion to one's distance
from the problem."*
John Galsworthy

When I was eleven, I turned on the TV and did a little channel surfing. It was quick work in 1960, with four channels to choose from. A special on the twenty-fifth anniversary of the death of humorist Will Rogers was airing. I got hooked. Before he died in a plane crash in Alaska, a reporter asked Rogers to explain his special bond with the American people.

Rogers replied: "I never met a man I didn't like."

I was struck by that idea. From then on I tried to find reason to like everyone. I can't say as a teacher that I *never* met a student I didn't like; but it was awfully close.

***

I worked hard to make clear to the young people seated before me that I did indeed like them. I knew what I did every day counted and tried to move students in a positive direction.

Yet, no matter how hard I worked or how hard peers labored, there was always more we wished we could do. Every day was different and every day was the same and you could not escape the Sisyphean challenge. You had to push the boulders up the hill. You could not rest. You could not quit. If your heart and soul were in the business you did not wish to quit.

You wished you had more strength.

Once I stepped into a classroom of my own, I discovered that education theory was often nonsense. Accepted wisdom in the late 70s and early 80s held that there was no such thing as a "bad kid." I agree there aren't *many*. I would also note that public schools are tasked with turning bad kids to good—if they can. But there are bad kids. Denying that only made, and makes, the job of frontline educators harder.

In those days we were told the best way—the only way—to teach was to take students "where they are" and let them "learn at their own pace." One authority suggested we stop using red for grading. Red was associated with failure.

Purple would be fine.

My first principal was a convert to The Way and liked to remind staff he steered to the "no bad kid" line. "Some of these kids have never had shrimp cocktail," was how he put it.

The boss was enamored of a weekly brochure titled *The Master Teacher* and put copies in all our mailboxes. In one brochure the author warned us not to wear green. (I don't remember why.) In another issue he said teachers should never accuse a child of cheating. Instead, we should suggest: "You are being less than honest."

Here we have *The Master Teacher* on how to motivate lazy students, although the Master Teacher would *never* call them that:

> In the process, we must always give smaller, more short-term assignments in which immediate success can be readily attained. We may even set up contracts with the students. And we should also give these students alternate work time—even if it's before or after school. Rewards for accomplishments must be given, or motivation may not continue.

Also:

> If you want action, avoid challenging the excuses students give you. Often, a student cannot admit doing anything wrong when confronted. Therefore, accept the excuse momentarily and go on. In the process, try this technique. Point out the merits and benefits of making the situation right or carrying out a task successfully. Remember, you're dealing with an ego

confrontation, so appeal to it rather than fight it and you can walk by excuse problems easily.

I couldn't see it. I wasn't going to bribe kids with rewards and it seemed cowardly to "walk by excuses." I wanted adolescents to stop making excuses and face up to what they needed to do to improve.

(See page 38: Excuses; Parris Island.)

Another big idea in those days was "positive reinforcement." We had an assistant superintendent who was mad for positive reinforcement. It was all-positive-reinforcement-all-the-time. One authority weighed in from a galaxy far away with a list titled "101 Ways to Say, 'Zowie.'" I no longer have my copy and recall only that he suggested we say to teens: "Keen-o!"

During one seminar Loveland teachers received a list compiled by a Dr. Kubany, a clinical psychologist with the Diamond Head Mental Health Center in Honolulu. The list was titled, "86 Ways to Say 'Good Job.'" Suggestions included:

That's really nice.
I like the way you're working.
Groovy.
Right on.
For sure.

We were instructed to use "positive reinforcement" even in matters of discipline. No longer should we chastise troublemakers. We should say, rather: "Oh, Anne, I appreciate how you're listening."

In theory, praise for Anne would make Buster take note. Buster might be thrashing classmate Andy, but in theory he would cease when he realized Anne was his model.

I remember thinking, "If Buster is pounding Andy perhaps we might praise Andy!"

Something along this line: "Andy, I love the way you're parrying all of Buster's blows."

Meanwhile, experts promised positive reinforcement would save kids, save schools, save a nation. We plastered pupils with praise, pickled them with praise, pummeled them with praise. It helped in some regards. It hurt in others.

Positive reinforcement, when applied with care, can be a powerful force for change. But in the real world positive reinforcement isn't always enough. One day a boy named Ralph told my fifth bell class he liked to trap cats in bags, hang them in trees, and set them on fire. I wasn't sure how positive reinforcement would help at that moment and couldn't tell if Ralph had ever had shrimp cocktail.

Maybe I should have remarked, "Keen-o!"

A few days later, Ralph began acting up during history. I took him to the hall and when he started talking back, blasted him verbally. To my surprise he had difficulty stifling a laugh. I bent to peer into his eyes. Ralph grinned vapidly, pupils huge, irises thin rings round two black holes. High on some mix of illegal stimulants, he was soon headed to the nurse's office.

Positive reinforcement: just one way experts say "zowie" and promise to fix the schools.

Positive drug tests: just one stumbling block secondary teachers deal with every day.

***

You might think, as long as I taught, I'd have more to say about administrators, but inside my four classroom walls I couldn't see what they were up to and rarely had cause for worry. It helped that Ed Lenney and Jane Barre, my second and third principals, who ran the school most of my career, were first-class individuals, always considerate of staff and dedicated to helping teens.

In some ways my first principal also ran a good building. Unfortunately, there were times he seemed like an administrator practicing to be a dictator. Even in matters of a sartorial nature, he was strictly regimented. Leisure suits were "in" at the time. He owned a closetful. He wore a powder blue leisure suit on Monday, a canary yellow leisure suit on Tuesday, a lime green leisure suit on Wednesday, a beige leisure suit the next day, and a white leisure suit with black stitching to round out the week. As for shoes: white patent leather was how he rolled.

I wore some ugly polyester in those days myself. So lime green leisure suits weren't the issue. The problem was that my first principal micromanaged everything. This meant he often got in the way. I've never had much sympathy for bad teachers and none for anyone I felt was lazy. Still, if I had a magic wand to wave I'd wave it to make it *easier for good teachers* every day.

What I learned by teaching was that for dedicated educators the Sisyphean challenge was all-consuming. There was never a minute you could afford to waste.

What you wanted, then, was help from above.

What you often got from my first principal was piddling interference and `paperwork to fill out.

My first boss seemed to think teachers were factory workers. He was prone to call after-school meetings on short notice and require attendance. We might appear Monday morning and find an after-school session scheduled and no excuse save premature labor good enough to get anyone home till he finished. These meetings often ran ninety minutes and featured the principal reading memos aloud, memos we already held in our hands.

Several sessions revolved around lunch policy, which seemed in no way related to moving students up the hill. The boss believed teachers should not set themselves above children, good late-70s/early-80s education theory. We battled over when and where and almost what we might eat and drink. At one point he wanted us to report to the cafeteria and sit with kids while we enjoyed our relaxing thirty-minute break. We balked and scored a rare win.

Next, he issued an edict forbidding us to eat or drink during class, water only excepted. We protested. He replied, "If you have coffee, kids will want to know, 'Why can't we have juice?'"

Easy answer we responded: "A teacher is going to miss a lot of lunches to catch up on paperwork, watch students serve detention, or talk to unhappy teens. We deserve freedom to grab a candy bar in class."

During one stretch I missed thirteen lunches in a row in an effort to squeeze work out of recalcitrant pupils. One day my victim was Cliff.

Or was my victim me?

We had been working on a map in class that morning. After twenty minutes I noticed Cliff had one item labeled—the Pacific Ocean—and placed it off the Florida coast. I kept him half his lunch and he nearly completed the work. Then I gobbled down a cafeteria burger in seven minutes flat.

Many of us considered the principal's attitude demeaning and lunch policy took on symbolic import. Our school sat across a wide, paved parking lot from McDonald's and there were days when staff wanted to pick up food rather than pack lunch or eat what the cafeteria offered. The principal said no. We couldn't leave school grounds.

"If you can go to McDonald's," he asked, "why can't students?"

Again, we thought the answer was obvious. We were—dare I say it—adults. No. Professionals!

Eventually, we turned to guerrilla warfare. We might say we were going to the post office. Then we gathered orders, drove down the road, mailed our letters, and hit McDonald's on the way back, hauling contraband into school in false-bottom briefcases.

On one occasion, Terry McCoy, our excellent association (union) president, tried a novel approach. He called McDonald's. Could they do him a favor? He would place an order and walk to the edge of school property with exact change, plus tip. Could someone come to the line and hand over the shakes? The manager agreed and the handoff was made. The principal had a fit.

***

The first few years I taught I was too busy to pay attention to what other staff members were doing. I had discipline matters to attend to and lessons to plan. Then I had lessons to re-plan when those lesson plans failed. I remember talking for half an hour, as best I could, with Regina, a girl so withdrawn I couldn't get her to fill in answers on a true/false quiz. I had bullies to chastise, and chastise them I did, but this took time. One day, I spent my entire lunch period helping a young man clean out his locker. It looked like he'd been saving for years for some school paper drive. But when a young counselor named Paula Dupuy joined our staff I had a clear view of what one truly dedicated professional could do.

Unfortunately, Ms. Dupuy had absorbed the implicit message of all college education programs. That is: if you, a mere mortal with a grade book, work hard enough you can save every child. Paula worked as hard as anyone I ever saw. Still, Sisyphus *was* mortal and even the finest educator can only do so much.

Consider the four siblings of the Norman family. Three had passed our way by the time Ms. Dupuy began her Loveland career. Each, in turn, had crippling attendance issues. Now she tried to convince mom and dad this mattered greatly and often drove out to the home to pick up the youngest child. Despite her efforts the boy missed 51.5 days out of 90 in one semester. Paula went to court four times to prod the family but legal remedies failed.

Another time, a young lady came to me before classes began and admitted she had been considering suicide. We had a close relationship and I told her I was glad she felt safe speaking to me. She was smart and sweet. I said teachers loved having her in class and I hoped my daughter, seven at the time, would turn out like her. I offered to listen whenever she needed to talk.

The girl seemed to feel better. As soon as she left the room, I began wondering what I should do. She had asked me not to reveal her secrets and it was clear she felt she had exposed her inner self to view, but danger altered any equation. When I asked Paula to intercede the girl was hurt initially, but the counselor won her over and provided the trained advice I could not.

Before long, the girl's mother was calling, frantically seeking Ms. Dupuy's help. The problem, as is so often true, was rooted in the home, not the school. Dad was drinking heavily and threatening everyone. On one occasion he punched the girl's twin brother when he tried to protect his mother from abuse. Paula managed to talk Mrs. Kinzel into taking the children and moving out of the home—and if this didn't cure the problem it reduced the danger.

That's the best even a great educator could do. Paula rolled the boulder up the hill. Only ninety-nine more to go.

Tracy was another difficult case. Her grades in my class, and every other, were awful.

When I checked files, records indicated she had an IQ in the gifted range. I took her aside and told her she was as smart as me and could easily succeed in college. We ended up talking through my conference period and on through lunch. Tracy appreciated my interest and we sat down several times for follow-up discussion.

I still couldn't convince her to give her best. Tracy had her own strategy of chess. She admitted that she enjoyed being class clown. "Last year I only had two close friends and this year everybody knows me," she explained. "I went from the 'bottom of the bucket' to somebody."

Her problems had nothing to do with what I thought or what the work in class was like or how hard I was pushing, trying to get her up the hill. Her parents were divorced and she had not heard from dad in over a year. Mom was raising Tracy and two younger sisters by herself, working the night shift. That much the girls might have handled; but when mom was home she was lost in a fog of liquor. Paula took Tracy on as a project and quickly won her trust.

Then she convinced mom to sign up for Alcoholics Anonymous. Another boulder up the hill. Only ninety-eight to go.

Some weeks later the program director called to say mom came twice and then quit.

Down the hill the boulder rolled.

Paula beat herself up over such "failures," but Tracy's problems weren't of her making. The task of Sisyphus is easy where parents push their children up the hill. Most parents do. Or they help. Tracy's situation was different. The roots of her problem—and any solution—would have to be found in the home where she and her sisters were orphans in all but name.

Like all good educators, Paula was blind to the clock. She told me once she was spending hours after school talking to kids, taking them to Saturday programs, coming back evenings to meet with parents when it was convenient for them. She wasn't complaining. She was simply trying to explain that no matter how hard she worked it was never enough.

I told her if she had nine clones they'd all be busy.

The next day I gave her a copy of one of my favorite quotes. It's from Jacob Riis, who devoted his life to cleaning up the New York City slums:

When nothing seems to help, I go and look at a stone-cutter hammering away at his rock, perhaps a hundred times without as much as a crack showing...Yet, at the hundred and first blow it will split in two, and I know it was not that blow that did it, but all that had gone before.

Why did I do it
I don't know, I figured
No one cared

Why shouldn't I try
My brother and sister did it
They didn't succeed
So I might be the first
The world would be happy without me

But now I know I'm over it
My life is coming back together
Except a few things
And thats nothing to discover

As a teacher you try to help every kid; but it's not as easy as it sounds.
Suicide note from a second student.

The good news is Paula kept hammering. That's what hundreds of thousands of educators do. They hoist their hammers and let them fall. They raise them again and let them fall. I worked with Sue Lundy for decades and she hammered rock like an extra in a chain-gang scene in an old Hollywood movie. I watched all kinds of dedicated older teachers when I started, and dedicated younger teachers when I finished, and saw them pound without respite. I watched Shawn Miller, a phenomenal choir instructor, and Hillary Pecsok, a fine French teacher, whack away at piles of rock. There were times Bruce Maegly, our band director, seemed to be swinging a sledge hammer, so adept was he at turning teens into musicians. I saw dedicated administrators and counselors and school psychologists and teachers' aides and others all try hard to crack stone.

146

My friend, Jeff Sharpless, might be the prototype for all the good teachers I ever met. One story sums up his philosophy and captures the spirit of all the educators I admired. A committed Christian, Jeff explained after school one day how he came to teaching.

For a long time he wrestled with a choice between education and the ministry. Finally, after turning to prayer, his choice seemed clear. "I think teaching is a calling," he said.

That's how he approached his work.

So: good educators hammered. They cracked diorite and granite and always earned their pay. There was a dark side though to the job those who don't teach fail to see. You slowly cracked the stone, but sometimes you broke your hammer, or you wore yourself out. And there was always another stone. You could not solve every problem in a classroom no matter how hard or how long you were willing to pound.

Every frontline educator must eventually come to grips with that awful, adamantine fact.

***

Ms. Dupuy came to us at a time when positive reinforcement was said to be the solution to problems in education. She encouraged staff to go in that direction, but without pontificating. She introduced a simple form called a "STAR Award" (Special Things Are Recognized), which I started using at once.

For two or three years most of our staff adopted the form; but when miracles did not occur, the practice faded. A friend of mine filled out STAR Awards for every student who scored an A or B on tests. Then she posted them outside her room. It was a good start, except that every citation read about the same: "Wow! You earned 100% on the Chapter 8 test! Good job!"

I thought this was a little like "mom praise," which was beginning to be a problem then and swamps our culture today. That is: we praise in rote fashion because we think we must.

Lacking sincerity, praising indiscriminately, and glossing hard truths, we degrade the power of our words and breed false confidence in the young. Children know mom's duty is to make them feel better. If you only have one date in high school (how sadly do I know), Mom must still insist, "Oh, you're such a handsome boy. The girls are sure to notice, eventually."

"Mom praise" rings hollow until girls *actually* start to notice. Generic teacher praise has the same hollow sound.

I believe in positive reinforcement. I also believe it is overdone. What I tried to do was make STAR Awards as meaningful as possible. If I was dealing with top students, that was never a problem. I could have given Jenny C. and Jennifer D. and Jennifer G. a STAR every single day. The problem was catching *every* student and catching them four times a year, my goal the rest of my career. Sometimes I had to keep my eyes and ears open, mouth shut, and wait for the moment. Meanwhile, if I saw something bad I had to address that too, sometimes in forceful fashion. I wanted my words to ring with truth and had faith in the resiliency of the young and their capacity for growth.

It didn't matter what the focus was so long as compliments were specific and sincere and students' knew I respected their talents. Tina earned a STAR for poetry and Erin for prowess on the basketball court, after I saw her play for our eighth grade girls' team. Joel received a series of five STAR's (he still has them thirty years later) because he was unfailing in his efforts and possessor of one of the kindest hearts I'd ever seen. I gave Travis a STAR for great hustle in soccer, even though the game had nothing to do with school. I happened to see him playing in a recreational league one Saturday morning.

And I love hustle.

The point was to focus on strengths and potentials and cultivate them any way I could. I might compliment artists for fine work and writers for fine stories and kids who worked hard for great effort—always my favorites. Funny kids made life interesting and I made a point to tell them so. If a girl failed three quizzes, no sense bitching. Catch her if she earned an A on the fourth and write out a STAR, and call her "perspicacious" while you're at it.

Students and parents often told me how much a few carefully-chosen words meant. Katie's mom sent in a funny note:

Katie was thrilled with the STAR Award. She brought it home and placed it on the refrigerator door. (She hasn't put anything besides fingerprints on the refrigerator door in two years!)

Joe's mom called me at home a decade after he passed my way. (Not "passed away.") Joe had just finished undergraduate work at Xavier and was headed to Notre Dame for further study.

"He still has the STAR Awards you gave him," mom explained, "including the one where you labeled him 'Mr. Conservative.'"

I had to laugh. Joe and I hadn't always agreed on politics, but I loved the way he laid out opinions, clearly, logically and maturely. His mother continued: "You always made him think."

I regularly hear from former students, even today, and many have told me how much STAR Awards meant. Heather's comment, via Facebook, is a favorite: "I don't have it anymore," she explained in a post one day, "but I know mine had the word stupendous. I remember because I seriously thought you gave me a STAR Award for being stupid.

"I was so happy to learn a new word!"

In any case, the last few years I taught, at the suggestion of a friend, I started making positive phone calls, sort of "phone STAR's," if you will.

I couldn't call every home and rave. That would smack of insincerity. I did manage to call 90% and it was not unusual to hear mothers cry, and even fathers, when I praised sons or daughters.

One evening, the girl I called *about* dissolved in tears. When Lizzy picked up the phone and I identified myself, she assumed she was in trouble. As she handed over the receiver to her mother, I heard her start to cry.

I assured Mrs. Nell as quickly as possible I didn't mean to scare her daughter, then proceeded to tell her what a cool kid she was raising and what a joy it was to have Lizzy in class.

***

Ideally, you want the rocks to move up the hill themselves. Good students always do.

The trick is to motivate others—to get them to test out their own pushing capacities. It was possible in Loveland during the first decade I taught to ask to have students back in class if they failed the previous year. It may seem counterintuitive but I always did.

149

In my class I started every year the same, so a student heard the same questions (and even the same jokes) the first week in 1982 they heard in 1981 and pretty much what they might have heard in 2002. When "repeaters" had hands up the first day, I made *sure* they shined.

Marty was a typical two-year man. The first day of his second year in seventh grade, when I asked: "History is the study of *blank?*" he raised his hand at once.

I pretended he was dead and called on one of those eager young ladies teachers love, the girl with the glint in her eye, who looks like she knows the answer and always does.

"The past," she said with confidence.

No, sorry. Not in this class.

Several more stars put up shots and clanged them off the front of the rim. Now the game was on the line.

Let's see if Marty can come off the bench and hit the winning basket. He still has his hand up, waiting patiently.

I call on him and he smiles and says: "People."

"Very good, Mr. Palmer," I reply. "In this class, ladies and gentlemen," I tell his peers, "history is the study of people. That's why history is always useful."

The others don't know Marty knows the answer from the year before. They only know Marty *knows*. As far as they can tell, Marty is the brain in class. Even Marty has that look, like maybe he is smarter than he realized.

I smile in his direction and tap the side of my skull with an index finger, as if to say, I knew you could do it.

Marty knows the answers again the second day and none of his classmates realize he has heard them all before. When the bell rings at the end of class I hold him back a moment and tell him he's off to a strong start, as I hoped he would be, and I'm not sure at that moment which of us is happier. I only know Marty worked hard all year and earned B's.

Researchers, of course, have shown it doesn't do much good to fail kids and often does harm. (It is true, if a student fails twice, say, second and eighth grades, the odds of graduating from high school at age twenty are extremely long.) But it depends in part on how teachers approach "failures" the following year and researchers rarely approach students at all. The real question is: Will the child who fails change his or her attitude? The concomitant question: Will educators help?

Years later, in the middle of one of my morning classes, there came a knock at the door. The gentleman standing in the hall looked to be thirty-five or forty. The face was familiar.

It dawned on me suddenly: Marty Palmer!

I asked how he was doing. Married with kids, I believe he said. We talked a few minutes but I had class and had to get back to work.

Sisyphus can't stop pushing because the boulders will get loose and roll down the hill.

Marty thanked me for taking time to speak. Before turning to go he said, "I just wanted to stop and say 'hello' and say you turned my life around when I was in junior high."

I didn't think of it until after he was gone, but dearly wish I had been quick enough to reply: "Marty, you turned yourself around and you should be proud of what you did."

14.

We All Enter by the Same Rectangle

"A stout heart breaks bad luck."
Cervantes

I made my share of mistakes as a teacher, but I never loafed. If hard work alone had been enough to save every child, I would have saved every child. Even while on vacation, I dragged unlucky family members along to visit famous historical sites.

On a hot day in July 1976, my first wife and I stopped to tour Valley Forge. The temperature topped 100° and a merciless sun beat down upon our heads. This made it hard to appreciate the suffering of General Washington's army that terrible winter of 1777-1778. When we retreated to the air-conditioned gift shop, however, I picked up a wealth of interesting material. Studying it at home, I realized the story of Valley Forge might have value for students.

***

The following November, when it was time to do a unit on the American Revolution, I was ready with a handout titled: MISERY AND COURAGE: WINTER AT VALLEY FORGE.

The reading opened with a young army doctor, seated in his tent:

Outside, bare branches rattled in the icy night wind. Guards in tattered uniforms shivered in the cold. Inside his tent, Doctor Albigence Waldo blew on frozen hands and tried to write in his diary. The canvas walls snapped and the candle flickered with every gust.

On this evening the 27-year-old Connecticut soldier was surprised to hear the sounds of "an excellent Player on the

Violin" coming from a nearby tent. It was a "soft kind of Musick" and reminded him of home. His distant wife filled his thoughts. "A thousand agreeable little incidents" of married life flooded his memory. Waldo couldn't help himself. In his neat handwriting he noted a few tears were "forced out."

Here my purpose was to humanize the men (and a handful of women) at Valley Forge, to show these people were no different than students now reading about them. Waldo set the tone.

Patriotism presupposes sacrifice. That meant my second purpose was to make clear the miseries Washington's troops endured:

Many of Washington's 11,000 soldiers were dressed in the scraps of uniforms. Hundreds were shoeless. Snow and freezing rain turned every step of the march to misery. According to reports Washington was preparing for Congress, "You might have tracked the army to Valley Forge by the blood of their feet."

I also wanted the reading to interest students in our nation's history and learning, generally:

…A guard was seen standing on top of his hat in the snow because he had no shoes. Soldiers in shredded socks and pants suffered the agonies of frostbite. "Feet and legs froze until they became black," reported one. Most had only one shirt, and these looked like rags. John Laurens, a wealthy officer, watched each day as his single pair of pants disintegrated. Dr. Waldo took sewing lessons and felt lucky to purchase a bearskin to serve as a blanket.

The story continued, focusing on food shortages. Soldiers were soon reduced to eating nothing but "fire cake," a mix of flour and water cooked over a fire. We returned to Waldo in our story:

Dr. Waldo jokingly described the diet. "What have you got for Dinner Boys?" he asked the men one afternoon: "Nothing but Fire Cake and Water, Sir." Again that evening he asked: "Gentlemen, the Supper is ready. What is your Supper, Lads?" Once more they shouted, "Fire Cake and Water, Sir."

We spent part of class discussing vocabulary and students were instructed to finish the reading that night.

On the drive home from school later, I began thinking about more creative ways to use the material. Instead of giving a quiz, I decided to do a short skit to start class the next day.

***

When students filed in and took their seats, I explained we would be having a "fire" in the center of the room. "Soldiers" would sit beside it, warming their hands and feet by the flames. We needed volunteers to discuss camp life. Hands shot up all over.

Good. Students liked the idea.

The first group to act out the scene started slowly and it looked like the plan might fizzle. Then one boy took off a shoe and threw it in the "fire," saying, "At least we'll have something besides fire cake to eat." His "comrades" nodded and rubbed their hands and looked dejected. A chronic complainer in class starred as a chronic complainer at Valley Forge.

Next bell, two volunteers in the group set their shoes aside before beginning and plunked down beside the fire in stocking feet. After a few minutes, one keeled over "dead." The other soldiers sniffed loudly, from cold or sorrow we knew not which. The dead man's best friend tugged off his socks and placed them on his "frostbitten" hands like mittens.

A third person in the skit exclaimed, "Dibs on his underwear!"

This brought moans and laughter from the audience and I knew we had stumbled onto something big.

The skit was the fun part, but I also had a serious intent. I thought we could use the story to address what I believe is one of life's central lessons. We started with some math. First, how many men did Washington have when he took his army into camp? Danielle answered correctly: 11,000.

"When spring came, how many were left?" I asked. Several hands shot up. I ignored anyone who might know. I wanted everyone involved and looked at a boy with his arms folded, leaning back in his desk. "I'm doing an armpit check," I told him. "Let me see yours." He raised an arm so I could see. I called on him to answer.

"I don't know," he replied defensively.

"Then why is your hand up?"

He gave me a funny look, lowered his arm, and started searching. Classmates jeered my stupidity.

"You are jealous because I am so funny," I responded. Then to armpit-boy, a hint: "Page six...."

He found the answer and said 4,000. Now he was involved.

I asked how many soldiers died that winter. A student said 3,000. "Okay, what happened to the rest? We're missing a few thousand troops." Someone said they quit. A girl in the front said they couldn't take it.

The essential question was now in view. This was the question Washington's troops had to answer and the question students would have to answer repeatedly in their own lives. Why, under nearly identical conditions, did some men stay while others gave up?

Bryce ventured: "The ones who stayed loved their country."

Kelsey disagreed. "They all loved their country or they wouldn't have joined the army."

Chrissie said the men who left probably missed their families. One of the girls said Dr. Waldo missed his wife. Why would he stay?

"One man had no shoes, so he had to stand guard on his hat in the snow, so I think that might be why he left," said a girl in the corner.

"Was it colder for those who left than for those who stayed?" I wondered.

Several students said no. The girl in the corner mulled it over.

"Then what's the difference? Why, under the same conditions, did some stay and others go?"

Kelsey raised her hand again. "The soldiers who stayed were more determined," she said.

I agreed.

155

"What is determination?" I asked. "Why do some people have it if others don't? Can you buy it in a store? 'Excuse me. I'd like a can of determination.'"

Armpit Boy, who rarely spoke, raised a hand. You have to call on guys in this situation. He said it was found inside a person.

"So, I should x-ray your head?"

He gave me a look again but smiled.

We have before us a question that interests the entire class, a question offering insight into human existence. That is my goal in one ordinary classroom, dealing with ordinary teens, on one ordinary day, in one ordinary school. This is learning in its purest form.

Students offer varied response. You have to set your mind to it. You can't quit. Hang tough. It takes determination. This takes us full circle but still makes sense.

"What *is* determination?" I ask again. "What color is it? What is its smell? Can it be tasted? Can you touch it? Where does it come from and which kind of individual are you?"

It isn't that I wanted to discuss Valley Forge in detail because students needed to know about Valley Forge in detail. I wanted them to think about what *kind of people* they wanted to be. Would they be the ones who pushed themselves? Or would they be the quitting kind?

I wanted them to consider the raw power of attitude, to sense that what they set their minds to do they might then do. I wanted them, even if I reached only a few, to be more determined and not quit when it was cold, or hot, or steep, or the load grew heavy five or thirty-five years hence. I chalked the word "perseverance" on the board once more, just as we did the first week of school. Then the definition again: "continued effort in the face of difficulty."

I asked for examples. One girl talked about how hard her divorced mother worked, holding down two jobs to provide for three daughters. "And she still has time to make dinner and talk if I need someone to listen," the girl added.

Two or three kids brought up Bruce Jennings, the one-legged cross-country bicycle rider. Good. One leg + determination = enough.

Bobby mentioned his uncle, who lost use of both legs in an automobile accident. He still rolled to the gym and worked his upper body to stay in shape. Even better. No legs + determination = enough.

***

It was a time when only men with perseverance could go on.

Could you have gone on under similar conditions??

Winter at Valley Forge (1777-78).

Eventually, I decided to expand the discussion. Now when we talked about Valley Forge every year I included the tale of the "best student" I ever had, excluding only her real name. I told classes I used to

157

get excited if I found mistakes on "Anna's" papers. Then I could do my part to see she improved. "Phenomenal student," I told the students seated before me.

"One day, I went to the office to check the records of a young man who was doing poorly in history. Right behind his file, I noticed Anna's.

"I decided to pull her record and see how high her IQ was. Anna scored the same on three tests in 2nd, 5th and 7th grades: 109, 109 and 109.

"Does anyone know what 'average' intelligence is?" I asked. A few kids offered guesses. I told the class people who studied the brain, at least in those days, referred to the 90-110 range as average.

"Look: Anna had high-average ability. She came in the same door as everyone else but earned straight A's. How was that possible?" I scanned the class. "You all come in the same door. How come some of you use your talent and some of you don't?

"Anna came in that same door. At least half the people in this class right now are almost as smart, or smarter, than she was. So how could she be the *best* student I ever had?

"The teachers come in the same door. How come some are good and some are not? Name a *good* teacher." I got a flurry of comments and names.

"Not you, Mr. Viall," someone joked.

(I think.)

I changed direction and asked how many ever had a teacher who was lazy? I had to add at once: "No names." Hands shot up. One or two students blurted out names every year, and since I asked the same question for decades I couldn't help hearing the usual suspects. I cut kids off at once. Still, I heard.

Now I threw in the story of an unmotivated colleague, by then retired. Every day, he assigned the same kind of reading and questions to start class. Every day he ordered students to go to work. Every day they toiled at their seats while he remained rooted in one spot like a stump, and with similar motivation. Often, while students busied themselves, he perused the sports page in an effort to keep his interest in learning burning bright.

When it came to grading he employed a novel system. At the end of every bell pupils passed in work and filed out the door. As soon as footsteps faded down the hall he threw everything in the trash. (I picked up

158

a stack of papers from my desk and dumped them in the wastebasket with a theatrical "thump.") He never graded anything. He just made up grades and stayed out of trouble by giving everyone A's and B's, or a rare C if he didn't like you.

"Think about every *good* teacher you ever had," I continued. "They came through the same door.

"You came in the same door as Anna. Why don't we get the same results? Are you determined? Or are you sitting here, like I used to as a teen, taking up space and breathing all this good classroom air?"

I singled out some boy or girl and said, "If you aren't going to do your best you can't have any of my air. Hold your breath! I mean it!" Most of the time, they went along with the joke and sucked in a breath and puffed out their cheeks.

I finished by asking: "Are you going to use your talent in life? Are you the determined kind or not?"

The next day I posted signs prominently in several places in my room. Each read:

WE ALL ENTER BY THE SAME RECTANGLE.

At first, students weren't sure what I meant. Finally, someone realized the rectangle was the door.

Our lesson was complete.

***

Skits like the one on Valley Forge only worked if students read and studied the material. Fortunately, most did. Once I realized how much kids enjoyed skits and how good they were at performing, we began experimenting. But it was a suggestion by a young lady in one of my morning classes that sent us digging deeper into a rich lode. This was early in my career. Lisa was one of Loveland's few minority students. Her grades were middling and she could be a pain if she disagreed with your pedagogical style. Still, the young lady knew how to think.

159

One day she approached my desk. We had just started a unit on the South in the years before the Civil War. She bent close and whispered: "I think we should do a skit about slavery."

Normally, I might have steered away from the topic, lest we seem insensitive. Now, Lisa's enthusiasm altered my thinking. We whispered back and forth before settling on a "panel discussion," including slaves and slave owners. Lisa agreed at once to play the part of a slave.

When I explained her idea to the class there were all kinds of volunteers. John, who liked to argue with Lisa anyway, agreed to play her master. We picked a second "master" and I explained that none of her slaves would be present for the skit. Then we selected two more "slaves." They would be from different plantations. Their owners would also be absent. This meant variety of perspective.

In years to come thousands of students performed in countless skits and took part in panel discussions and debates and it was often subtle touches that made performances great. In Lisa's case she wore a blue bandanna round her head and adopted a field hand's manner of speech. She also ran the kind of chain you use to secure a dog in the yard round her wrists and through belt loops and jingled it whenever John claimed to be a "good master."

John picked up on every cue and threatened "trouble" when they returned to the plantation. He even carried a whip that he snapped occasionally to emphasize his point. Lisa refused to be cowed, saying if he beat her, "like always," she was not afraid.

Finally, John claimed slaves sang in the fields because they were happy. Lisa objected and explained how music lightened the sorrow bearing down upon their souls. She sang a few verses from a Negro spiritual and explained the meaning behind the words, making her point in vivid fashion.

This panel discussion, the brain-child of one creative teen, was the first skit ever designed to last an entire period. Lisa and four classmates held center stage for forty-five minutes and all earned A's or B's.

Again, I should note that I never managed to save every child. Yet, I never lost sight of the fact there was potential in every head and it was my job to tap it.

When I first met Craig, close to the end of my career, he had already been held back twice. In other words, he had a reputation for failure. A tall, thin kid, he favored Gothic clothing, and on first glance appeared to be the kind who might cause discipline problems. As it was, he rarely did homework and test scores were low. But he was quick-witted and funny and had a maturity, partly based on age, that gave him an edge in discussion. I sensed he'd be a natural in skits and encouraged him to join a group preparing for a presentation on Pilgrims and Indians.

The day of the skit, when everyone else was ready, Craig insisted he needed more time. My heart sank. I thought he meant he hadn't studied. No, he said, he needed time to dress. I sent him to the restroom. Five minutes passed. We sent a scout to find him. The scout returned.

No Craig.

I was starting to think he must have skipped out the back when an old lady in full-length black dress and lace collar, gray hair pulled back in a bun, entered the room.

Granny sported blue-tinted hippie glasses.

For the next forty minutes "Granny Craig" was as good as anyone I ever saw in a skit. He knew why the Pilgrims went to Holland in 1609, before coming to America, and why they left. He knew what weather was like when they arrived on these far shores and cackled as he explained. Sometimes he stumbled over answers, but only in character, as if memory was fading with age. He said he was shocked when those natives mooned the settlement (see page 103)—and said it like he meant it. Once he hiked his dress to show a little Pilgrim ankle and called in my direction: "Hey, baby, give me a call!"

Classmates were enthralled.

When the bell was about to ring we ended a minute early so I could tell everyone what a wonderful job they'd done. I singled Craig out for praise. "How many think Craig deserves an A+?" Every hand went up and we awarded him a perfect score by acclamation.

In the late 80s the State of Ohio began tinkering with curriculum as part of an early effort to raise standards in the schools. Over the next decade Ohio focused on a battery of Ninth Grade Proficiency Tests. Government was stressed. So social studies teachers increased government coverage. At one point, I interviewed a Hamilton County commissioner and put together a handout on county government. Next: over to Clermont County to talk to the county prosecutor and create a handout on the civil and criminal justice system.

I kept adding material and by 2000 my unit test on government had grown to 150 questions, requiring two days to complete. That spring, Becky, a top student, came to me with a fantastic idea. Why not do a skit on the three branches of government? I told her I could have scratched my head a thousand years and not come up with that idea. But I could see the possibilities a soon as she broached the subject. The next day we put her idea out for every class to consider.

In seventh period Kimball approached to ask if he and three friends could volunteer. What was his plan, I wondered? He said he would be one of four superheroes, known as Executive Man. His friend Evan would be Legislative Man, a third boy would be Judicial Man, and the fourth would portray People Man, representing the citizens of this fine nation.

I gave the go ahead with a smile, but could not have imagined the creative fashion in which four young men would put plan into action. The day of the skit they dressed in capes and t-shirts, lettered "P" for People Man, "E" for Executive Man, and so forth. One boy wore shorts and red tights. Evan played Legislative Man as a hero with a split personality, half House of Representatives, half Senate. If he answered for the Senate he faced one way. Then he turned the other direction to reply, often disagreeably, as the House.

I can't remember who the other two boys were, but know this: The quartet was working from a list of 150 review questions for the coming test. Not once did they make a factual error and it turned out to be a hilarious way to review local, state and federal government.

Of course, school reformers are never satisfied. This year's reformers always have better ideas than the last. Once No Child Left Behind was enshrined in law, the State of Ohio dumped the Ninth Grade Proficiency Tests. Success would now be measured according to performance on a new Ohio Achievement Test.

The experts demanded that schools measure what students were learning. So the OAT would cover three years of social studies material and do it in fifty questions.

I had been trying to hold students accountable for three times as much material on a single unit test. As was often the case, I studied changes in education and couldn't see how this represented progress.

15.

Poison Ivy Dilemma

"Three factors over which parents exercise authority—student absenteeism, variety of reading materials in the home, and excessive television watching—explain nearly 90 percent of the difference in performance between high- and low-achieving status."
Richard Riley, U. S. Secretary of Education

You don't have to teach long to discover that some problems "in" schools have deep roots outside your classroom, where you are unable to take an axe in hand and cut them.

A call I took at home late one June reveals an obstacle that sits square in the path of every plan to "fix the schools." Classes had ended two weeks earlier. I was lounging on my couch, dressed in flip flops and basketball shorts. The ringing of my phone interrupted my reverie.

Mrs. Featheroff was on the line. (I always handed out my home number to parents and students.) She wanted to ask about Mike's history grade. Mike had failed history for the year.

Mike had failed math.

Also science.

Mike had failed Language Arts, art and gym. Now he had been retained in seventh grade and mom had just received notice.

I remember asking: Didn't you see his grades all year? No, she admitted. Mike owed a fine and our school wouldn't send report cards home or release records if library fines or fees were owed.

I never liked that policy. Still, I wanted to ask: Do you think the fact he was absent 106 days hurt? Only my Dad taught me to be polite. (In Ohio the school year is 180 days.)

Well, what she really wanted to know was, "Is there any way Mike can still pass history?"

Keep this in mind next time you hear low test scores blamed on men and women at the front of every room. Mom had not seen a report card all year and had never bothered to inquire. She had allowed her son to stay home, on average, three days a week. Sending multiple letters home and citing her to court had had no discernable effect. I called home once each quarter, myself, to warn that Mike was faring poorly. No doubt other teachers phoned as well. My door was open before school, during lunch, after school, any time Mike cared to make up work.

Assuming he showed up for school at all.

I liked Mike too; but I have talked to teachers, counselors and administrators who have gone out to homes like cowboys in an effort to round up strays. Where excessive absenteeism is involved it makes more sense to say we're going to "fix pediatrician's offices," than to think fixing schools is the imperative.

In recent years, schools have done more and more to ensure parents have access to their child's records. In Loveland, we started posting grades online in the late-90s. Teachers made more and more phone calls home. More and more letters went off in the mail. You still had a certain percentage of parents who wouldn't have paid attention unless you hit them in the head with a plank.

***

Of course, the idea teachers possess some sort of magical power is not new. When I began my career, liberal thinking dominated academic circles. I'm a liberal, too, but that meant there was plenty of liberal baloney for everyone to chew. I recall administrators who insisted in good faith and with straight faces: "If a student fails, the teacher fails."

I always wanted to ask: "If a teacher fails, does that mean administrators fail?" Alas, it would be several years before I gained tenure and could unleash my sterling wit.

Here's what I realized early on. Kids sometimes faked sick, stayed home, and ruined their chances for a quality education. One day, Harold, a boy in my first bell class, was missing when I took attendance.

"Has anyone seen Harold?" I inquired, before sending an attendance slip to the office. He might be at his locker. Perhaps someone had seen him on the bus or in the hall.

A girl exclaimed, "Harold's absent today because he said he didn't want to take his science test."

(Later, a check of records showed he missed 39 days the previous year and showed up tardy 26 times.)

It didn't take a genius to realize this was a problem and not one of mine or other educators' making. If students missed thirty or forty or fifty days annually, or even a hundred, maybe the fault was in the student or in the family. If a child failed to get a good education because of chronic absenteeism, maybe teachers didn't fail at all. Maybe parents failed.

Or alarm clock companies.

Suppose we really want to make improvements in U. S. education. If that's true our leaders are going to have to admit there are challenges beyond schools' control and see them as the societal problems they are. They're going to have to consider issues like the "Poison Ivy Dilemma." They're going to have to understand students often fall behind in *school* because they're not *in* school.

And they're often not in school because they choose not to be— and their parents don't do anything. Or their parents *are* the problem. Do kids choose to skip school? They do. A friend of mine once told me that when she was in fifth grade she discovered a perfect way to get out of going to school. She was allergic to poison ivy. If she wanted to stay home for a few days she rubbed her arms and legs with leaves and no one was the wiser.

As early as the mid-80s, my colleagues and I were concerned enough to collect examples and submit them to our school board and administration. Referring to the chart that follows (next page) might help the reader grasp how vexing this issue is for every educator. Mary, an eighth grader, was pregnant at the time we drew up the chart and rarely made school. Zach would end up in drug rehab. Aaron would pile up 452 days of absence during nine years in the Loveland City Schools. Casey's mother wanted him to go to school but admitted during one meeting she tried to get him up every morning. He was twice her size and prone to violence.

165

Appendix A

Name

Shannon 24 1/2 + 8

Amanda 38 + 3

Kallie 36 1/2 + 14

Bobby 53 1/2 + 5

Mary 81 1/2 + 4

Noah 36 /1/2 + 2

Candace 16 + 27

Aaron 39 +2

Zach 40 + 31

Wendy 34 +13

Imelda 31 + 19

Karen 34 + 20

Chart shows absences and tardies, January-March only.

X = full day absent; / = half day absent; T = tardy.

Totals at left indicate absences and tardies for year, to the end of March.

"When I try to make him get out of bed," she said, "he looks like he's going to hit me."

At that, she started to cry.

As you might guess, there was no dad around. That's another problem that has had a highly negative effect in schools. In 1950 only 6% of U. S. children lived in one-parent homes. By 1995 the figure was 24%. By 2012 it was 35%, including two out of every three young African Americans.

The issue only looks uglier when we broaden it out. By 2003 the future of every public school and every public school educator in America was tied to "standards" under No Child Left Behind. One benchmark was attendance—which seemed insane.

Another "standard" by which schools were measured was graduation rate, meaning educators took a legislative cuff on each ear. If a young man or young woman stayed home, say 35 days a year, and scored poorly on standardized tests, teachers and administrators took the heat. If they continued to miss at the same rate and "solved" the problem—that is, a disinterest in getting up and going to school—by dropping out, educators got faulted for that too.

The term "dropout factory" became a staple of the Big Fixer lexicon. The implication was that those who worked in schools were *purposely* creating dropouts when, in reality, they had limited control. In Ohio a teen could not legally drop out till age eighteen—or age sixteen, if they had a full-time job and *parental* permission. The law proved unenforceable. In a typical year more than 23,000 underage teens simply walked away from schools and never returned.

Nor could I help notice while working on this book that even the Big Fixers had failed to solve the Poison Ivy Dilemma. When Mayor Michael R. Bloomberg ran New York City and Joel I. Klein was his school chancellor they were unable to dent the problem. In April 2010 *The New York Times* noted that 140,000 public school students in the city missed a month or more of classes every year. Another source, in 2012, put the figure at 200,000.

Michelle Rhee also failed to deal with the issue when she ran the Washington, D. C. schools. The *Washington Post* could report in 2014 that one of every five D. C. students had at least twenty days of unexcused absence annually.

And that didn't include excused absences.

In Chicago the story was grimmer still. Ron Huberman, a former beat cop—which ought to tell you something—vowed to fix the schools after he was tapped to head the district. Ironically, these were the same schools Secretary Duncan "fixed" a few years before.

According to newspaper accounts, Huberman was planning a new approach to violence that had seen scores of youngsters killed or wounded and turned poor Chicago neighborhoods "into precincts of terror and despair." In a two-year period 500 school-age children were killed or wounded in shootings across the city. Research showed students most at risk attended 38 of 140 schools. Those most likely to fall victim to gun violence were absent 40% of the time.

(That would be 72 days per year.)

In the toughest neighborhoods kids were dealing with gang turf wars. School leaders hoped to create "safe-passage lanes" so they could come and go without suffering harm.

Huberman planned to remake the worst schools, even though Duncan had already won acclaim by remaking them when he was superintendent. There would be increased counseling, more effective training for security guards, and changes to a discipline system reporters described as designed to throw "children" out of school "as quickly as possible."

The most chaotic schools, attended by most high-risk students, were different from better-run schools. Or so reporters said. They suspended and expelled more kids and were quicker to "involve police in minor skirmishes, like shoving matches, that then go unresolved."

I remember reading that story and thinking reporters had no idea what they were talking about. Neighborhoods were precincts of terror and despair. It wasn't safe to *come* to school. Kids at greatest risk were roaming the streets 40% of the time. Most school-aged children getting shot were getting shot by other school-age children.

These weren't problems rooted in schools and focusing on "fixing schools" seemed absurd. How absurd? There are 17,000 "school resource officers" presently at work in the halls of U. S. education. That's a euphemism for "cops."

And that fact reflects directly on problems in society rather than problems in the schools.

In December 2009 the Chicago Public Schools began assigning advocates to work one-on-one with students most at risk. They often served as replacements for missing parents. They tutored, consoled, advised and visited hospitals when kids were wounded. One helped a boy's family move to a safer block.

This plan acknowledged a fundamental truth. Troubled youngsters "are often on their own. So trying to reach them through their families can be futile."

Despite efforts aimed at *school* reform, the carnage continued the following school year, with dozens of young people killed or wounded. Pick up the paper, though, and what solutions are people like Bloomberg, Duncan and Rhee peddling? They insist we can fix education if we give more standardized tests—hold teachers accountable—if we "grade" schools.

For obvious reasons, this kind of blindness makes real educators sick.

***

Do I have suggestions to offer, other than hiring teachers with telepathic powers? Short of creating residential schools for children who are chronically absent, I'm not sure I do.

I know the Poison Ivy Dilemma is there, a problem to a greater or lesser degree in every school, and that we ignore it to the detriment of young Americans.

In the spring of 2012 Johns Hopkins University released a scholarly report titled: *The Importance of Being in School: A Report on Absenteeism in the Nation's Public Schools.* It was said to be the first effort to quantify chronic absenteeism at the national level. Based on statistics compiled by Bob Balfanz and Vaughan Byrnes, it was estimated between five and seven-and-a-half million students missed a month of class or more and did it every year.

Huffington Post summed up findings:

Chronic absenteeism—defined as missing at least 10 percent of school days—is more prevalent among high-poverty students. In New York City, 200,000 students, or 20 percent, were chronically absent in the 2010-2011 school year. In Baltimore, one-fourth of all students missed more than a month of school during the same year...[Balfanz and Byrnes] estimate that between 10 and 15 percent of students nationwide miss at least one in 10 school days.

"This is how poverty impacts kids' performance in school," Balfanz said. "They have to get their sister to school, and that makes them late, so they just pretend to be sick rather than getting in trouble. Or they need to earn money to help the family. Or there's gang violence they're avoiding."

As some education advocates push for more rigorous academics and teacher accountability, Balfanz argues they fail to ask a basic question: Are kids actually in school?

A basic question indeed!

You wonder why it took a study to identify a problem any real educator sees.[11]

---

[11] As a young teacher, I thought I knew it all. I felt, for example, that Loveland administrators could *solve* problems like attendance.

I apologize to superintendents Dr. Charles Waple and Mr. Ron DeWitt. Time would prove that problems I thought they should do something about were far more intractable than I realized in the fervor of youth.

16.

The Iceberg

*"Train up a child in the way he should go,
and when he is old he will not depart from it."*
Proverbs 22:6

As far back as 1983, I was beginning to see that school reformers had no earthly clue. It was hard to fathom how they ignored the fact that problems rooted in the outside world spilled over into every classroom in the land. But they did.

They still do.

I recall one newspaper article from that period in particular. A college professor was quoted, insisting we were wasting time with all the changes being made in education. The problem, he insisted, was teachers. Everything else was "rearranging deck chairs on the *Titanic*."

That was the first time I heard that line, now a cliché. I thought the problem was the iceberg.

***

From my seat behind a teacher's desk, I saw the danger daily. The bell rang one morning to signal an end to fourth period. When the class exited I noticed a purse some girl had left behind. I opened it to look for the owner's name and out fell a pack of cigarettes.

No wallet.

I pulled out a note to see who it was from or who it was to. I couldn't help but notice a sentence in which the author called a former boyfriend, then in drug rehab after a near-fatal overdose, a "lying, fucking bastard."

Finally, flipping it over, I saw it was signed, "Love, Marissa."

Moments later the owner returned, best friend in tow. I said, "Here's your purse, but I'm keeping the cigarettes." Both girls spoke up like lawyer clones, insisting I had no right.

Later that year, a student teacher found another note from the same girl, after it fell out on the floor. This one was written during third bell English while everyone else was watching a movie:

John,

Hey, I'm in school again! I was in the psyco ward! Boring. Of course you know I ran away…How's school coming along? Me. Sucks. I told my mom I smoked and slept with K. J. She didn't like it much, but she didn't get pissed off.

She asked how John's baby was doing and wondered, "Are you off house arrest?"

Then she finished defiantly: "Partying, rock n' roll, and guys (especially you) is going to rule my life still. Man dude you're so fuckin good looking, a total babe! Man, we're getting lectures on finishing school. I'm gonna go now."

I couldn't see how teachers were the problem if I had talked to the young lady's dad by phone and he told me he "washed his hands" of the girl. I couldn't see how schools were failing if the girl had been to drug rehab, had an abortion, and tried suicide by end of eighth grade. I liked her very much and we talked about her troubles. Marissa had great potential and when grounded for low grades read *A Raisin in the Sun* in a single sitting for my class.

It wasn't just Marissa, though, and I worked in a solid community where such stories were comparatively rare.

Holly was a bright young lady, but the year before I had her she was retained after missing too much school. Her second time around in eighth grade I discovered she was a gifted writer. We talked about getting to school regularly, tapping her potential, being a success in life. A check of files proved her intelligence, I told her, and indicated she had college ability. Now she was absent for the third time in a week.

I thought back to a note she had given me after our last discussion:

Dear Mr. Viall,

I'm writing to apologize. This is all very hard to put into words. I guess I'm also trying to say thank you. You're the only teacher who took the time to look at my record and speak with me. You gave me the sense that you cared. And whether you know it or not that means so much to a student. Just knowing that someone cares. What I want to apologize for is kind of complicated. You expect good work from me and I haven't given you much of that....

I'm the only one who really knows what's going on and I guess I'm a little scared to talk about it. I'm hoping within time things will look brighter. If not I'm not sure what will become of me. Things really look bad right now and it's hard to concentrate on school and keep my mind off my personal problems. I will try harder. I hope you understand.

Holly was sweet to have in class but her troubles didn't begin with school or end with me.

She would soon come to me again to explain her fears. At fifteen, she was entering the fourth month of an unwanted pregnancy.

***

In the last decade the focus on teachers as the fount of evil has increased to an alarming degree. The Big Fixers, in large part because they rarely set foot in a classroom to see what goes on, have failed to realize the iceberg is *there*. They have focused on "teacher accountability" when many of the worst conditions in schools reflect conditions in the society surrounding. If we're going to address the most serious needs of students in the schools we're going to have to figure out how to get around the iceberg which floats in our path.

Consider Ray, for example. The young man came to us midway through eighth grade and on his first day made a lasting impression. He had not been in our building fifteen minutes before easing up beside

Katherine, standing at her locker. Katherine was a pretty blonde, one of our top students, and gathering books and materials for the day ahead.

The new guy wanted her to know who he was. He asked her to "go with him." She hesitated. Ray added in what he apparently believed was impressive fashion, that she should go with him because he had a "big dong."

Ray earned his first in-school suspension.

Ed Lenney, then our principal, met with teachers who would have Ray in class and told us the young man had been the victim of sexual abuse at home. In weeks ahead we tried our best to educate him but he earned suspensions for telling girls to suck his dick, for bragging his dick was a yard long, for swearing at a substitute and for mooning members of our staff.

I did what I could. Once, late in the year, when Ray heard he could still pass history, he volunteered to come in during study hall and catch up. He worked hard and stayed through his lunch and mine. Another day, when he had after-school detention, for calling me a "pussy," I had him complete makeup work. He finished three assignments and earned three A's. I forgave his trespasses and filled out a STAR Award for a young man who desperately needed praise.

It was clear from talking to his mother that she could not control him and dad was long gone.

How was I supposed to save Ray?

How was I supposed to save the girl in baggy clothes? She sat quietly in history every day, hunched over her desk, long black curls falling in cascades to obscure her face. Over the years I prided myself on getting every student involved. In this case, nothing worked. I tried questions which required "yes" or "no" answers. The girl wouldn't look me in the eye.

She appeared friendless and alone and grades were poor. I tried engaging parents. I called home several times and said I was worried. Their daughter seemed depressed. They insisted everything was fine at home. "She just doesn't like school," dad assured me.

By end of first semester teachers were so worried we insisted on a face-to-face meeting with mom and dad. The father was professionally dressed, articulate, and seemed concerned. The mother was supportive. We told them the girl was suffering great emotional pain, surely in need of counseling. The parents thanked us for our interest and said they would take matters under consideration. When they stood to leave dad smiled and shook hands all around.

I called home periodically the remainder of the year. The girl was miserable and we met with parents once more in spring. Again—we contacted them—they didn't contact us. In the end the girl barely managed to pass.

The next year Mr. Lenney made sure to provide an aide to work one-to-one with the young lady.

The aide and the girl formed a bond and she admitted she was being sexually abused by her father and older brother. Dad got arrested. The brother went to juvenile detention. And if you're any kind of teacher, or even a decent human being, you wished you had seen the situation clearly from the beginning.

***

Sometimes, I saw what I saw and had to wonder. Was I crazy? Was I the only one who recognized such problems?

Even then, in the late 80s and early 90s, reformers far removed from a world where Ray and the black-haired girl struggled to survive had achieved universal agreement. Drastic action, *focused on teachers*, was needed to save education.

The first year the State of Ohio released scores on its new battery of Ninth Grade Proficiency Tests, results were grim. Critics rained down condemnation on teachers' heads.

I picked up the Cincinnati *Enquirer* one morning and saw an editorial by Robert Clerc (*"Schools Failed Proficiency Tests"*) and knew it couldn't be good. Clerc hated teachers' unions like Bible prophets hated sin.

He believed the solution to every problem was a voucher system. Each parent would receive a voucher equal in value to tax dollars spent to send a child to public school. This could be used to send a son or daughter to any private school they preferred. The idea was to break the public school "monopoly" and introduce competition in education. Oddly enough, private schools could still charge more than the voucher was worth, could reject students they didn't want, and kick out those they didn't like after they took them on a trial basis.

(You can pretty much predict that no elite private school was ever going to enroll Ray.)

Clerc had studied test results and said they proved educators, not students, and not families, had failed. Teachers could do the job if they wanted. They just didn't like to work.

"There is ample time in the school calendar," he fumed, "to teach what should be learned in a year."

I saw a disconnect because I had Elliot in class later that same morning. Elliot was no "problem" in the conventional sense. He laughed at my jokes and understood I had a low tolerance for fools. The battle was trying to keep Elliot awake to listen to my jokes, or anything else, on the off chance he showed up at all. The boy was absent or tardy three or four times every week, which did slice into my *ample time* to teach what should be learned.

One Friday, the young scholar arrived twenty minutes late for first bell history. I explained what everyone was doing and got him started. A few minutes later he was slumped over, sound asleep. I woke him gently. He remained briefly alert. When I turned to help others he conked again. I woke him a second time. He went under a third. I woke him again and called him back to my desk. Was he sick? No. Mom let him play video games till 4:00 a.m.

I had him take a seat on the floor, hoping cold hard linoleum would jumpstart his cognitive functions. I answered several questions from classmates and then glanced in his direction. His head was twisted to one side, resting against the light green concrete block wall. His eyes were shut, mouth agape. His history papers had slipped from his grasp and he let out a snort.

Elliot came late again Tuesday when we had a test. He didn't have any supplies. So I wasted my ample time to fetch him a pencil. Five minutes later, having colored in answers, A, B, C and D, at random, Elliot was done. He laid down his pencil—my pencil—laid down his head—and was soon fast asleep.

By the time the year ended Elliot's mom had been arrested for an altercation with our school resource officer. Elliot had served a suspension for drug possession. And the young man had been absent or tardy 107 times. Once again, I could see the iceberg dead ahead.

Why couldn't critics?

We had fewer of these problems than most schools; but Elliot's situation was far from unique. We had, for instance, a case where three eighth graders brought cocaine to school to sell.

It wasn't just students, either. I remember talking to one young man about his father. Was dad interested in how his son was doing in school?

The boy responded, "My father is a useless meth head."

Or you had a case where Joe Rutkowski, one of our counselors, tried for months to convince mom and dad their son was abusing a variety of substances. Despite his efforts, the parents refused to admit there was a problem.

Finally, their child overdosed and nearly died.

Another day, Steve and Alec, by that time high school students, stopped by my room after classes had ended. We talked about what they and other former students were up to. Diane, they said, was pregnant at sixteen. Leslie's father beat her. Charlie had dropped out and was selling drugs.

That last detail was corroborated several years later when I picked up the paper to read that James, another former student, had been murdered in a drug deal gone wrong. Charlie was by his side, had been badly beaten, but was expected to survive.

***

If chapters like this sound disheartening, I believe they illustrate several critical points. The naïve belief that teachers can fix all problems and save all children obscures a cruel and horrible truth. We don't do nearly enough to aid children with severe problems *outside* of school. We ignore the iceberg to their peril. Once they come to class, teachers may be nearly powerless to help.

Do I offer solutions? I'm not arrogant enough to say I know how to fix problems as complex as these.

According to Fox News, the war on drugs has already cost our nation $1 trillion and we're not winning. In 2010, for example, 19,000 mostly young Americans died as a result of opioid misuse, 15% from heroin, the rest from pain killer abuse. In 2013, twelve months before the promise of No Child Left Behind was supposed to be fulfilled, one in every fifteen high school seniors admitted smoking marijuana daily.

Could we do more to help all kinds of kids?

We absolutely could.

If I could wield a magic wand, here's a change I'd make. Any student in grades 6-12 who ran into serious discipline problems would be tested for alcohol and drugs. If they were abusing, I'd wave my wand again and make sure they and their parents got free and mandatory counseling.

Next, I'd stop jailing people for non-violent drug offenses.

I'd pour the money saved on enforcement and incarceration into services for children. I'd bring social services into elementary and secondary schools. Rather than save the *Titanic* after the hull was gashed, I'd place the professionals, psychiatrists, drug counselors, and more, right next to classrooms.

I've already said where I think the battle to save children is being fought.

***

I'd send heavy reinforcements into schools.

17.

WWAD (What Would Abe Do?)

*"Always bear in mind that your own resolution to succeed
is more important than any other one thing."*
Abraham Lincoln

So the iceberg was there—and the Big Fixers missed it—and when the ship had a hole torn in its side they blamed teachers. I couldn't believe it. (I still can't.)

At times, it seemed like educators were being asked to save every child from *everything*. In the late 80s, with obesity spreading across the land, there were calls for added time devoted to gym. Richard Simmons, the fitness guru, "called on education officials to require students to exercise for an hour a day and to take a nutrition course."[12]

At various times the State of Ohio mandated drug deterrence programs to go with AIDS prevention lessons, topped off by efforts aimed at building self-esteem, and for older kids, raising awareness about dating violence. There was a period when the state expected us to provide alternative job training for eighth graders, and also a time when we were told to offer classes in Life Skills, including cooking and electric wiring. When school shootings became a plague one lawmaker suggested adding gun safety classes to the curriculum.

***

[12] Today, with a relentless focus on testing in reading and math, 44% of administrators admit having cut "significant amounts of time from physical education" during the school day.

Time for music, art, and even social studies and science has also been reduced.

No matter what we did, the problems of the world seeped or poured through our doors. And the Fixers kept putting forward plans to fight the flood with pitchforks and spoons.

In September 1991, *Time* magazine ran an article on U. S. Secretary of Education Lamar Alexander. Walter Shapiro reported:

> The crisis of the common school, the American public school, is that all too commonly it fails to educate. By almost every measure, the nation's schools are mired in mediocrity—and most Americans know it. Whether it is an inner-city high school with as many security checkpoints as a Third World airport, or a suburban middle school where only "geeks" bother to do their homework, the school too often has become a place in which to serve time rather than to learn. The results are grimly apparent: clerks at fast-food restaurants who need computerized cash registers to show them how to make change; Americans who can drive but cannot read the road signs; a democracy in which an informed voter is a statistical oddity.

This seemed like shallow assessment and I thought Alexander should have known it and said something, too.

Then again, like most men and women who head up the Department of Education, Alexander had *zero* teaching experience. His first taste of life in the nation's capital came not as an educator but as a legislative assistant to Senator Howard Baker. He did meet his wife during a softball game for Senate staffers, though, so that was kind of cool. Later he went on to success as Tennessee governor, winning fame for reforming schools, though none of the reforming was done by his hand. As a result, he was elevated to a cabinet post under President George H. W. Bush.

If a frontline educator had been in Alexander's shoes he or she might have told Shapiro, "We need security checkpoints because guns and knives and drugs come from the outside into schools."

Teachers don't foster the geek idea, either. That one can be pinned on American culture.

Voters are uninformed? They aren't crippled. If they want to be informed they can hoist a news magazine and try reading.

Time would be a good place to start.

The article went on to list various features of the "Better Schools Program" instituted by Governor Alexander. (Naturally, in his zeal for fixing public schools, he sent his son to private institutions.) When it came to discipline, "Trouble makers booted out of regular classes are sent to designated rooms. There, they must continue to study under the guidance of a disciplinarian like the football coach, or someone else with a touch of intimidation."

"This way, getting kicked out of class is not a free ride," Alexander told the writer.

See: Problem solved!

I rubbed my eyes and when they cleared still saw what every teacher sees.

We had tried the in-school suspension approach in Loveland. I, for one, liked it. If Chuck Battle, a former college football player, or someone like Mike Rich, an imposing Phys. Ed. instructor, was in the room guests remained quiescent.

Of course, your toughest teachers can't man the in-school suspension room all day. They have other duties. So in-school is sometimes staffed by the middle-aged math lady who gets flustered trying to keep order even in a regular class. Then the program becomes a "free pass" of a different sort.

Consider Ray, mentioned in the chapter preceding. On one occasion Mr. Lenney ordered him to in-school after Ray made outrageous sexual comments to a female classmate. Ray's "free ride" was over but Ray didn't know it because he didn't read *Time*. In fact, if Secretary Alexander tried manning an in-school suspension room, Ray probably wouldn't listen to him.

Ray decided he didn't like in-school suspension. He would rather take an out-of-school punishment and get on home and play video games or nap. He started an argument with another resident of in-school and applied the finishing touch by spitting on the other boy's shirt. A donnybrook ensued and the flummoxed math teacher had to call for back-up before someone—but not a reporter or reforming Secretary of Education—got a little killed.

In the 90s, editorial writers studied unsettling social trends and came away dazed and confused. Once again, the Cincinnati *Enquirer* wagged a finger at teachers and offered fresh recipes for success:

> Efforts to raise the academic quality of American schools are unlikely to have a long-term effect unless the schools also take major steps to develop good character in their students, a group of scholars and educators warned Tuesday.

Editors cited rampant youth disorder, including rising rates of teen suicide, teen homicide and out-of-wedlock births. A panel of experts signed off on the need for character education. This was no garden variety panel, either, but one stuffed with professors from Stanford, Harvard and Cornell.

The State of Ohio jumped on the bandwagon and legislators began tom-tomming their vote-for-me drums. Before you could say "Mickey Mouse" or "Donald Duck" (which was what students actually brought up whenever the topic of "character" was first broached), schools were hard at work developing character education programs. The Ohio Department of Education decreed we would teach "basic American values" like compassion, courtesy and responsibility.

(Ray, are you listening?)

Thomas Gephardt, editor of the Opinion page for the *Enquirer*, weighed in on the topic. He noted with approval efforts by the local Princeton City Schools to draw up a list of qualities that should be taught:

Honesty and integrity
Trustworthiness
Civility and compassion
Loyalty
Wisdom
Freedom
Justice
Equality
Diversity and tolerance
Responsibility

Unity
Self-discipline and courage

I liked teaching values. I did. But didn't churches once shoulder this burden? Didn't I learn character by observing my Dad? Don't media forces contradict any message schools deliver—daily—hourly—every minute of the four seasons—and one day extra during Leap Year? Schools don't color society nearly so much as society colors schools. Indeed, it often seemed teachers were cast in the role of lifeguards and forced to swim against powerful tides.

There are even those who insist there can be no turnaround till we put prayer back in schools. I'm no minister and have no degree in theology but since people who don't teach offer all kinds of school fixes I should put forth my plan to "fix the churches," instead.

In May 1989, a chart in *Time* showed a drop in Sunday school enrollment from 14,000,000 weekly to a little over 6,000,000 from 1965 to 1987. So forget putting prayer back in school. If you want children to learn good values put them back in pews Sunday mornings.

I even have a name for my bold plan: I call it "No Sinner Left Behind."

***

Sarcasm aside, I was happy to do my part for character education. Every spring we spent an entire class discussing a handout I prepared on Abraham Lincoln's early years. We began with "compassion."

It is not generally known that Lincoln served as captain of volunteers during the Black Hawk War, waged against Illinois tribes resisting encroachment on their lands. But I liked the story for what it showed about one of our great leaders, even in his formative years. Lincoln missed all the shooting and in self-deprecating fashion noted that the only blood he ever shed was during a mosquito attack. Nevertheless, his great heart was in evidence in 1832:

One day his soldiers caught an old Indian wandering near camp. Labeling the poor man a "spy," they made plans to kill him.

Lincoln was outraged and "dared anyone to lay a hand on him."
The men backed down.

I thought it was important to introduce the concept that even in times of war humanity should prevail. I wanted students to consider that Lincoln's greatness came from deep inside. I wanted them to search for similar qualities in themselves.

We turned to Lincoln again to illustrate the quality of "self-discipline." I loved the way he earned his education:

Lincoln spent no more than twelve months in class all his life. Yet he showed a burning desire to improve himself and was always "hungry for books." His stepmother often watched him copy long passages from authors he liked, writing on boards if paper was not handy. Another time he used several blank sheets to make a "book" and practice math. Carefully—patiently—he worked out problems like "4,375,702 divided by 2,432." Even when plowing the fields he took a book. Whenever he stopped to rest his horse, the young man threw himself to the ground and read what he could. Neighbors complained that he neglected chores like killing snakes. Still, they were impressed by his thirst for knowledge.

Now I asked students to write out self-improvement plans of their own. At first, most were confused. "Look," I said, "Lincoln was interested in creating a better version of himself."

"We could all do that, couldn't we?" Kim asked.

"Exactly," I replied, "we can all create better versions of ourselves."

That concept, that we could all be better than we were, proved fuel for spirited discussion.

You can teach character in history and you should. You can focus on Susan B. Anthony, who met defeat at every turn in the fight for women's rights but could not be deflected from her course. You can look at Edison, who said the key to success was "the ability to stick to a thing"

184

or the Wright Brothers who tried hundreds of wing, engine and propeller designs before finding success.

Carmen, one of my top students, saw me working at a table in the school library one day. She stopped to talk and told me she had started reading more after learning how Lincoln took books along when he went to plow.

We discussed my recent sale of all my handouts to a major textbook company, paid for but never published. I told her I planned to keep writing.

"The Wright Brothers, huh," she responded simply.

Carmen got character education.

Another day, thinking to stir a little interest, I told my classes a quick story about Robert E. Lee. A young woman, with babe in arms, approached and expressed admiration for the general's devotion to the Southern cause. Lee, a humble man, was embarrassed by such accolades.

The mother wanted to know how she might ensure her infant son turned out to be a man like General Lee. "Teach him to deny himself," Lee answered, then tipped his hat and went his way.

It was apparent when I finished most kids had no idea what Lee meant. Deny *what*, they wondered?

"Obviously," I said to one of the girls, "he doesn't mean you should say, 'I'm not Jamie.'"

"Glory?" Jamie guessed.

Morgan tried "comfort." Close. The room fell silent. Suddenly, students were interested in solving a riddle.

"Mr. Viall," Jamie asked, "if you say 'comfort' is close, then does he mean 'deny being lazy?'" Close, very close. Jamie is hesitant as she tries to find words to explain.

Cassie thinks she knows. "Lee is saying you have to deny yourself comfort. You have to do what is hard."

Jamie adds: "He means you have to do what you don't want to, even when it's hard."

I am thrilled to see they grasp the point. "Yes," I say, "you have to deny yourself the easy path."

For reasons newspaper editorialists can never grasp, real students are intrigued. We turn to examples. I throw out my Walter Payton story, or some story like it. Payton, one of the greatest running backs in NFL history, once said during the off-season he ran up a sand dune behind his house, not one time, not ten, but three hundred times every day.

"You have to work hard, to build strength, if you want to be a better player," I added. I picked on Cassie again. She was an excellent student. "Cassie, I know you love doing homework!" She had a wry look. "Don't lie, I know you do."

"No, I don't. I hate it."

"Then why do it?" I asked.

"Because I want to get into a good college."

"What about dads who don't pay child support and dads who do?" asked Jeremy. "Don't dads who do deny themselves?"

I loved his comment and told him so.

The discussion took various twists and turns, which is why teaching is always rewarding and, I think, hugely important. Cassie talked about how hard swim practices were. Kurt, a member of our school's incredible jazz band, said hours of practice were required. Jared explained how his grandfather worked every day in his auto body shop and helped the family financially.

Finally, Cassie summed it up. "If you want to be good at anything you have to put in the work."

One of your most critical jobs as a teacher is to foster the growth of a wide variety of abilities. I might compare a good teacher to a gardener burying seeds and bulbs and roots of every kind. You plant carrots and corn and dozens of flower varieties. You start ivy and place rose bushes and do a little grafting. You bury acorns and hope they grow into oaks long after you're gone.

Measuring "success" with a standardized test is like counting nothing more than the number of bushels of oats produced. If all you care about is *oats*, it's a great system.

If carrots and roses matter...and oak trees...well, not so great.

Calvin gave me this brief note one day late in the school year. It's one I cherish:

You have influenced the way I act in school in many ways. If it wasn't for you, I'd probably be failing every class. In some ways you have 'taught me to deny myself.' I think I learned a lot in your class, but for some reason I still didn't do too well....

186

P. S. Am I passing?

He was.

***

The mid-90s marked the heyday of character education. But teaching character didn't fix the world.

(Standardized testing would knock it out of the curriculum almost entirely in years to come.)

By 1995 the Cincinnati *Enquirer* could report that one in every four American children was living in a single-parent home.

Reporters explained:

...more than half the children whose fathers did not live with them had never been in the father's home...and 42% had not seen their fathers at all in the previous year.

Making a hard life harder, say policymakers, is the alarming number of fathers in all income brackets who abandon financial responsibility for their children. Only about one third of the nation's 8 million divorced or separated fathers provide court-ordered child support.

Yeah. We needed character education, alright. Maybe just not so much in the schools.

18.

The Mom and Pop Effect

"You are the bows from which your children
as living arrows are sent forth."
Kahlil Gibran

I can't say I ever envisioned including Michael R. Bloomberg and Justin Bieber in the same chapter about teaching. Most Americans recognize Bieber by name, a troubled young singer, beset by legal problems. What does Bieber have to do with education? More than you might think.

As for Bloomberg, minus the title of "mayor," his identity likely escapes most ordinary citizens. If you pay close attention to education news you know he's one of the biggest names in school reform. Harvard graduate, successful businessman, humble bazillionaire, he wrapped up his third term in charge of New York City in 2013.

Of course, most Americans *don't* pay close attention to education news. So I should point out that the mayor gambled his legacy on a promise to fix the city's ailing schools. Despite his best intentions, progress was slow and the mayor's nerves began to fray. In a speech to a conference at M.I.T. in November 2011, Bloomberg let rip. His *plans* were perfect. That he knew. This meant grading schools and opening up more and more charter schools.

If his plans were perfect—and weren't working still—there had to be explanation. The man who never worked a single day in a classroom in his life knew where the blame must fall.

It was those *teachers*.

At one point, he sniffed to his audience: "We don't hire the people who are at the top of their [college] class [to teach] anymore. In America, they come from the bottom 20 percent and not of the best schools."

If you're a public school teacher you've heard this shallow analysis before. When I was new to the profession, I remember reading about problems in schools and an author who explained that, yes, problems boiled down to bad teachers. We were a collection of losers "culled from the bottom of the intellectual barrel."

Critics have long relied on this quotation from George Bernard Shaw to put a point to such stories: "He who can, does. He who cannot teaches."

You wonder, though.

Did Bloomberg or any of the other critics ever consider this quotation, also from Shaw, whose father was a raging alcoholic? "Parentage," he once wrote, "is a very important profession but no test of fitness for it is ever imposed in the interest of children."[13]

***

Before we spend the next decade like the last, talking in tight little circles focused on schools, we need to face the fact not all parents are equal. We need to understand that mothers and fathers determine to a very great extent, in small ways and great, what happens to children even after they head for school. In my experience, Beth, Brian, John, John and Lauren were wonderful to work with in class because their parents were educators and set high standards at the dining room table. Troy had a learning disability. But mom and dad taught him to work hard to overcome any difficulties. Kyle, Gina, Lisa, Cory and Kristin, all school board members' kids, entered through the same rectangle, took their seats, and

---

[13] There are *bad* teachers, of course. I worked with one gentleman so lacking in motivation he could have been replaced with a cardboard cutout of himself and students wouldn't have noticed for a week. I worked with two young women who snuck off at lunch and smoked pot in a car in the teachers' parking lot.

There *are* bad teachers and we need to do more to get rid of as many as we can.

Unfortunately, even if we got rid of them all, we still wouldn't have addressed the most pressing problems many kids deal with both in and *out of school*.

buckled down without fail. Sonya was another favorite, born to a 15-year-old mother, but a teen mom determined to see her daughter made none of the same mistakes.

I suspect, if Bloomberg and a few Big Fixers would only sit at a teacher's desk, they might realize a child is typically a reflection of his or her parents, for good and for ill. During a parent-teacher conference near the mid-point of my career, I sat across the table from a bright, polite, worried mother. Her son was a straight-A student, polite like her, and hard-working, probably like her or her husband, or both. The boy was quiet and mom was concerned.

I offered assurance. Her son had plenty of friends, all good kids. He was a pleasure to have in class.

She was perplexed. "I don't know what to do," she said in the tiniest voice I ever heard coming from adult lips. "He's so quiet and shy, especially around girls."

I remember another occasion when Mr. Lenney had to discipline a volatile young fellow for fighting on the bus. This was not the first time the teen's temper had landed him in trouble—but his mother loved him and always made excuse.

Now mom had to come to school to pick up the young man after he was suspended once more. Something the principal said set her off and she stormed out of the office, shouting as she went, "Some of the people in this building should have been on the Space Shuttle!" This was a month after Christa McAuliffe, the first and only winner of the "Teacher in Space" contest, perished along with the entire *Challenger* crew in a fiery explosion.

The first time I ever tried to measure the "Mom and Pop Effect" was on Open House Night in 1984. Attendance at Open House is probably the easiest way a parent can show commitment to a child's education and for me the night began on a high note. Mrs. Broughton stuck her head in my door and told me how much David loved history the year before. "No one else in his life," she continued, "has ever had as much impact on him as you did."

(Not counting mom and dad, of course.)

The evening was disappointing in other respects. In those days we tracked kids by ability. In my weakest class ten students were already behind in their work. *One* parent appeared to represent the group, the mother of Jenny, a young lady who failed the year before but now carried an A- average in history.

When seventh period parents visited, for our "gifted" class, thirty adults crowded the room.

I didn't bother checking every year, but on Open House Night in 1986 I tried a different measure. I had 44 students in 1st and 3rd periods. Fifty parents showed up. I had 54 kids in 2nd, 6th and 7th periods. Eight parents appeared. That same day we had a test. In periods 1 and 3 there were 29 A's, 13 B's, and 2 C's. Periods 2-6-7 produced 4 A's, 11 B's, 8 C's, 16 D's and 14 F's, with one girl absent.

Fifty parents for forty-four kids showed up and their sons and daughters averaged 3.66 (B+) on a 4.00 (A) scale.

Eight parents for fifty-four kids showed up and their children averaged 1.53 (D).

The next year, I had a long talk with a woman who was tutoring Roberto, a young man faring poorly in every class. She mentioned that his parents had told her: "You're our last hope."

That afternoon and evening we were holding parent-teacher conferences. Our policy was to send letters home and let parents who were *interested* call to schedule appointment. Teachers had 24 slots to fill. To make room for as many mothers and fathers as possible, I filled in the half-hour block allotted for supper. I was happy to sacrifice a meal to create two extra fifteen-minute slots.

How much difference do mothers and fathers make? Again the evidence was stark. Fifteen parents who came to conference had sons or daughters with A or B averages. Eight had C's. Three had D's. None of the parents whose kids were failing called for appointments. Not one.

Not even Roberto's mom or pop.

In 1992 we adjusted our conference setup. We began asking specific parents to attend. That year, I had seven failing students, but only one parent bothered to show up.

After giving invited parents first crack, we opened the schedule to everyone. Eight parents went out of the way to see how sons or daughters might be faring, even though they had A averages. Seven came for B students, five for C's and only two for D's.

I didn't check the correlation again for years because it seemed obvious. In 1998, when we organized teachers and students into teams, and

I was tapped as team leader, I retested the premise. I compared attendance at Open House (early September) with grades at the end of first quarter (mid-November). At least one parent was in attendance for 73% of kids who earned A's. For B students the figure was 70%, for C students 52%, for D students 26%. A parent appeared to represent one of twelve students with failing marks, 8%.

The following year I checked again and the numbers were virtually identical.

And remember: Attending Open House is just about the easiest way to show commitment to a child's education. All you have to do is hop in the family car and aim for the school.

Even my last principal seemed to believe the "Easy" button to push in education was to ensure teachers kept in touch with parents. She required us to keep phone logs, proving we called home about problems, and collected them quarterly, like swabbing for DNA.

I never had a problem calling home if students were faring poorly. I graded hard and knew it. So I put in place every safety mechanism I could, including handing out my home number to parents and students. There were pranks occasionally and one young perfectionist who called— no exaggeration—two or three times nightly. I talked with the occasional mom or dad who made me wish my number was still unlisted. But most parents wanted to help. If we were working from *both ends* we almost always saw results. The student had to do his or her part, too.

I was totaling year-end grades once when I realized Tabitha was one step from repeating eighth grade. I had been checking progress and calling home to sound warning for months. Now she had failed three of four main subjects. Her only hope was to pass history, remain eligible for summer school, and have a chance to advance.

Earlier that day the history exam had been offered. She had 36 wrong out of 105, a mark of 66%. This meant she failed history too, although it was close. She had a 68 average for the year. Had she earned a C- on the exam she would have had a passing mark (70 D-).

I decided to cut her a break. I had told her more than once she had college potential. On one unit test she scored a 98. My exams weren't any harder, only longer.

I hiked down to the office, checked her schedule, and headed for the great outdoors when a student informed me Tabitha's gym class was playing softball. Tabitha wasn't "dressed out," which figured, since that also boiled down to motivation. She sat uselessly atop the bleachers.

I climbed the steps and said I wanted her to retake the exam. Tuesday, the next day, was the last day for students. Teachers had to come in Wednesday to wrap up paperwork. She could come in anytime and have another crack at the exam. I handed her a study guide filled out by one of my top students, a boy who had already earned an A on the test. Now it was up to her.

As I headed back inside I noticed a bird had shit on my elbow.

The Romans would call that an omen.

Tabitha came in on Wednesday, after I called mom and dad to explain her dire situation. I'm not sure what they said or did but when Tabitha showed up to retake the test she did not miss 36 again. She missed 35, though, and ended up spending an extra year in eighth grade.

The older I got the more I talked to parents like a counselor, not a teacher. Usually, I told mom or dad to call me weekly. Or we discussed grades and ways to handle teens. One night a mother told me she could not make her daughter abide by rules. Noelle was sneaking calls when grounded (this was before cell phones), riding her horse when grades were supposed to keep her dismounted, and refusing to go to her room when ordered. Mom admitted she had to pull her by the hair one evening to make her listen.

Dad was often away on business. So I told mom, in speaking to teens, to keep something Anatole France said in mind: "The more you say the less people remember." She should tell Noelle what she wanted done but should not beat her up over details. Nagging was counterproductive. Noelle had talent. I told mom to catch her being good and break the cycle of argument and recrimination. Mom took my advice, the fever abated, and Noelle's grade rose from a D to an A in history and their battles were greatly diminished.

I averaged 400 school-related phone calls every year, roughly a third positive in nature. There were nights when I spent two hours on the phone and listened to variations of a theme: "I don't know what to do " "Karl is lazy here at home." "I can't get Kathy to listen."

When I told one father his son was failing he admitted, "I don't know what to do with him. He don't care about nothin."

I got on the phone another night and recorded results in my diary:

Spent 1½ hours on phone tonight with five parents. Bill -----'s mom has him in AA three nights a week and says he's rated chemically dependent. (Carol, his sister, is also in the program on a limited basis.) Bill's dad started him drinking at six—Bill got into his father's cocaine. She says Walt and Luther [two other eighth graders] are dealing.

Sometimes, a phone call home isn't even an option. As a speech therapist in the public schools, my wife Anne worked with children with every handicap you can imagine. Early in her career she had a young boy in therapy named Ted. Ted had freckles, brown hair, and terrible language problems. At age 11, he was in a severe behavior unit. Once, when he was hooked up to a recording device for a hearing test, he lost his temper. Unhappy with the beeping commands, he picked up the machine and threw it against a wall, smashing it to pieces.

Ted had reason to be angry. His parents were long gone, and his only hope, so to speak, was Uncle Buster. At one point they spent months living in a rusted-out station wagon.

"What's Uncle Buster like?" my wife asked one day. Ted stammered a little, then pinched thumb and index finger together and made a loud inhaling sound, international sign for "dope smoker."

(The Department of Education estimated that during the 2008-2009 school year there were nearly 1,000,000 homeless children in this country.)

***

It may be Mayor Bloomberg had trouble getting a look at the real world, where kids like Ted barely get by, because his view was blocked by giant piles of money. Sitting at a teachers' desk, I learned that in classrooms up and down the halls there were good teachers hard at work in most and bad teachers, sitting on their asses, in a few. I learned just as surely that most parents were good and cared about sons and daughters, and those children had far fewer problems in school. I saw quickly, too, that some parents were weak—and a few were terrible—and their children were the ones who usually suffered most of all.

You don't have to go to Harvard to grasp this point. It is *possible* to teach any child. But when children come from dysfunctional homes chances are tragically reduced. Obstacles are magnified and multiplied.

Remember Ariel Castro, the Cleveland, Ohio man who held three women hostage in his basement for a decade? He had a child by one victim —a reminder that even the worst human beings can produce sperm or egg and send children to school burdened with unfathomable emotional baggage.

Race and poverty are not determinative factors. Race is neutral to learning and parenting, though cultural attitudes are not. Poverty is most a problem where *root causes* like dad's drug addiction or mom's mental disorder drive the family downhill. And the damage done by bad parents can be seen across the racial and economic spectrum.

Consider Justin Bieber and his family. According to *Rolling Stone* magazine, Pattie Malette, his mother, "endured years of sexual abuse from several molesters, including a friend's grandfather" when growing up.

(There are an estimated 3,000,000 cases of neglect and sexual abuse annually in the United States, effecting 6,000,000 children.)

Pattie's own mother was sixteen when she had her. Her father skipped out when she was two and played no role in her upbringing. By the time she was a teen she had serious drug problems. Her mother had her committed to a psych ward.

(More than 11.5 million American adults suffer from debilitating mental illness.)

Luckily, she found religion, and luckily for Justin, met Jeremy Bieber at a high school party. By the time she was seventeen she was pregnant. But the day she delivered, dad was nowhere to be found. He was in jail.

(An estimated 2.7 million American children have at least one parent behind bars.)

When Jeremy did get out he and Pattie argued violently. Divorce followed. Justin's father had a drinking problem. One day Pattie "smashed a beer bottle against his mouth, and he shoved her into a wall and spat on her face."

(Children raised in single-parent homes are more than twice as likely to drop out of school.)

Jeremy soon disappeared and continued absent from his son's life for many years. Dad struggled with drug addiction, took an interest in martial arts, did time again on an assault conviction.

After Justin began to make a name dad reappeared in magical fashion. When last seen, father and son were traveling together by charter flight, smoking marijuana in such copious quantities the flight crew decided to don gas masks.

(At least 23.5 million American adults are addicted to alcohol or drugs.)

Justin, of course, has millions, which means a pile of money is there to cushion any fall. He's out of school, too, but we need to remember there are millions of kids, raised amid worse difficulties, usually lacking the buffer of unusual talent to pull them through.

One more example should be enough. When classes ended one day a concerned mother appeared at the school where my wife was working. She insisted on seeing the principal.

Good. Mom was "involved."

She told the secretary she was "tired of being followed." Not good at all. But the secretary had trouble concentrating on the message because the messenger was wielding a large knife.

The principal overheard their exchange and stepped from her office to see what was wrong. Mom lunged at her. The principal ducked and dodged and mom chased her down the hall and out the front door and through the parking lot screaming.

Luckily, the principal was faster than the mentally ill mother. Unluckily, in the real world where real children live, the mother *was* mentally ill.

So, the next time you hear some billionaire like Bloomberg, or Secretary Duncan, talking about what must be done to *fix the schools*, stop them between syllables. Ask them: "Are you blind? Do you not see the iceberg? What do we do to help children when *parents or problems outside of school* are paramount issues?"

As a society, the real question is what do we do? What do we do to help *these* kids?

19.

Think Horses, Not Zebras

*"There are countries in which the ignorant have respect for learning.
This is not one of them."*
I. F. Stone

I apologize if the tone of some of what I'm saying sounds gloomy. But I warned from the start I don't believe in "fixing schools." I do believe a teacher can exert a *powerful influence* for good and advance learning in innumerable ways. I believe *students* have a similar power. Parents, too, play a critical role.

There are changes that can help in any classroom and some that can help in any school. Some programs, structurally, are better than others. Nevertheless, the factors that trump all structure, all policy ever written, and even fiscal realities, are easy to see. Go back a few pages and consider how Abraham Lincoln got his education. Go back to the map test failed by thirty-six students (see page 72). What happened when they took it over? How did it happen?

If we wish to improve learning outcomes we need to keep in mind what Roger Fouts, who spent years studying animal behavior, once said: "Good science is parsimonious—it seeks the simplest explanation."

We must remember this medical school adage: "If you hear hoof-beats, think horses, not zebras."

***

In the early 80s, with the U. S. economy slumping and Japanese industry starting to dominate in autos and electronics, politicians and pundits freaked. The media did a little shallow digging and uncovered the ugly "truth." The roots of our malaise could be traced to differences in systems of education. Japanese kids scored higher in science and math. What other conclusion could be drawn? Japanese schools were better. Problems in U. S. schools were the cause of our decline.

The more you read the more you noticed factors that might be cultural. First, Japanese students attended classes 225 days annually. U. S. students did 180. That would be equivalent to giving one runner a lap head start in a mile race. You figure he *should* finish ahead.

In 1983, when *A Nation at Risk* was issued, *Time* set out to uncover the secrets of Japanese success. Professor James Shields outlined their approach this way:

> "The whole culture is pervaded by the ethic that with true effort you can succeed; that if you're not achieving, you haven't tried hard enough."

> Although a Japanese high school student may have five hours of homework a night, worried parents often send their children to afternoon juku, or cram schools.

> "Sleep four hours, pass," went one well-known Japanese saying. "Sleep five hours, fail."

In August 1987 *Time* reported on Asian American students attending the same "failing" U. S. schools that made critics weep. Asian American kids were kicking red, white and blue butt. Asian American kids "spend more time on homework…take more advanced high school courses and graduate with more credits than other American students. A higher percentage of these young people complete high school and finish college than do white American students."

"To put it plainly," Harvard professor Jerome Kagan admitted, "they work harder."

By 1990 the idea that U. S. public education was in ruins was pundit gospel. Once a year you could pick up the newspaper and see charts showing average SAT scores, always pointing down. Average reading scores on the SAT had fallen to their lowest levels yet.

Oddly enough, Asian Americans attending the *same schools* that were failing were somehow succeeding. In a typical year, 28% of 18-year-olds in the U. S. took the SAT. The figure for Asian Americans was 70%.

Normally, the higher the percentage of any group taking the test, the lower the average score. In math Asian American kids beat their classmates by 43 points.

Theories abounded. Asian Americans were the offspring of an educated elite. Good genetics, not good schools or good effort, equaled good results. Arthur Jensen, a Berkeley professor, threw in the towel and the flag with it and said Asian people were just smarter.

Others wondered if the explanation was to be found in Confucian ideals, with a stress on family loyalty and education. The story of Hoang Nhu Tran was entered in evidence. Hoang's parents fled the communist takeover of South Vietnam in 1975 and brought him to the U. S. when he was nine. Resources were slim and they lived in a trailer park. As soon as they saved enough for a small house they moved to be closer to the best junior high in Fort Collins, Colorado. When Hoang reached ninth grade they moved again, closer to the best high school. Hoang ended up as valedictorian, attended the United States Air Force Academy, and went on to be awarded a Rhodes scholarship.

Asked to explain how this was possible, his father replied: "You have to bend the bamboo when it is young."

In 1991 *NEA Today* ran a chart comparing how U. S. and Japanese high school students spent time. American kids had an hour more of household work per week. It was a surprise to see Japanese high schoolers watched more television: 17.7 hours per week vs. 14.2 in this country.

The other numbers told a tale:

Hours spent

	U. S.	Japan
IN SCHOOL	26.2	41.5
STUDYING	3.8	19.0
READING	1.6	3.3
PLAYING GAMES/SPORTS	7.0	0.7
SLEEPING	60.3	53.0

If you totaled the first three categories, our kids put in 31.6 hours weekly on educational activities. Japanese kids devoted 63.8 hours to similar tasks.

Two Legs Suffice

Time revisited the "mystery" in an article in March 1993. Asian American kids made up 1.5% of the U. S. school-age population but held down 10% of places in the Harvard entering class. Only 15% of California high school graduates qualified for admission to the prestigious University of California system. Among Asian Americans the figure was 40%. A Chicago-area administrator highlighted the differences. Asian American students had almost no discipline problems. He explained: "Our Asian kids have terrific motivation. They feel it is a disgrace to themselves and their families if they don't succeed."

I heard the same hoof-beats in my classroom and saw the same horses thundering past. One day I handed out a test on Colonial America to my fourth bell class. James, a native-born student, went sailing along, not bothering to read the pesky questions, marking A, B, C, D and E for fun. (E wasn't even a choice on the test.) When I graded his work that evening he had 8 out of 50 correct.

Somehow, I don't think he felt he'd disgraced his family.

Two weeks later I gave a quiz in the same class. This time I noticed in particular that Rena, a Japanese girl, planning to remain with her family in the U. S. for only three years, scored 100%. James decided not to bother reading the questions again and scored 4 out of 40.

Another day, I got on their class after most did poorly on a test over the American Revolution. (O, sweet irony!) As proof of lackadaisical effort, I noted that almost everyone missed the word "militia" even though both **word** and **definition** were in bold in the textbook.

"Militia" was listed on the **study guide**. So it **had** to be on the test.

When I pointed this out a student interjected, "Mr. Viall, you never **told** us the definition."

I happened to be looking in Rena's direction and saw her roll her eyes. Somehow, Rena **found** the answer and earned an A.

That spring she invited me to the Japanese School she attended almost every Saturday. "It would be an honor if you would come," was how she couched the invitation. Sessions started at 8:40 a.m. and ended at 3:00 p.m. in the upper grades. Curriculum, the principal told me, included 130 hours of Japanese language, 88 hours of math and 44 hours of social studies.

How much would Program for International Student Assessment (PISA) and SAT scores of all students in this country increase if they devoted 88 extra hours to math instruction, grades 7 thru 12? Check my multiplication if you're a product of our "failing schools" and remember how. Isn't that 528 extra hours? Maybe if we want U. S. students to score like the Japanese we need to pile them out of bed on Saturday morning and ship them off to school.

That extra time would be equal to *four years* of math in a typical U. S. secondary school.

So there you have it—a flock of horses!

***

We don't need to keep scanning the horizon for zebras if we want to understand why some nations *appear* to be better at educating the young. In 2011 *Time* ran a story about daunting problems, not in American schools, but in South Korean. Internationally, Korean kids rank near the top on all tests. So what could be wrong?

It turns out after-hours tutoring sessions, paid for by 74% of all Korean parents, were dragging on late into the night. Fourteen-hour school/extra-study days were typical. Authorities were trying to rein in the frenzy.

I was already three years into retirement but found the numbers compelling. In my experience it had been a battle to uphold high standards even in what was increasingly a top-notch district like Loveland. When it came to homework, I favored more, not less, because I believed it allowed me to extend the learning day. We had 8,000 minutes in class. If I could get kids to do thirty minutes of history at home, say four nights a week, it added 4,320 minutes to the academic process. That was a gain of 54%.

Unfortunately, many American parents and even some educators don't know their own minds when it comes to the sacrifices required to achieve excellence. We all want children to excel. We just don't necessarily want them to have to exert great effort to do so.

Go to any bookstore and you can find new releases on education, insisting homework is wrong because well it can lead to family strife. That's true. It can. Asking kids to do anything, from sorting laundry to raking the front yard, can lead to family strife.

If you want a perfect example of the difference cultural attitudes make, pick up *The Case against Homework* by Sara Bennett and Nancy

201

Kalish. The two women advance the kind of argument that could never gain traction in Japan or Korea. They claim homework makes kids fat.

> We believe that because homework is such a sacred cow that it never really occurred to most researchers that it could be a cause of obesity. Once we brought it up, however, every single expert we interviewed agreed there was a connection.

Here's their math: A child doing two hours of homework burns 100 calories. A child free to play outside burns 400. Figure the child does homework five days a week and you have 1,500 calories not burned. One pound = 3500 calories. So a child doing homework will pack on fifteen pounds per year.

(Remember kids: next time you don't have your homework, tell your teacher, "I'm on a diet.")

During a decade as team leader, I fielded a number of homework complaints. Occasionally, parents called me at home. Others went to the principal, to ask Jane Barre or Erica Kramer, my last boss, to see what was happening.

Jane or Erica would visit my room or call me to the office. "Could your team be giving too much homework?" they'd inquire.

I would promise to look into the matter.

In the next couple of days, I would find time to say to my classes, since every student on the team had me for history, that I was curious. "I just want to know how much time you think you're spending on homework on an average school night." I didn't say why I was asking. I was "curious."

"Take out a piece of scrap paper," I continued. "Give me an estimate."

"Do you mean studying for tests, too?" someone always inquired.

"Yes, tell me how much time you spend doing any kind of work for school. But don't count flossing."

One year we received a complaint from a mother who said her daughter was doing two to three hours a night. I asked my classes the usual question a few days later, kept a rough tally, and came up with these results:

40 students said they were doing less than an hour
46 averaged 1 hour +
34 averaged 1 ½ to 1 ¾ hours
 8 did 2 hours or more
 3 did more than three hours a night

     I kept checking every year and our team always hit around 1 ½ hours (average). I'd report back to Jane or Erica and when possible talk to parents, but never asked my team to lighten the load.

     Another year we fielded a series of complaints. One father said there should be *no* homework. "Teachers should do their damn job at school," was how he so eloquently put it. Finally, we received an anonymous tip from a parent who said her child was doing 5-7 hours nightly.

     I decided to send a letter to parents:

     …I don't believe in "busy work," nor do other members of our team. We feel that homework is a valuable extension of the school day and a reinforcement of what we do in class.

     Speaking as a parent, I want my children to have work to do at home. Nevertheless, homework can seem a bit like the tale of "Goldilocks and the Three Bears." My oldest daughter once studied twenty hours for a calculus final. My son seemed to think he could finish high school without studying twenty hours total.

     My second daughter had almost no homework in seventh grade and the next year had a heavier load. I was happier with more rather than less. I felt, for example, that her eighth grade Language Arts teacher did her a great favor by requiring her to read several excellent novels.

     My last daughter is now in seventh grade. Between soccer practice, band, show choir and homework she puts in many long nights. Some evenings I feel sorry for her. Other nights I'm glad she's not wasting time typing away madly at some Internet messaging site.

When she's reading I'm almost always happy. I suspect the time she puts in now will help her when she heads off to college.

I had long heard hoof-beats at home, just as I did in my classroom. My younger brother speaks five languages and likes to multiply triple-digit numbers in his head for fun. Growing up, he finished in the bottom half of his high school class, in the same nether region where I was content to reside. A generation later my son Seth upheld the hallowed tradition.

We're all three very hard workers today. We just came to our senses slowly.

My older brother and three daughters, with similar brains and the same last name, had different attitudes. My older brother put in time and effort in the classroom and did quite well. Abby, my oldest child, studied at length, as already noted. When Sarah graduated from high school she devoted a hundred hours to preparing for an Advanced Placement biology exam. That was the kind of effort that eventually led her to do graduate work at Yale.

The last few years I taught, Emily, our youngest, by then a high school student, studied in the same home office where I worked. I'd often be stuck grading papers till midnight and finally inquire, "Are you about done?"

"Maybe another hour," she'd reply, and keep working, and I'd head for bed.

I noted repeatedly in my diary that she was doing four hours, five, that one afternoon she got home from drama practice at 5:00 p.m., gobbled down a snack, and worked straight on to midnight.

There's nothing complicated in this. When we hear hoof-beats in education we must understand we're hearing horses. We're not hearing aardvarks.

We're not hearing zebras.

***

Five thousand students walked through the same rectangle that opened on my room and most listened to the hoof-beats my daughters heard so clearly. Angie and Dale heard them in one generation. Her daughter, Toni, and his son, E. S., heard them when they sat in my class twenty-five years later. Anjuli, Bart, Brandon, Doug and Jon heard hoof-beats. Elissa heard them loud.

And I tried to ensure others—who didn't seem to hear—learned to listen. Effort was always the key.

Consider Tom, a young man "fresh off the boat" when I met him early in my career. His family had fled from South Vietnam when communist forces poured over the border and toppled the U. S.-backed government. His English was spotty but he had the same "good attitude" my daughters later displayed. Ed Lenney, then our assistant principal, asked Dave, another good student, to help Tom out. Dave not only kept up with his work, he taught Tom to ask for pizza in the lunchroom and say he had to go to the bathroom when he did. [14]

What Tom did was pick up every scrap of knowledge he could. I remember the day he turned in the most precisely drawn map of Ohio I had ever seen, far surpassing the work of Ohio-born peers. Five years later he stopped by my classroom one afternoon to say hello. He smiled and said he had been awarded a scholarship to pursue an engineering degree at the University of Cincinnati.

---

[14] Again, I wish I could fill a hundred pages with stories about good kids. Each name I pick reminds me of ten I might have selected. Tom reminds me of Kwok Ling and Helen. Angie makes me think of Sherry, and Toni makes me think of Elli, Sherry's daughter. Elissa conjures up memories of McKenzie, and McKenzie's red hair reminds me of Alyssa, Elaina, Evan, Jason and Tina, all fine students in turn.

Jason, also being funny, reminds me of Alex and Taylor, and then I realize I haven't mentioned Michelle—funny, yes, and as honest a young person as I ever met. Then I realize I haven't included Dominic, who moved to Loveland midyear. On his first day in class he found $40 on the floor and handed it over at the end of the bell without a moment's hesitation.

And what about Noah and his brothers? What about Bob, Bobby and Thomas? And Sarah, and Lindsay, and Lindsey? Or Darin, or Bryan, or Ryan, Kyle or Courtney?

Or Leah! Or Jacquelyn? Or Mandy?

I wish I could list them all.

Dave #2 might serve as a template for what good students are like. We were reviewing for the final exam one year when I noticed Dave, who had an A average, taking copious notes. Not all classmates were following suit.

When the bell sounded I called on Dave and several others to stay behind. He showed me seven-and-a-half pages of detailed notes. Matt, a C-student, had 3/4ᵗʰ's of a page. Scott, with a D average for the year, had five lines.

"Why do I need notes? I've already passed for the year?" he offered with the same dim logic I would have used at a comparable period in life.

A third boy, teetering on the verge of failure, had nothing on paper, no so much as a doodle.

So: if you want to grasp the fundamentals of education this might be a good place to pause and reflect. What *most determines* success in a classroom? You can say it in Spanish for variety, as the great educator Jaime Escalante once put it: "Gana." Desire.

See?

Si´!

In Missy's case, she was blind from birth. Yet, in every class, the young lady earned straight A's. She carried a Braille machine with her to take notes but it was noisy and she preferred not to use it, listening intently instead. A friend made copies of any notes and Missy's mom would Braille them at home when it was time for her daughter to study.

Missy's mom always did the Brailling.

Missy *always* studied.

Wes and Steven took the same kind of approach—although both had serious reading problems. In this case, the Sisyphean challenge for teachers might have been formidable, save that both young men placed their backs to the boulders and pushed. At the start of seventh grade, Wes was reading at the third grade level. He "solved" his problem by reading all his history materials twice, three times if necessary. He wasn't an A student—but earned B's—and won my abiding respect.

If Wes struggled with the printed page, Steven could barely decipher text. After providing a rocky start in life, his parents vanished, and his aunt took over in their stead. The year I had him for history she was reading every assignment to him when he got home and all I had to do was give oral tests and quizzes the next day. Steven—with a huge assist from his aunt—earned A's every time.

In Erin's case, I was lucky to have her two years in a row, in seventh and eighth grade. That meant I saw her in action 360 days, and on 359 she was probably smiling. It wasn't just her demeanor I liked. What I admired most was her drive.

One day I gave her class, a top track group, the first essay test I think any had ever seen. My plan when I collected results and took them home was to grade hard on purpose. You know: Give the best students a jolt. By the time the red ink massacre was over only one member of the class had higher than a C. Erin told me later she studied six hours. Her grade: 106 A+.

She was smart, but not the smartest kid in the room. She beat everyone when it boiled down to gana.

Horses.

See.

POSTSCRIPT

Whenever I hear experts talking about America's "education crisis" and what must be done to solve it, I think of Erin and a thousand like her, and recall this line from Herodotus:

"In soft regions are born soft men."

In 2010 *Time* magazine surveyed public sentiment in regard to improving the nation's schools. One pie chart highlighted responses to the following question: "What will improve student performance most?"

52% of respondents said more involved parents
24% said more effective teachers
6% said student rewards
6% said more time on test prep
6% said longer school day
6% didn't know or gave no answer

I noticed immediately that increased effort *by students* was not a choice. That's a glaring omission. Yet, in six years spent working on this book, I saw that omission repeated without end.

So, where do we stand today, after decades of school reform, after all the Big Fixers' fixing? At least *on the surface* we have good news to report. For the first time, in 2013, U. S. high school graduation rates surpassed 80%.

Oddly enough, a survey conducted by UCLA shines a light on other interesting developments. In 1966 only 19% of entering freshman graduated from high school with A or A- averages.

By 2013, 53% did.

As late as 1987, half of U. S. high school kids reported doing six hours of homework weekly. By 2006 that figure had dropped to less than a third.

The high grades only piled higher at colleges and universities. In 1960, only 15% of grades awarded to undergraduate students were A's. In recent years that figure has swollen to 43%.

Again, studies indicate that students at this level are doing well when it comes to grades, while doing relatively little work in the process. One report finds that today's undergrads study, on average, only 10-13 hours per week. Another puts the figure at 17 hours.

A third reports a decline, between 1961 and 2003, of roughly ten hours of average study time per week, at the college and university level.

Higher grades? Less work? Soft lands, indeed. We're not just ignoring horses.

We're chasing unicorns instead.

20.

Two Legs Suffice

"They can because they think they can."
Virgil

Ed Lenney, my second principal, was a natural gentleman, unfailingly considerate of staff and students. (Except for the "gentleman" part, the same could be said of Jane Barre, my third principal.) Generally speaking, I would argue that an individual should teach at least a decade before claiming to understand the nature of education. Twenty years is better. That way you know there are always plans afloat to fix the schools. If you work in education for forty years, as Ed did, or Jane, you find the same plans coming round in successive generations.

No doubt some expert insisted centuries ago that if Aristotle would stop walking about the Lyceum as he discoursed with students test scores for Athenian kids would soar.

***

In the early 90s experts insisted that "discipline plans" were the fix for what ailed schools. We tried fresh approaches to age-old problems. For a time all members of our staff recorded student infractions in a four-step system. First and second steps led toward detention. A third step triggered a phone call to parents. The fourth step was detention.

Discipline improved a bit. But the paperwork was burdensome and no "system" short of explosives is ever a permanent solution. One day I gave an obstreperous scholar a "step" for causing a disturbance.

He responded matter-of-factly: "I don't care, that's only my second step."

I was tempted to make the third step a "noogie," but instead made note in my discipline log.

209

Record keeping did allow us to form a picture of our dilemma. The "middle school" movement was catching on at that time and Loveland would soon make the switch. (The "middle school format," combining grades 6-7-8 in one building, was also going to fix education.) Now, in our final year as a junior high, we had 369 seventh and eighth graders; 271 made it through first semester without detention.[15]

On the other end of the spectrum, twenty-eight pupils accounted for more than *half* of all infractions. Sixteen were suspended at least once. And those sixteen young people had, almost without exception, the worst grades in the building.

The next year we added a sixth grade and became Loveland Middle School. This change helped in some ways and hurt in others, but the same families that had problems at home still had problems at home. The same good teachers still worked hard and the same bad teachers still tried to get by with minimum perspiration.

Discipline records for first semester, 1990, showed the usual pattern. We had 614 students; 391 had *no* detentions. Another 108 had one or two. That meant 499 kids totaled 157 detentions.

In the same period the top-ten offenders amassed 183.

In light of such figures, Ed agreed to set up a "disciplinary board." We began calling students and parents in for conference. Most meetings were held evenings, when it was convenient for mom and dad to attend. Ed and members of the faculty took turns giving time to make the system work. During meetings we tried to outline problems and suggest ways kids might change.

To put a little steel in the system we implemented stiffer penalties for repeat offenders. Once a student received an eighth detention in a semester any additional infractions triggered automatic suspension.

For at least 95% of our student body this made no difference, save perhaps for the better.

Parents and children who came to conference ready to make excuses often had the impression we were too hard on kids. One look at statistics surprised even teen offenders. With adolescents, of course, you had to eliminate excuses before you saw improvement.

---

[15] Most junior high schools include grades 7-8-9. Ours was 7 and 8.

Hauling students in front of a board also made it harder for a child to say to one teacher: "You don't like me." Or to another: "You're too mean." It was hard to explain, if a teacher was mean, how the majority of peers stayed out of trouble.

During most sessions I took notes:

This past week we met 12/2 and 12/3; a group of teachers stayed until 7:00 and I was proud of them. But on the first day Mrs. James cannot make it; [her son] is the first place detention man. Bill Dalton has a father who is an alcoholic, as Debbie Pomeroy [a teacher] knows from a life in Loveland; same with Rob Kidd, who comes in next; then the third in a row is Harold Loeb. Harold's mom called Ed Lenney last week and told him she was leaving her husband because he drank all the time—and so did Harold, who has been coming in [to school] at 1:30 and 2:00 on school days. She only relented and called Ed again after finding apartments too pricey.

The new system had a positive effect, though not as pronounced as hoped. Discipline boards helped the way it helps to lose seven pounds when you need to lose thirty. One young lady, with eight detentions on her record, never got another the rest of the year. Students with four, five, six and seven were wary. Top offenders slowed down, too, but still racked up infractions. Now we sent them to in-school suspension or kicked them out for several days. Dan, who led all others in violations, was suspended several times.

I still have my notes on a meeting that seemed to go exactly as we hoped:

Last night we talked to Geoff Sampson; now in legal custody of aunt, Mrs. Arnoldson...Geoff's mother abandoned him to foster care at age four; doesn't want him back; her boyfriend has no kids (and sells drugs), says Mrs. A. Geoff's father had him for two years but she says, "Geoff basically told him what to do."

Geoff faces charges for stealing a car and was caught driving, though he looks to be 4 feet, six inches tall.

Danielle Balanda [later: Vogt], Joe Rutkowski [two members of our staff] and I tried to be positive and still emphasize that he must improve his self-discipline. I think we were all sad (and hopeful) about what came out of our discussion. Danielle told Geoff he'd really improved in her class. I told him I'd talk to him if he needed to talk about divorce, how hard my own kids took it. Joe was impressive in his comments.

I tried to end on a positive note by betting Geoff a milkshake he couldn't go a week without DT—but telling him I expected to lose. Danielle said she'd make the same bet for a second week. Joe asked what flavor Geoff liked and we all laughed when he answered emphatically, "Strawberry."

Before she left Mrs. A. thanked us, and cried a little, saying the stress of having Geoff caused her to "go back on her heart medicine."

I patted Geoff on the shoulder as we left and think all of us went home feeling hopeful.

The next day, he asked to leave class to retrieve a book from his locker. I let him go and while he was gone he stole an Ohio State jacket from another boy's locker. By noon Geoff had been caught and police summoned.

Research shows, of course, that suspensions don't help those suspended. In this case research is doubtless correct. What no study shows is how Geoff or other disruptive students affect the learning environment of peers or how much it helps when their negative influence is removed. That's because people who do studies in education don't usually come within two rivers and one mountain range of such young men if they can avoid it.

Every good public school teacher would tell you it's our duty to help Geoff and every other child like him. At the same time we have a duty to the *society* of students. So the question has the feel of triage. How much must be done to save a handful of kids who damage the learning environment for hundreds of more serious-minded peers?

This is a question advocates of vouchers and charter schools leave unanswered. That is: What do we do with Geoff? Private and charter schools don't face this problem. The "worst" kids rarely wish to attend private schools, even more rarely can afford to, more rarely still are able to gain admittance. Often they have parents who don't care what institution they attend—public—private—charter—or some school in the Ninth Circle of Hell.

In Loveland top administrators met the discipline dilemma head-on and blinked. Mr. Lenney was told to stop issuing "so many suspensions" and received a slap on the hand for his efforts. Staff went back to issuing detentions as a bottom line and the same few kids continued to disrupt the school.

Going into the 1991-1992 school year we settled on a new approach. I suggested taking students who caused the most trouble and isolating them in a single room, a sort of academic quarantine. Rather than allow them to travel, to spread the infection so to speak, we would send teachers to them and add a second adult to the room. In an isolated setting you could handle minor problems with a more lenient approach and the second adult would bolster the other and allow us to double the help available to kids who needed help most.

Ed liked the idea and so did staff. It became a question of drawing up a roster. Dan, with 81 detentions, was in; Thomas, with 50 +, was next. Jerry, who had been kicked out of his house and spent a week living in the woods, made the cut. Maris was the only girl.

The academic record of the fourteen chosen students was bleak. In the four main subjects (Language Arts, math, science and history) the year before, they racked up almost 100% F's.

This plan wasn't going to work unless we had the right people to implement it. It was my idea. So I volunteered to take the group for history. We got lucky with the other three teachers, all excellent young women: Karen Gowetski (now: Clary) for Language Arts, Cindy Taylor for science and Jennifer Windau for math. In months to come the kids would learn to view these three like older, wiser sisters and three good teachers would prove central to the success of this new class.

The key was Stan McCoy Sr., hired by the district to serve as program director. Stan was a former teacher, football coach and administrator, a no-nonsense old-timer, like some character from central casting. He would take no grief and yet would show he cared.

None of us knew what to expect when school started in August. The new class was known as SPARK, for "SPECIAL PROGRAM FOR AT RISK KIDS." But it wasn't going to be special unless we made it so and Stan was the man we needed. He was the stern father these kids never had, but one who showed them love and respect and wanted them to succeed. If Jerry didn't show up for class Stan went to his home, banged on the door, and if that failed, went round the side to rap on a bedroom window. "Come on out," he called, "I know you're in there!"

Jerry started coming out.

Stan and the rest of us quickly found there was plenty of talent in the group. We were all good teachers. It wasn't like we were surprised. Under a redneck exterior and a mullet hairdo, Logan had a first-class mind. Dan kept asking Ms. Taylor to marry him, but when you got past hormones you could see he was extremely bright. Thomas was quick-witted in discussion and with a break or two you knew he could end up in college.

It wasn't always easy to handle the SPARK crew, even with two adults in the room. If Jerry or Ralph or Greg got angry they might let loose a stream of profanity. In this setting you said you'd heard it before, calmed them down, and went on with business. Thomas had trouble getting along with peers. Ralph told us his father disappeared when he was little. His mother disappeared into the bottle on weekends. Substance abuse was a defining issue in one student's case, probably in at least two others. So, life was just as hard as ever for these youngsters.

All we could do was try to help.

The low point for me came early in the year when I tried to settle the group and get them going on an assignment. Logan and Thomas were arguing and Dan was egging them on. I told them to quit acting stupid and find their seats.

Logan bristled, "You can't tell us what to do. You can't tell us anything!"

Thomas switched allegiance and agreed. Dan threw in his chips. "Yeah, why should we always have to work," he grumbled. "That's all you care about."

"Fuck you," a spectator interjected.

They weren't talking to Dan.

Logan was puffing up and looked like he wanted to come at me. "Line up and I'll kick all your asses, starting with you," I said. I glared at Logan and glared at the others.

They found seats but were clearly offended. Logan said bitterly I was like every other teacher. Peers agreed. I think I could have won them back but it wasn't necessary. Stan had already shown his commitment.

Now he cashed in a few chips.

"Quit acting like a baby," he told Logan. "It's your own fault." To the rest of the group he added: "Mr. Viall is trying to help you and you won't sit down and work. What *do* you want? Do you want us to give up on you? Well, Mr. Viall isn't about to give up and neither am I."

Dan looked hurt.

Logan turned pensive.

Several members of the class nodded. They knew Stan had faith. They knew I had been telling them I could see their potential. Stan buried the dagger. "Mr. Viall comes in here and tries to help and you just want to screw around. You ought to be ashamed of yourselves, not mad at him."

I picked up from there. I told them they were as smart as any class I had. They had great ideas in discussion. They weren't afraid to speak their minds, either, including now. But were they willing to work—do *their* part—and what might they accomplish if they did? The storm dissipated and we turned to our lessons.

The next day, I made a point to tell Logan I thought he had leadership ability. I believed it then. I believe it now.

***

A few weeks later, we were discussing Lincoln's background: a poor boy made good. I thought the SPARK kids might relate. I decided to combine our discussion with the story of Bruce Jennings, the one-legged bicycle rider, and throw in Anna, my old star student with the high-average IQ. (See page 158.)

Now I used examples to make a special point for the SPARK crew. How many of them, I asked, thought they could bicycle across the United States? Logan smiled and said: "Maybe." Greg said no way. The rest agreed.

"Count your legs," I said. The class looked at me like I was speaking in tongues. "Count your legs," I said with emphasis.

I pointed at Greg's lower extremities. "One. Two." I looked down, as if discovering a secret, and in astonishment counted again: "One. TWO! Oh my god, I have two legs!

"Maris?"

"Two......." she answered.

Coach McCoy knew immediately where I was going. From his desk in the corner he offered gruff admonition: "Pay attention. This is important." He said no more. The SPARK class would have to figure it out.

"We all have two legs," Thomas said with a hint of exasperation. Clearly, he had no idea where we were headed.

The trap was baited. Now to spring it. We turned to Lincoln. How had he achieved success? "He read a lot of books," someone offered. "He was president," a classmate noted. (Okay, not everyone got it.) "He walked six miles to borrow a book on grammar," Maris added.

"Two legs," I noted. "Lincoln had two legs."

"He wanted to be smart," someone offered.

"We all want to be smart," Thomas interrupted.

"We all want to be pretty, too," I countered. "Of course, some of us already *are*." I raised and lowered my eyebrows like Groucho Marx and fluffed my hair. Several kids made puking sounds.

"Lincoln *made* himself a better person. Anyone can do that," I insisted. "I could be a better version of myself. Logan could be a better version of Logan. Maris could be a better version of Maris. People can always do more than they think...."

"Yeah," Greg agreed. "Our grades sucked last year and now they're good."

"Two legs," I added cryptically.

The class wasn't sure where we were going, but they were interested in finding out.

Now I told them about Anna. The first fifteen years I taught, I said she was the best student I ever had. She did perfect work and did it enthusiastically. I explained how I checked her records and discovered her IQ was high-average. I looked at Dan and said: "I've checked your record and you're way smarter." (This was true.) I added, "I think several of you are smarter than Anna, or at least as smart. (Also true.) You just don't work as hard." (Truly true.)

"Yeah, until this year, we never studied," Jerry said. There was general agreement.

"Two legs," I offered. "Some people use one leg and ride a bike across the country. Others have two legs and figure they can't. You have to realize if you have two legs you have to *use* them.

"The same is true if you only have one."

The class was listening intently. "Last year, you had the brains. You just didn't use them like now. I bet if you studied for the next history test you'd all get A's and B's. You have to make yourself do more—like Lincoln—like Anna. You have to make yourself something better than you are."

Then, carried away by my own rhetoric, I made a stupid offer.

The kids knew I played a lot of basketball and tried to stay in shape, but had heard me complain about advancing age and fossilization. I explained the deal: "If you all get A's and B's on the next history test I'll run to school from my house."

"How far?" the class wondered.

"I'm not sure. About fourteen miles."

***

In days to come we reviewed as always for the test, but the SPARK guys were fired up.

Sure, they wanted to make me run.

What they really wanted was to prove something about themselves. Now, when they had free time, they quizzed each other on facts. As soon as they came in after lunch they shared answers and checked with me to ensure they had the right information. If someone reverted to form and started screwing off, a peer might remark, "Don't be a dumb ass!" And they'd get back to work. Coach McCoy did his part—he always did—and drilled them when I was away.

The day of the test thirteen kids were present. Coach warned, with a hint of pride: "These guys are *ready*."

217

I passed out the tests and the kids went to work. Dan finished first and slapped his paper on my desk. He claimed to have "aced" the test. Greg was next. Logan laid his paper down third.

When the last test came in the class called on me to grade them. Coach held the fort and I dashed down to the office to run the answer sheets through a grading machine. If a test was bad a staccato sound indicated all the mistakes. As I fed in the sheets, the machine was mostly quiet. By the time I walked back to the room I had flipped through them all and knew the results.

"How did we do?" the kids clamored.

"Two legs," I deadpanned.

There was a moment of confusion before anyone caught my meaning. I smiled a huge smile and said, "All A's and B's!"

It was an electric moment for us all. For Stan, who so wanted to save these kids. For the three young female teachers who had done so much to shift the kids' perceptions. Certainly, for those students. I was thrilled and told them so.

"Better be ready to run!" someone shouted. "You're going to DIE!"

Then it dawned on us: Phil was absent.

"What about Phil?" they asked in worried tones. Yeah, he had to make the grade too. That was the deal. Some groaned, knowing Phil was perhaps the weakest link in the chain, a young man beset by drug demons.

The next day, he was back, and promised to be ready by seventh bell. His peers kicked into gear and drilled him on facts. Turning point of the Civil War? "Gettysburg." Dates for the war? "1861 to 1865." Document which ended slavery? "Emancipation Proclamation."

Seventh bell, the SPARK study hall, Phil sat down to take the test while the others waited. As soon as he finished they wanted to know how he thought he had done. Good he said.

"Grade it! Grade it!" the class demanded.

I began hand-checking answers. He missed two out of 25 on the front. Then on the back he missed four in a row. At number 42 he missed a seventh. One more, eight out of fifty questions, and he dropped to an 84 C+. A wrong answer on 43 was erased and corrected.

I thought to myself: if he misses another one I'll pretend I didn't see it. I wanted these kids to win as much as they did.

218

No ploy was necessary. Phil got the last six correct and earned his 86 B-.

The class erupted with shouts of joy. "OOOOOOOH, Mr. Viall, now you're REALLY DEAD!" someone warned.

Mostly, I believe they were amazed by what they had done. These young men and one young woman, so unsuccessful the year before, had matched my best classes, the "smartest" kids in the school.

I didn't want to start my run to work in the dark. A few days later, with Mr. Lenney's permission to arrive late, I set sail to pay my bet. I was in fair shape but hadn't been doing much distance running. The first six miles weren't so bad. By the eight-mile mark I was sweating impressively. At the ten-mile mark I had to stop and walk. I ran a little, walked a little, ran, walked, and broke into a speedy shuffle, feet lifting imperceptibly from the pavement.

Finally, two miles from school, I picked up the pace and finished strong. Once I arrived I took position under the open windows of the second floor SPARK room and shouted to announce my presence. The kids stuck their heads out the window and whooped and hollered.

My legs hurt for three days.

I was happy for those kids and they worked hard for us the remainder of the year.

***

Fixing a car is easy. The notion that you can "fix the schools" is a false construct. It would be akin to saying you were going to "fix cars" to end bad driving.

So time spent designing plans to fix the schools is time and opportunity wasted. Put thirty teachers in a room and ask what they feel needs to be done to fix the school and one will go off on a rant about discipline. Five will chime in and agree that discipline is a problem, but there will be no agreement about what must be done to fix it. If the principal isn't in the room someone will hint that the principal is a moron. Enthusiastic young teachers will have ten plans to solve every problem and ten crabby old teachers will have ten reasons none of those plans is worth trying.

Almost all comments will be anecdotal.

One stumbling block is that we insist on going into every meeting and planning session and expect to come out and change a few rules and suddenly miracles will transpire. Instead of trying to conjure miracles we should focus more narrowly on improvement.

We should focus on people—on individuals—on how best to motivate them or help them or save *as many* as we can.

The demise of the SPARK program is a good example. Stan, the three young female teachers and I—and those fourteen kids—were justly proud of what we'd accomplished. Yet, other teachers, who weren't involved and couldn't see what was happening, spent time in staff meetings complaining because the SPARK guys were rude in the *halls* between classes.

That's true. Too often they were. There were occasions when their behavior was totally unacceptable, as when two or three boys made sexual remarks to an attractive new female teacher.

Save for the attractive new teacher, who had every reason to be upset, I thought there was too much useless grumbling. I remember thinking of some of my colleagues, "We have removed the worst behavior problems from your *classes* and you're upset because you have to deal with the toughest kids for a few minutes every day in the halls."

It didn't matter that we had made progress. None of the SPARK crew had walked on water.

High-level administrators were also counting dollars at a time when Loveland was chronically strapped for funds. You couldn't *prove* the SPARK program was cost-effective. So when Stan asked for health care coverage the second year his request was denied. I remember him coming to me, almost in tears, to say the time and energy he was devoting to the program were causing health problems. For his sake he had to resign the position.

Losing Stan knocked the program sideways on its foundation. He was replaced by a well-intentioned young lady straight out of college and for budgetary reasons we lost our separate room.

If that wasn't bad enough, one member of the second SPARK class had the longest criminal record of any juvenile in Hamilton Country. Another had the earmarks of a future sex offender and from what I heard his comments to a new math teacher who joined the program were shocking beyond belief.

You'd think the Big Fixers might someday realize how hard it is to save these kinds of kids. Every year, in every secondary school, you had teens with drug problems or teens who had suffered terrible abuse, whose dads were long gone, whose moms were gone mentally. And you had to try to save them. You went home nights and had a glass of wine or a beer because you knew every day you were failing to save someone—and you tossed half the night wondering if you might see a solution if you studied the problem anew.

But you never saved them all.

I know I was unable to save Drew, another member of the second SPARK class. Drew was a kid for whom even society seemed to have no cure, no solution. By the time he was in eighth grade he was sixteen and had been labeled as having a "severe behavior disorder."

In class one day, a fraction of a second late, I saw him shoot a paperclip with a rubber band. A peer, also a student with severe behavior problems, took a hit right above the eyebrow.

I escorted Drew to the hall and told him he had detention. He denied everything. I rubbed my eyes like a cartoon character seeing a ghost. Was I imagining? Was the other boy's welting an illusion? Drew turned bellicose.

"Fuck you," said Drew. Ah. Drew was a philosopher.

I told him he could do fifty pushups or go to the office. Take your pick.

"I'm not taking this shit," Drew replied with a hint of menace.

Now I had no choice. I couldn't grab him and shake him, which might have helped rattle his thinking.

No. I had to haul him down to the office; and I knew when I got there what was going to happen.

He was going to get kicked out of school.

By now I was shaking with anger—and frustration—because I had no good way to address the situation. I was also wary. In this country, 800 educators are attacked by students (or parents) every day.

Once we arrived, Drew took a seat in the office but didn't like what he heard.

"Fuck you," Drew told the principal.

"Fuck you, too," he told the assistant.

Having outlined his case, he stood suddenly, preparing to bolt. I suspected this might happen. So I had my right shoulder on the right doorjamb, my left foot in the lower left corner of the frame, and my left arm on the left doorjamb, chest high. Drew saw no way past and sat back down, muttering colorful vocabulary words. I had my say and headed back to class. From what I heard he soon spied the open route and stormed from the office and out of the building.

Jane Barre, then our assistant principal, told me one day when she brought Drew to her office and made him call his mother, he loomed over her and threatened to hit her with the phone receiver. He was "shaky," she said and she had to talk him down.

(Around this time she attended an in-service program for administrators. "One speaker suggested we position desks in our offices in such a way as to provide 'escape routes' should students turn violent," she told me.)

The day Drew returned from his suspension, he had a run-in with one of our female science teachers. Classes had ended for the day; but the problem escalated. He boiled over and she told him she would write a referral to the office and submit it the next morning.

"I'll just have to kill you," he responded.

Drew wasn't smiling.

The teacher wasn't sure how to respond, but Rodney, one of our janitors, appeared and offered assistance. He escorted the boy out of the building. In the parking lot Drew told Rodney to "fuck off."

Rodney was an interesting guy. He told me one day he was a former barroom brawler and said he regretted some of what he'd done in the past. I studied his arms, tattooed and big as hams. He looked like Popeye with a dustpan.

I figured he didn't lose many fights.

Drew was a wiry fellow and you wondered what made him feel he was safe to spew such venom.

Rodney couldn't do anything but stand there and listen. None of us had an answer. Drew could spew. He could dig himself deeper into a hole he might never get out of and we couldn't stop him from shoveling.

So, no, the SPARK program didn't fix every kid and didn't fix our school. I did what I could. So did my colleagues. But we fail as teachers. We failed, not because we were in a union, or weren't committed, or because we were hiding behind tenure, all the reasons school reformers ascribe as roots of America's education malaise. We failed the way cops and ministers and drug counselors fail, because saving every student isn't as easy as people like Arne Duncan want you to think.

Does that mean the program was a failure? I know, via Facebook, that Greg and Dan are doing well today. I used to talk to Karen and Cindy, who worked with the SPARK kids both years. Would they do it again, particularly if it was set up the same way as the first year?

"In a minute," Karen replied.

"Absolutely," Cindy agreed.

- # Bottom Line

Pushups

"Pride trumps most other impulses in young men."
Nathaniel Fick

When I began my career corporal punishment was allowed—but it would take another chapter to describe my experiences in that regard and explain why I'm not in favor of putting the paddle back in schools.

I also discovered that different discipline styles worked for different people. Sue Lundy, one of our very finest teachers, was like a mother to students. In my case, humor proved useful, even when it came to discipline. And when all else failed, my bottom line with boys was to require them to do Marine Corps pushups. Pushups were more immediate than detention; and I was able to avoid sending kids to the office, if transgressions would normally merit suspension.

My time at Parris Island informed my thinking. If some youth was disruptive I required him to do twenty-five pushups. If he was defiant—or profane—I demanded fifty.

There were a few, like Drew, who refused to swallow the Cod Liver Oil. They were exceptions.

At the start of every year the threat of "pushups" was greeted with disdain by some of the biggest troublemakers. They might scoff openly, insisting, "I do a hundred pushups every night at home."

Like Mona Lisa, I offered an enigmatic smile.

Here's what none of my charges understood. Most young men who do a "hundred pushups" every night take the position and lower their bodies a few inches before rising again. Or they bend their elbows, dip their bodies, and bob their heads.

The Marine Corps pushup requires one to go lower and exert far more effort to rise again.

"Let's see *you* do fifty," the occasional malcontent would sneer.

"Okay," I'd reply, "but if I do *more* than fifty you have to match."

You only had to do 56 or 58 once to prove that history class was not the best place to fool around.

Out of respect for the fragile psyches of the sinners we usually went to the hall to perform penance, unless the transgressor volunteered to try in front of class. Then both of us had to drop and do fifty, to the delight of a teen audience.

Most of the time, we headed for the hall so the young men might suffer in private. Out in the hall, I lay on the floor and made a fist. Now the rules:

- When you go down your *chest* and not your shirt must touch the fist.
- You may catch your breath and rest, but only in the *"up"* position.
- You may not *jackknife* your butt in the "up" position. Hips and shoulders must remain level.
- You may not drop to your knees till *finished*.

Okay? Ready?

Go!

Somewhere, around twenty-five, most young men began to labor. At thirty-five or thirty-seven, most were huffing and puffing, like engines pumping blood. If they continued to display a bad attitude before starting, and we were out in the hall, I might bait them. "Come ON! I can do fifty! You don't want to get beat by an old man!"

If they seemed contrite, I complimented them (in or out of class) if they hit, say, thirty-nine, telling them, "Well, not many guys can do that many."

If they made a good effort I tried to make it clear they had earned a little respect. To me it all came down to attitude. Build some up. Knock some down.

Do whatever it took to change attitudes for the better.

If I liked a boy's demeanor, I might say after thirty-nine, "Take a break." Then the young man could fold up and finish after a respite. Or I sat up a moment and we discussed ways to stay *out* of trouble. I told most "victims" they were stronger than I was at the same age, which was true. I only wanted them to understand they *could not disrupt* my class.

225

I also hoped to establish a bond, to let them know if they stayed out of trouble we were cool.

Only three young men ever completed fifty pushups without taking a break, including Joe, who wasn't in trouble and volunteered to try. It was a humbling experience, and to my mind the best punishment I could devise.[16]

Of course, the bloated fly floating face down in the ointment should be obvious. For decades I had to keep practicing those damn pushups. And I hate pushups.

I did it though.

It was worth a little extra sweat to keep kids from getting suspended, to have a bottom line punishment that was effective, one that kept most of the toughest teens within bounds. I needed the exercise, anyway.

---

[16] A decade later, Joe enlisted in the U. S. Army and served with an elite Ranger battalion.

21.

Not English Class

"Write, write, write. It's a wonder I have any arm left."
Dorothy Parker

The last social studies curriculum I ever saw, implemented by the State of Ohio after passage of No Child Left Behind, included all sorts of standards, benchmarks and indicators. Starting in 2003 eighth grade teachers would be expected to focus on how the new U. S. government dealt with war debt under the Articles of Confederation. You're kidding, right?

Who cares today?

Worse, there was no room in the curriculum for 2,000,000 words of adolescent prose.

***

Like all sensible American history teachers, in years before bureaucrats got their hands round our throats, I wanted students to take a long look at the first settlers who came to New England. One of my earliest ideas for interesting kids in the story of the Pilgrims was the best.

We began by focusing on the importance of religion in the *Mayflower* passengers' lives. For those who came in 1620, I noted, nothing mattered more.

I put three questions on the board:

1. On a scale of 1-10, rank religion, 10 being highest. How important it is to you?
2. Do you believe there is a heaven? If so, describe what it's like.
3. Do you believe there is a hell? If so, describe it.

Students took a few minutes to write out ideas. Then I asked for volunteers to share thoughts. The first time we tried this lesson Randy was perfectly clear. He said people seemed religious, but sat in church being "preached *at*, not preached *to*." Kathy asked what proof of God's existence there could be.

Phyllis responded: that the way everything in the universe worked so well was proof enough. Her comment reminded me of William Paley's "watch-maker theory." I threw the concept into the mix. "Suppose you walk down the street. You see a watch lying on the sidewalk. What do you know exists?"

Answers varied. Time? A watch? You exist? A sidewalk? Your feet? Finally, Diane waved a hand and said: "A watch maker!"

The intricate way the universe worked, like a fine watch, I said, was proof of God's existence, proof to Paley, anyway, who posited the idea.

Chad countered immediately: "It could all be luck. If the planets were in some other order and we turned out differently we would think that was normal, too."

Over the years I noticed during this discussion that religious kids often sounded apologetic, like it wasn't cool to have conviction. I'm not religious, but liked to hear what committed students had to say. The twenty-fifth year I used this lesson, J. C. spoke up about his faith: "We believe you have to accept Jesus Christ personally if you want to be saved."

I asked: "What about those who don't, who aren't sure, will they make it to heaven?"

He answered politely, trying not to sound judgmental: "No, my church believes they won't."

I thought it took a bit of character to put that out in front of peers and imagine it made a few kids take stock. Hope he's wrong, I remember thinking, before moving on to the next question.

The following year, and the last time I used this lesson before switching to a new subject, Rachel commented from a different angle. She raised her hand to answer some query and said, "I think God is like an imaginary friend for grownups." An astute observation, whether you agreed or not.

We finished the lesson the same way every year. If students believed there was a heaven—and almost all did—how did they propose to get there? That was the one question the Pilgrims cared to answer.

I used an analogy first noted in the writings of the Venerable Bede (c. 637-735). Bede told the story of a priest who tried to make clear to his congregation what "eternity" meant. Suppose you had a giant boulder. Once every thousand years a bird flies past and brushes its wing across the rock. How long would it take to rub the rock down to a pebble? That's like eternity.

As for life on earth: imagine the same bird flitting in the classroom door, across the front of the room, and back out a window on the other side. That was like our time on earth. To the Pilgrims, then, it made sense to focus on the condition of their souls.

Naturally, in a discussion about religion the less the teacher says about his or her beliefs the better. What I thought in this case didn't matter. I only wanted students to think.

***

Starting in 1981, and every year after, since my plan worked, we did a unit on the Puritans, who came to New England next and deeply influenced American thought. We began by reading a section aloud from our text:

To be sure that children learned to behave properly, some Puritans wrote rules for them to follow:

If thou passeth by thy parents, bow towards them.
If thou must speak to them, be sure to whisper.
Argue not, nor delay to obey thy parents.
Go not out of doors without thy parents' permission, and return when they say.
Quarrel not with thy brothers and sisters, but live in love and peace.
Grumble not at anything thy parents command, speak, or do.
If thy parents speak anything that thou knowest is mistaken, correct not, nor grin at hearing of it.

Repeat not over again the words of thine parents that asketh thee a question.

Thinking we might spend five minutes on the subject, I asked what rule would be hardest to follow. Almost everyone threw up a hand. One boy put up both and waved them in concentric circles. Getting along with brothers and sisters, most agreed. One young man told us his brother got back at him after an argument by filling his deodorant dispenser with cream cheese. That one made us laugh so hard it was some time before we could continue.

The next step was to pass out an eight-page handout on the Puritans. This meant going far beyond standardized tests which might have one question about the Puritans (and more than likely none).

To put it another way, what we were about to cover was either a waste of time because standards matter or standards were an idiot fix because of what standardized tests measure. It has to be one or the other and we desperately need to get this right. A wrong answer imperils education.

In ominous fashion, I warned the class that what we were about to read was so shocking students might faint dead away. We turned to page six and looked at the story of a young, law-breaking Puritan couple. "Aubrie," I said to one of the shy girls, "Be ready to catch Mike when he faints." Aubrie brightened at the attention. Mentioning her by name helped bring her out of hiding. "Okay. Get ready. I don't want anyone jumping up and running out of the room screaming."

Then in mock seriousness I began:

One shocking crime involved Jacob Minline and Sarah Tuttle, a young couple in New Haven, Connecticut. Court documents show they became "familiar." Indeed, they bent the law so terribly that we hardly dare quote from the record:

"Amanda, you might want to cover your ears. Aubrie, keep your eyes on Mike. He's looking pale."

They sat down together…[I pause] his arm being about her…[pause] and her arm upon his shoulder…or about his neck…[pause] and hee kissed her [gasps from students]…and shee kissed him [more gasps]…or they kissed one another, [horrified gasps fill classroom] continuing in this posture for about half an hour.[17]

The kids took it from there. "They'd have to arrest my brother and girlfriend for sure," said one.

"I was at King's Island [Amusement Park] last year," said another. "It was Gay Pride Day. Guys were holding hands."

"The Puritans wouldn't like that," I noted. "They believed homosexuals should be executed. They also believed young couples who had sex should be forced to marry."

We ran out of time right about there. I told everyone to finish the reading for homework. In my class kids had plentiful homework because I believed it allowed me to extend the learning day.

At our next meeting we turned to Puritan attitudes in general. I explained that the first Viall in America was a Puritan, and said I loved their emphasis on hard work. This was the famous "Puritan work ethic," which went into our notes. Students groaned and said it figured. Sometimes they thought I was a little nutty when it came to piling on the work.

"What else did you learn that surprised you?"

Sammie noted that parents "whipped" children who lied. "The punishment I thought was weird was when they tied restless kids up in a ball and kicked them around the floor," she continued.

We turned to page four to look at the paragraph:

If a youngster talked too much they might have a special wooden plate clamped between their teeth and tied in back. If a young boy was too restless he might be tied in a ball, with knees round his chin, to be "booted back and forth" across the floor by adults. A child learned to call older men, "Sir" or even "Honored

---

[17] Misspellings are in the original document.

Sir." Youngsters of either sex were expected to bow to parents, eat after adults, and speak only when spoken to.

The contrast with modern society could not have been starker. Student reaction took me by surprise. Zach said he thought most modern parents were too easy. Classmates agreed.

"I saw parents let their daughter throw a temper fit in Thriftway because she wanted candy and her mom wouldn't let her have it," one of the girls said. "So she lay down on the floor and started crying and kicking her feet and hitting her arms on the floor and then the mom got the candy if she would get up."

"One time," another girl said, "my friend was supposed to be grounded. But she went to the mall with another family and used her mom's charge card to buy $300 worth of clothes."

"What did her parents do?" I asked.

"Nothing really. They yelled at her. She had to go to her room…but she kept the clothes."

I posed this to the class: What should her parents have done?

Brian offered a classic response: "I'd make her walk back to the mall and return everything and follow in the car."

"Yeah," I added, "and you could bump her every time she moved too slowly." The class roared and when everyone stopped laughing, I awarded Brian a "free A." (The "free A" could be used to replace any quiz grade or missing homework and I granted them liberally, for incisive thinking, superior effort, and as a motivational tool.)

What about clothing? What were some rules the Puritans followed? Krista said the poor could not wear lace. Short sleeves were illegal. Keith quoted the law: "No garment shall be made with short sleeves, whereby the nakedness of the arm may be discovered."

I called several young ladies by name: "Amanda! You criminal scum! Aubrie! Oh my god!!!!"

Keith caught on and exclaimed, "Oh, I think I'm going to faint! Her *arms* are showing!" His friend leaned over and fanned him with his paper. Keith just did manage to recover.

We turned to a crime the Puritans called "misspence of time." Students gave examples. You could be arrested for beachcombing or playing cards or shuffleboard.

"What did Puritans think you *should* be doing?" I asked.

"Praying and reading the Bible," several students responded.

In what ways, I asked, would Puritans say we "misspend" time? Kids fired off ideas: video games, Saturday morning cartoons, watching football on Sunday.

Shane summed it up: "Just about everything we do."

I asked if anyone spent more time watching TV than praying and going to church. Almost everyone admitted they did. "The Puritans would say we're all bound for hell," I concluded. That wrapped the second day.

Day Three: we turned to a reading based on the diary of Judge Samuel Sewall. The judge discusses fights with Indians, the deaths of young women in childbirth, smallpox epidemics and (briefly) his role in the Salem Witch Trials. He also reports fining a defendant for cursing.

"Imagine what he'd think of rap music," said one of the kids. Students threw out names of celebrities the Puritans wouldn't like: Dennis Rodman, Eminem, everyone on reality TV, responses depending on the year of discussion.

We turned to Sewall again. In the same months witches were hanging in Massachusetts, he mentioned his four-year-old son Joseph. Students could relate:

November 6, 1692: Joseph threw a knob of Brass and hit his Sister Betty on the forehead so as to make it bleed and swell...I whipp'd him pretty smartly. When I first went in...he tried to shadow and hide himself from me behind the head of the Cradle.

The problem now was not getting kids interested but avoiding a situation where we used up an entire period relating tales of family mayhem. If it could be hoisted and hurled, some child had thrown it, including one boy who watched a Rubik's Cube ricochet off his sister's skull.

When I was a young teacher I read somewhere that only 10% of all writing assignments given out by English teachers at the secondary level were more than a paragraph in length. In other classes the figure plummeted to 3%. So, for thirty years, I did my part to turn the tide.

The Puritan setup was now complete.

Here was the plan: to ask teens to write a 500-word story about Judge Sewall coming to modern times. Their job would be to show him around. "Take him anywhere. Show him a hospital, bring him to school, take him to your church, or to the movies," I explained.

"Can the story be funny?" someone asked. Yes, definitely.

"Then I'm going to take him to Hooters," Josh exclaimed. I wagged a finger at the young scholar but everyone cracked up, including me.

The kids did fantastic work. The first year, in one girl's story, Sewall sees a car go down the street. He asks his host: "What was that armored horse I just saw passing by?" I loved that line and the kind of thinking behind it and felt this was an excellent way to get in writing practice.

In another story Sewall attends a pro football game, shockingly on Sunday. He is horrified by the profanity in the stands; but the cheerleaders prove too much. When he races onto the field to cover the "nakedness of their arms" (and other body parts) he ends up being arrested and enjoys a tour of the modern justice system.

A third student comes home to find him hiding in a closet. "I don't want the witch to find me and put a spell on me," he explains. "I see there are several people trapped in that little box!" The judge points to the television.

As the years passed and Loveland became increasingly wealthy and more of our graduates went on to college, it seemed wise to do what I could to help as many as possible learn how to write. On this one assignment, I asked 4,000 students, over a quarter century, to do 500 words.

Then I read and red-lined 2,000,000 words of adolescent prose.

***

The talk today is all about getting "back to basics," when good teachers have been stressing basics and *more* for three thousand years. In my class we wrote extensively and I graded hard. I told students I would

234

stop counting for neatness and accuracy when one of them could come back someday and tell me, "My boss says he pays me extra because I do sloppy, careless work."

One of my favorite activities was to ask students to learn history by conducting interviews. I turned this into a major assignment resting on two assumptions:

1. Students would find an individual sixty years old or older for a subject.
2. They would write up an interview of a thousand words.

At first classes howled. A thousand words! And where were they supposed to find anyone so old? Then it dawned they might start with grandma or grandpa. Two young ladies wondered if they could go to a nursing home to find subjects. I particularly enjoyed saying yes to that idea. Jean asked about interviewing great grandma. John wanted to know if he could choose someone from his father's congregation.

Yes, yes.

I wish I had a tall stack of interviews to quote, because the work was almost always good, often phenomenal. John went to his father, pastor of one of Loveland's largest churches, and turned in a 4,000-word report on a 94-year-old woman. The same year, three classmates found subjects who were 92. Suzanne summed up the assignment best when she wrote: "Mrs. Smith is an 83-year-old history book."

In this way students dived deep into the past. They learned about Loveland's separate school for blacks and hard times for all during the Great Depression. They heard about the details of life: 5¢ ticket prices at movies, football games when "big" players weighed 190, first homes that cost $2,000. You had family history, too, grandpa on his first date with grandma and how they met and fell in love.

Even I was impressed by how much work our ancestors did when young. Deana had this to say about her grandfather (b. in 1918):

When he was young, he would help around the house and farm by gathering firewood, kindling and bringing in coal. He would help his mother wash clothes on a washing board in a tub and help her with the dishes. He would help feed the chickens, hogs, cows, horses, etc. and would help to milk the cows, by hand, twice a day. In the summer time he would go with his father to help in the fields at his farm. They would start to work at 7:00 in the morning and would not finish till 5:00 that evening.

Times had certainly changed, even if people hadn't. Bryan's essay on Melvin A. Lakness (b. in 1914), referred to his first grade teacher, Mrs. Harmon: "One day Mr. Lakness came in with a dirty face, so Mrs. Harmon whipped him and washed his face for him."

Almost every interview proved a pleasure to read but Annette's still stands out. She began by noting that her subject was her grandfather on her father's side. She skipped over his childhood and said she chose him because he fought bravely in World War II. Grandpa was born in 1921, joined the army at 18, and lost a leg in combat six months later.

I knew instantly those dates didn't add up. The U. S. entered the war in 1941; so she had her grandfather wounded too early, or born too late. My heart sank. I was going to have to speak to one of my favorite students about careless work, if not outright fabrication. Then a third prospect dawned. What if *grandpa* was lying? What if he was making up stories to impress Annette?

I had trouble concentrating.

Then on page two the detail that clarified everything: Grandpa was born in Germany and was wearing the field gray of the Wehrmacht when he lost his leg in Poland.

***

My efforts in school when I was a teen were far from impressive. Still, I had several fine teachers.

Now, in my own classes, I borrowed a lesson from my numbskull past. Junior year of high school, I had a superb English instructor named Lee Smith, a fanatic for clarity in writing. Indeed, Smith forbade the use of the words "thing" or "things" in formal writing. If he found either the penalty was harsh and irrevocable. He circled the word and slapped an F on your story.

236

I adopted the same rule (modified for a modern world in which parents might suffer apoplexy if I flunked a child). Then I explained to students why. I told them my friends and I learned to comb stories, looking for the offending words. In the process we found other mistakes. Smith forced us to think about what we were trying to say. So I would use his rule: only allowing anyone caught using "thing" or "things" to recopy and resubmit for a higher mark. When students began substituting "stuff" for "thing/things" I added a third word to my list of taboos.

"Don't tell me you left your 'stuff' in your locker," I explained. "If you left your marijuana stash, say so. Say exactly what you mean."

Of course, grading writing is a daunting task. One evening I looked up from my desk at home to see I had spent ninety minutes going over ten 1,000 word interviews. I kept plowing, believing students would be thankful someday that they had learned to express themselves with greater facility.

The very next evening a mother called, interrupting another grading marathon to complain. I had a second ironclad rule. Any assignment not broken into paragraphs would be returned with a failing mark. Mom was mad because I gave her son an F when he turned in one giant globular paragraph, a thousand words in length.

I said he had the option to break up the essay and return it for a better mark.

Mom was irate. "I don't see why he should have to do the essay over. This isn't English class, after all." (I wrote that down while we were still on the phone.) "It's only history."

I told mom her son had a choice—thanked her for her call—and hung up the phone.

Headaches aside, the need to do more writing seemed clear. Another good lesson began with a look at Iroquois culture. First, students completed a brief reading on Iroquois life. Twenty-five topics were covered, one paragraph each, including homes, food, clothing, marriage and government.

The second step was to ask students to write twenty-five paragraphs focusing on modern American life. Once more, the kids responded with gasps. They felt better only after I explained there were no right answers—they should only try to be descriptive. "Don't just say

'Americans eat a lot of junk food.' Give examples. Anyone have any?" I asked.

"Ding Dongs and Twinkies," Chris volunteered.

"Perfect."

"Little Debbie Snack Cakes," Rafael laughed.

Okay, now students had the idea.

In terms of history, I wanted them to be familiar with a highly advanced native culture, which in the 1600s gave women control over property and a say in government. So they read:

7. In many ways, Iroquois society was controlled by women. Females "owned" the homes and the right to use certain farm lands. Older women in each clan chose the sachems, or chiefs, and could remove those who failed. It was said, then, that they had "put a chip in his mouth," ending his right to speak in Council.

A boy described our culture in response: "Women control the credit card but men control the channel changer."

Students read:

10. Hunting was the man's job. When a warrior was about to shoot he asked the animal for forgiveness. Then he cleared his mind so the creature didn't "hear" his thoughts. After he made the kill he put his hand on the body, saying, "Brother, thank you for giving your life so that my people may eat." Sometimes large hunting parties built a long V-shaped wall, and started fires to drive game towards the "point." There the animals were trapped and slaughtered.

Steff made this comparison:

A lady walks into the clothing preserve, a determined look upon her face. She spots a promising rack and the hunt ensues. She spots a perfect prey. The lady snares it and runs with it to the clerk. She pulls out 5 green bullets, hands them to the cashier, and she has done it. The lady has finally bagged the elusive shirt.

Another student read about Iroquois eating habits and focused on a modern American ritual: "The man takes the top and bottom disks and twists in different directions to reveal the cream center. He then licks the cream and eats the disks later. Sometimes he dips the disks in a glass of milk."

Yes! The mighty Oreo!

Sometimes, artistic kids asked if they could draw instead of write. On one occasion, Randi turned in twenty-five full-page color illustrations. She said she had devoted ten hours to the assignment. Considering the quality of what she presented, I had no doubt she was telling the truth.

***

During the second half of my career I was blessed to work with a dozen fine student teachers. Anne Dollenmeyer came in one afternoon, a week before her placement began, to get a feel for what kind of kids she'd be handling.

She happened to sit in during my seventh bell, a class sprinkled with comical kids. Two of the funniest, Shelby and Nathan, sparred verbally every day.

"This is Ms. Dollenmeyer," I explained by way of introduction. "She wants to be a teacher. So, pretend you're normal and try not to scare her away."

Nathan replied, with perfect timing: "You might want to take Shelby out of the room, then."

Anne cracked up. So did everyone else, including Shelby, and by our laughter we credited Nathan for his wit.

What Ms. Dollenmeyer and all my student teachers found was that if you cared to listen, every adolescent had a "voice."

Julie Cohen, who came to me from Miami University, had an interesting writing assignment designed to bring it out. The "I Am" format, as she called it, was simple and adaptable in all kinds of ways. Students began by filling in spaces at the top in order to make clear what they were writing about:

The Lewis and Clark Expedition

History Date:
Description of Event You Chose:

I am _____.
I wonder _____.
I hear _____.
I see _____.
I want _____.
I am _____.
I pretend _____.
I feel _____.
I touch _____.
I worry _____.
I cry _____.
I am _____.
I understand _____.
I say _____.
I dream _____.

The first time Julie used the idea a young man in fifth bell approached for clarification. Could he write about anybody on the expedition?

Julie said he could.

Sam was only an average student but buckled down to work. When Ms. Cohen called for volunteers, he was first to raise a hand and say he'd read. Then he marched to the front of the room and told his story through the eyes of the Indian guide Sacagawea's baby.

Sam was a big kid, which greatly enhanced the comic effect. Some of what he wrote fit the history perfectly. For "I feel," he turned to humor: "I feel something squishy in my diaper." When he got to "I cry," he had: "waaa, waaa, waaa," which he delivered in a pitch perfect sniffling tone.

Julie and his classmates applauded. Sam looked like a young actor accepting a Golden Globe.

Sam opened up more the rest of the year. His overall work improved slightly, from C- to C+, thanks to Ms. Cohen's creativity. But we all teach in the real world, where miracles are in short supply. You try to reach kids but they don't always stay "reached."

Sam died three years later, choking on his own vomit, one young voice silenced forever by a drug overdose.

***

I adopted Ms. Cohen's idea and used it the rest of my career. After switching to Ancient World History in 2004, we used the "I Am" format with a reading on the Black Plague.

To capture the fear people felt in the 1300s we began with modern examples. One was an article on MRSA, called *"A Menace in the Locker Room,"* taken from *Sports Illustrated.* It opened with a high school wrestling coach who noticed a small red mark on the back of his right calf. Probably nothing. Maybe an ingrown hair. The spot grew. The pain intensified. The coach went to the doctor, received antibiotics, and headed home. The pain redoubled. A second doctor prescribed higher doses. The leg swelled to twice normal size. Soon the coach was fighting for his life. A foot-long incision to drain fluid was made. Later a second was necessary to drain his hip.

In college they tell you to capture student interest at the start of a lesson but this was too easy. The picture of the coach's leg with a long line of stitches brought gasps from the audience.

Next we talked about the spread of drug-resistant bacteria and the causes. The article mentioned eight linemen for the St. Louis Rams who contracted MRSA in 2003. The head athletic trainer at Georgia added, "You would be hard-pressed to find a football team at any level—pro, college or high school—that hasn't had to deal with it one way or another."

I assured students that antibiotics killed most staph infections. But some bacteria resist. In fact, anti-bacterial soap backfired, killing weaker bacteria and clearing a path for the hardiest, most dangerous strains to multiply.

"How many of you have antibiotic soap at home?" I asked. Hands (clean) went up all over. "Does anybody know what it says on the label?"

"Kills 99.9% of all bacteria," came a chorus of response.

"Yeah, it's that 0.1% you have to worry about. Next time your mom tells you to wash your hands, look at her and say, 'You're trying to kill me, aren't you?'"

The comical kids promised they would—and were proud to tell me the next day they had.

We turned to AIDS, which terrorized Americans in the years before these teens were born. I explained that in the early 80s people had no idea how AIDS spread and thought saliva and tears were infectious. Coughing and kissing, even arm-to-arm contact was feared. "Imagine AIDS could be spread by coughing," I continued. "That's what it was like when Black Plague struck."

A question came up, unexpectedly, about smallpox. I said the last case in history was in the 70s, but there were still two specimens in existence. One was kept in a test tube in a lab run by the Center for Disease Control, the other in a facility controlled by the Russians.

We had fifteen minutes left and I put everyone to work on the reading. It was titled: "SO GREAT WAS THE CRUELTY OF HEAVEN," a line taken from the words of a plague survivor.

Students read:

> Victims showed black swellings in the groin or armpits. These swellings or "buboes" oozed pus and blood and could be the size of an egg or an apple. This was followed by the appearance of black splotches on the skin. As the disease developed other symptoms made their appearance. Those infected had a continuous fever. Some spit up blood.

Bodily fluids—clothes—bedding—anything touched by victims—seemed to carry the plague.

With five minutes left, I asked everyone to finish the story at home and do an "I Am" related to sickness, injury or health for homework.

Once again the work kids produced was wonderful. Many focused on plague, but the variety of response gives hint why teaching can be so much fun. Chelsea chose to write *as* the immune system, an imaginative leap I could never have made. Drew took the perspective of a tick responsible for Lyme disease. Ian was chicken pox incarnate, "begging to be scratched."

Brent was a virus in a laboratory:

I am small pox.
I wonder why I am bad.
I hear that I am a terrible disease.
I see that little kid that is scared of me.
I want to be set free from this container.
I am small pox....
I touch glass.

Darren wrote about what it was like to have A.D.H.D.:

I wonder why I have it.
I hear people laughing.
I see problems and can't pay attention.
I want to get better grades.
I am a teen with A.D.H.D.
I pretend that I am normal.
I feel dumb.
I touch my head and try to think....
I say I am smart.
I dream I really am.

Others attacked the assignment from a comical perspective. Meghan wrote about a tragic paper cut. Michael described the time his dog Finch gobbled up a corn dog, complete with stick. First, Finch realizes unguarded corn dogs are in view on a kitchen table:

I am panting to get attention.

Later, post-surgery, Finch considers the error of his ways:

I understand that I am a dumb dog.

243

I say that wearing a lampshade to keep me from ripping my stitches is worth it.

Amy, a reserved but brilliant young lady, wrote about a period when her father, a native of Germany, was diagnosed with colon cancer and passed away:

I am Christopher ----.
I wonder how long I have left to live.
I hear Amy talking about sports, trying to cheer me up.
I see my family's saddened faces.
I want to fight this cancer.
I am weakened and can hardly walk.
I pretend to slip into a deep sleep but stay awake and listen to conversations.
I feel my life slipping away.
I touch the hand of my daughter.
I worry about what will happen to my family when I am gone.
I cry knowing I may never see my family again.
I am slowly losing my life.
I understand that my family will miss me dearly.
I say that I love my family.
I dream the place I will go will be like Germany.

Allyson turned in an equally poignant response. She was quiet in class, rarely speaking. For her subject she chose the car wreck in which her mother died, her father at the wheel, and the psychic damage done to every surviving family member. Her father was overwhelmed with guilt and having a hard time raising three kids and he was drinking. Allyson carried the burden of holding the family together. Her grades suffered as a result.

I failed to keep a copy of what she wrote; but the simple act of admission seemed to break a logjam in her heart. She began pouring out her feelings in her writing. If she still didn't talk much in class, she smiled more, and I told her what a fine writer she was.

22.

Songhai Trade

"It is the ignorant who are the sufferers of ignorance, as truly as the blind by want of sight."
Plato

Nothing the foot soldiers say ever alters the planning of the education generals. Once No Child Left Behind became law there was no stopping the steamroller of "school reform." Change was coming, even if the steamroller was heading in the wrong direction, crushing everything in its path, including much of what was best in U. S. education.

By 2014, every child was going to be proficient in reading and math.

I have faith in kids, but only in America could lawmakers promise perfection without pain or sacrifice.

***

Here's what NCLB meant on the classroom battlefield. In April 2003 my last principal, Mrs. Kramer, called together the social studies department to inform us the big switch was coming in August. Under the new State of Ohio curriculum, Jeff Sharpless and I, as seventh grade teachers, would switch to Ancient World History, covering 1000 B. C. to A. D. 1750.

Having taught American history for twenty-nine years, I was stunned. To teach a subject properly you must know the material. Most of what I had once known about ancient history was now forgotten. It was like leaving work Friday afternoon as a carpenter and arriving Monday morning to be told you were a plumber.

Once the shock wore off I made a beeline for Borders Books and plunked down $202 for materials, including Thomas Malory's *L'Morte d'Arthur*, the original King Arthur saga, *India: A History,* and John Reader's *Africa: Biography of a Continent.* King Arthur turned out to be fun to read. The book on India proved excruciatingly dull. And the first chapter of Reader opened with shifting tectonic plates four billion years ago.

I had *a lot* to learn.

Even bureaucrats tucked away in cubicles in Columbus must have realized this switch was too drastic. The move was postponed till August 2004.

That meant sixteen months to learn plumbing. I had time to read the Bible, Koran and Popul Vuh too. It meant knocking out a book a week: *Japan: a Short Cultural History, Everyday Life of the Incas* and *Chronicles of Froissart,* a contemporary account of the Hundred Years War. My oldest daughter and I took a course in Greek Literature at the University of Cincinnati and it struck me Homer's work might be adapted for middle school. I purchased Tacitus and Livy and Plutarch's *Lives* and read the Roman historians with pleasure.

In terms of modern-day lawmakers, who passed No Child Left Behind with little input from teachers, Plutarch offered wise admonition:

"Laws must look to possibilities."

***

When time came to switch I was ready. New standards stressed the use of timelines. So we started with that. Since most seventh graders are twelve or thirteen, I asked them to cover events from 1991-2004. I also made up a timeline of my own to serve as template, employing a rather greater scale. Above a line marking my 55th birthday, I drew a cake, stuck full of candles like a flaming pin-cushion. The event for 2000 was a bicycle wreck which left me in the hospital. I labeled it: "My head bounces off pavement. This explains a lot."

Students came through with creative responses. Jerika glued her kindergarten picture in the upper left-hand corner of her timeline. For 1994, when she was three, she had a picture of a shoe and the caption: "Learned to tie my shoes." At age four she had a picture of an eating utensil and a tragic description: "Tripped and fork gets stuck partly in head." Elliot had this for 1992, when he was one: "Walking is now a possible way of transportation."

I could see at once the rich possibilities of my new subject. But now I faced an existential dilemma. The pressure to teach to the test increased steadily, from August 2004 until the day I retired, and has only increased since. In my view teaching to the test was malpractice.

The correct approach is simple. The more you learn the better. Or, as Poet Laureate Billy Collins put it:

"…no matter what size the aquarium of one's learning,
another colored pebble can always be dropped in."

There's no way of knowing how much the state spent when it unleashed its phalanx of bureaucrats and drew up the new curriculum. Whatever it cost, the money was wasted. Seventh grade social studies teachers were now expected to cover twenty-eight centuries of human history. Students would be judged proficient based on the score for a single test.

Worse still, the social studies section of the Ohio Achievement Test (OAT) would consist of fifty questions spread over material from sixth, seventh, and eighth grades. So my success or failure would boil down, roughly, to answers students supplied on 16 and 2/3rd's questions.

I thought this was lunacy.

One problem, to start, was that the official standards were vague to the vanishing point. Take Geography Standards, Benchmark A: "Identify on a map the location of major physical and human features on each continent."

Under this benchmark there were two Indicators. One: "For each of the societies studied, identify the location of significant physical and human characteristics on a map of the relevant region." Two: "On a map, identify places related to the historical events being studied and explain their significance."

At that point, teachers had no clue what would end up on the social studies section of the OAT. So what should we teach about world geography? It would be useful to know that England is an island. It turned out, when I gave classes a map of Europe to fill out, plenty of kids thought

France was England and England was France. I thought it might help if they could find Ireland and Spain on the map, because so many of us trace our roots back to those countries—with a stop, via Mexico, for some.

If it was up to me, I would have asked students to know what nations sell us oil. I would have expected them to locate Saudi Arabia, Iraq, Iran, Israel, Pakistan and Afghanistan on a map. It would be useful to locate Jerusalem and Mecca and know why those cities are still important. Current events matter, right? Too bad they can *never* show up on a standardized test.

When we studied the collapse of ancient Kush civilization, due to environmental degradation, we might have spent time looking at world population trends: 1927: two billion; 1976: four billion; now: seven billion. We might have discussed strains on land, air and water this growth will cause.

The problem, of course, is that we haven't yet included *historical* places and you can get 16 and 2/3rd's good questions out of the paragraphs above and 16 and 2/3rd's questions from the seventh grade curriculum are all the OAT can "measure."

Here's another Benchmark: "Explain reasons that people, products and ideas move from place to place and the effects of that movement on geographic patterns."

Does that mean we should cover the slave trade that stripped Africa of 9,000,000 human beings? John Reader describes slaves flowing out of the continent "like blood from a stab wound." That's a great line that will stick in kids' heads. We use it in class and spend a day on this inhuman traffic.

In the spring of 2005 the State does not ask about the slave trade on the OAT. Technically, that means we "wasted" a day addressing the topic.

Suddenly, I have to worry. Should we focus on Vikings? Or Hun raiders and China's Great Wall? Or when Rome flattens Carthage and spreads its culture, instead of the reverse? You can spend two days on Rome and Carthage but if there's no question on the OAT you might as well save your breath, as Seneca once said, "to cool your porridge."

The question now becomes: Which pebbles should we pick up from the vast streamed of knowledge?

Until we see the first OAT we have no clue. Once we do see it, and see it a second year, social studies teachers rub their eyes in disbelief.

These are among the basics the State of Ohio says students must know:

- The first year they must select the proper definition for *mercantilism* (picking A, B, C or D).
- They must answer two questions, one the first year, one the second, about *Shay's Rebellion*.
- The single geography question (not a bad one, but the only one) on the first test is to know what river is shown on a map of Africa and indicated by a number. (It's the *Nile*).
- The only map question on the practice test posted on the state website to provide guidance before the second test is to know on what continent the *Gobi Desert* is found.
- Students are asked about *Songhai* trade the first year—and asked again the second year.
- The only question on Roman history the first year goes something like this: "What *language* did the Romans speak?"

(FUN FACT: I once testified in front of the education committee of the Ohio Senate. I asked if any member could define mercantilism. No one could. No one had ever heard of Songhai, either.)

If the state asks only a few questions it's no longer a matter of what we should *cover* but what we're wise to skip. Once we begin to get a grip on what the test includes and how it's designed, we know Julius Caesar is dead where the OAT is concerned. There's no point going over the story of Pompeii, nor the tale of Nero and the courage of early Christian martyrs. Interesting stories aren't what these tests are about. Courage can't be measured. If students can find Rome, Italy, Greece and the Mediterranean Sea on a map those are not "basics."

Only the Gobi Desert matters.

It's a simple concept. From this point forward, if it's not on the test it doesn't count as knowledge.

***

Forced to pick between a standardized vs. broad-based approach to learning, I chose the latter. In good conscience, I couldn't bring myself to do it any other way. The first unit my classes did, my first year in Ancient World History, focused on Homer and the *Iliad*.

Naturally, if you ask seventh graders who "Homer" is you hear the same answer every time. He's that cartoon character. At least one boy is sure to imitate Homer Simpson's trademark: "Doh."

"Doh," indeed!

I didn't expect the state to ask a question about the *Iliad* but the epic worked with teens on several levels. First, we had a love story and war story rolled into one. Second, we could tie the *Iliad* to current events and look at issues that will merit attention as long as humanity survives. One handout I prepared included these questions for consideration:

1. Why would a young man (or young woman today) wish to be a soldier?
2. How might the story of soldiers in Iraq or Afghanistan be like the story of the Greeks and Trojans?
3. What is a hero?
4. What is a celebrity?
5. What is the difference?
6. Do you believe our lives are governed by "fate?"

Indeed, those who preach the saving grace of high-stakes testing ignore a cardinal tenet of education. That is: our first task is to impart a passion for learning.

I began by having kids explain how their parents met, an idea I swiped from my friend and colleague, Mr. Sharpless. Some didn't know. Those who did were anxious to tell. A girl said her father got off an elevator on the wrong floor and had to seek direction. The first woman he saw provided guidance, struck up conversation with her father, and later they married.

"Imagine your father pressed the correct button," I said. "None of us *has* to be here. None of us has to survive this day. Is it fate that we are? That we do?"

This led to a final question:

7. Do the gods (does God) step in to help or hurt individuals? When and why?

When we finished our discussion we were right where I wanted to be. Was "fate" random or did God (the gods) lend a guiding hand? Like Homer and the Greeks, the kids couldn't know for sure.

To make this unit work I had to trust teens to see that Homer was timeless. They did. When we turned to the poem the next day, students realized the *Iliad* was a superhero tale. Achilles was Superman, his heel his kryptonite. Helen first appeared in the synopsis I prepared dressed in "shimmering garments," headed for the palace to hear the news. It had the same feel a viewer might have watching the red carpet on Academy Awards Night.

Since the names and vocabulary were challenging, we began the reading in class. It was hard to keep all the warriors straight. But that was never the point. The point was to expose teens to classic literature, which would make them better readers and writers in the end.

Homer did the hard work, capturing teens' interest with battle scenes like this:

…the son of Phyleus, the spear-famed, closing upon him
struck him with the sharp spear behind the head at the tendon,
and straight on through the teeth and under the tongue cut the
    bronze blade,
and he dropped in the dust gripping in his teeth the cold bronze.

Other times, students were moved by passages like one, where Hector, who has just donned his helmet, warns of dark times to come. For his wife, Andromache, and their infant son, the future might be bleak:

So speaking glorious Hector held out his arms to his baby,
who shrank back to his…nurse's bosom
screaming, and frightened at the [look] of his own father,
terrified as he saw the bronze and the crest with its horse-hair,
nodding dreadfully, as he thought, from the peak of the helmet.
Then his beloved father laughed out, and his honored mother,
and at once glorious Hector lifted from his head the helmet
and laid it in all its shining upon the ground. Then taking
up his dear son he tossed him about in his arms, and kissed
him….

Down the hall, Jeff Sharpless was using the same handout. He stopped by my room the next day and suggested putting together a comic play, based on Homer's tale. The focus would be a contest between Jessica Simpson (big on TV at that time) and Helen of Troy, for title of "the most beautiful woman in the world." Helen would brag about having the face that launched a thousand ships.

Jessica would counter: "I have the face that launched a cheesy reality show."

Jeff and I wanted learning to be fun. So we put together a comedy and asked for volunteers. The response was overwhelming, even though tryouts and practices would be held after school. So many kids showed up and were so excited, we decided to create two entire casts.

The play changed as we went along, mixing Homeric lyrics, modern tabloid gossip, and absurd sight gags. One narrator, Homer in our play, came up with the idea of reading her lines as "Hillbilly Homer." Her role was twice as funny her way. In another scene Homer described mighty Ajax, who "carries his shield like a wall." One of our artists suggested making a large, rectangular, plywood shield and painting it like a brick wall. So we did.

In another scene Greek warriors stripped the armor from Hector's corpse. The actors gave it a twist. When one warrior removed the dead man's helmet another pulled out a hidden pair of boxer shorts and lifted them in triumph, redefining the term: "Greek tragedy."

Jeff, who played guitar in a rock band in younger days, organized a "Greek chorus" and handled set design. One song in the play followed the tune from *Yellow Submarine*:

> In this town that's under siege
> Lives a girl, who's really neat
> She is Hel-en of Troy
> She is hot, oh boy!

> So we fight the filthy Greeks.
> Every one of us thinks they're freaks.
> If our city falls some day
> We'll be killed or enslaved.

CHORUS

> We all live in a city known as Troy,
> A city known as Troy,
> A city known as Troy.

> We all live in a city known as Troy,
> A city known as Troy,
> A city known as Troy.

Finally, our production concluded with a rendition of Highway to Hades, based on the classic AC/DC tune.

Jeff and I got fifty kids involved and did it three years in a row. Each year they gave up twenty or twenty-five afternoons after school to rehearse. We generated great enthusiasm and when we put on "Jessica of Troy" for our classes the actors, artists, singers and audience (even a few parents who came to watch) enjoyed the show. A hundred and fifty kids got acting and drawing and singing experience.

Too bad you can't turn that into a question on the OAT.

***

It only gets worse. On the OAT there won't be more than one question about the Greeks in a typical year. So it would make sense to stick to basics. After all, one idea right on the test is greater than a *thousand* ideas right, if we have them in our heads, but they do not appear as questions.

One of a set of water colors done by Amanda for a project on the Trojan War: "Paris leaps from the ranks of the Trojans."

The new State of Ohio curriculum required us to focus on the roots of democracy. That at least made sense. But the only question the state asked the first year on the standardized test went something like this: "Who invented democracy?"

All you had to know was it was the Greeks.

In my class, by comparison, we addressed the inherent limits of democracy and threats to our rights, not just from government, but from our neighbors. We began by defining the terms "minority" and "majority." Then we put up this quote from John Adams:

"Absolute power in a majority is as drunk as it is in one."

I asked kids to name minorities that could not protect their rights through votes alone. "Blacks would be one," Andrew replied. Ella noted that women could not protect their rights until they could vote.

"Does anyone know when women earned the right to vote in the United States?" I inquired.

Someone did: 1920.

I informed the class this would be on the next test, not because the state might put it on the OAT the following spring, but because that date highlighted an important point. "My mother was in kindergarten by the time American women were deemed capable of casting a ballot.

"Just think," I said to Danae, singling out one of the brightest students in the room, "you would have had fewer rights through all the long ages of history than the *dumbest man* who ever walked the face of the earth!"

This riled up Danae and all the other girls and kept discussion rolling.

A young man surprised me when he asked: "What about gays? They can't protect their rights with votes because there aren't many of them." It was a good comment and opened up all kinds of possibilities.

We could now go in a hundred directions. Each had merit. But which—if any—would the State of Ohio test? We might look at what happened to Japanese-Americans in 1942. After Pearl Harbor was bombed 110,000 people were sent to relocation camps.

"Most were full citizens, with the same rights as you and me," I like to remind students.

Given a chance, thousands of Japanese-American men eventually fought under the Stars and Stripes, winning praise for their courage. I always felt the following story summed it up:

Daniel Inoyue was fighting in Italy when he and his men received orders to charge a German position. Inoyue led the way forward, was shot in the stomach, and kept going. A grenade nearly blew off his right arm. Inoyue cut down the German who tossed the grenade, by throwing one of his own left-handed. Then a bullet hit him in the right leg. Still, he kept going, personally destroying two enemy machine guns. Twenty-five German soldiers died in the action—and Inoyue received the Distinguished Service Cross for his courage.

On his way home after the war, however, Inoyue was denied a haircut in a San Francisco barbershop. In uniform, with his battle ribbons and medals clearly displayed—and his smashed arm in a sling—he was told: WE DON'T SERVE JAPS HERE!

JAPS!

Inoyue was no JAP.

Neither were thousands of others imprisoned during World War II. They were Americans, even if others refused to treat them as such.

In a pre-standardized world, Inoyue's experience could be used to raise questions about the nature of prejudice and why it's most potent when people are afraid. (Think: Muslims in America after 9/11.) If we didn't want to use that example, we could focus on the Greeks' fear of excessive power in the hands of government. (Think: Tea Party Movement.) We could have jumped sideways, to the Bill of Rights, and discussed why this list is critical in protecting basic freedoms. (Think: everybody.) Unfortunately, if you're going to test *basics*, teachers are wise to stick to *basics* and hammer them into student heads.

It's a paint-by-the-numbers approach to learning and a pitiful way to go about raising standards.

Ignoring the straightjacket the state wished to impose, we spent another day looking at examples of Greek wisdom and trying to figure out what ancient thinkers meant:

"The wise are doubtful." Socrates

"He must be ready to suffer more hardships than he asks of his soldiers, more fatigue, greater extremes of heat and cold."
Xenophon (on leadership)

Ideas matter, and we concluded by considering a line I first heard in ninth grade, on some rare occasion when I was interested enough to pay attention. The Roman poet Juvenal summed up the "Greek Way," saying their standard was:

"…a sound mind in a sound body."

We defined "sound" briefly. Then I explained that I had tried to live according to that standard. I asked kids what plans they had to develop both their minds and bodies. Corey said she thought you could be excessive about working out, like professional body builders. Kasia said if you were a bookworm that could be bad. I introduced the odd notion, coming from a teacher, that you *could* study too much. Others admitted they needed to start running or get outside and shoot baskets.

When time came to wrap the discussion I told each class I planned to bicycle across the United States someday. Kids thought that was cool. I told them what mattered was that they set their *own goals*.

It was time for the bell and I left everyone with a final word from Aristotle. One day he was asked how much superior educated men were to the uneducated. "As much," he replied, "as the living are to the dead."

Aristotle.

What a dumbass.

He failed to mention standardized tests.

***

Of course, you can "teach to the test" and still cover material worth covering; but every good teacher has more than enough valuable material to fill 180 days and then fill them twice over, even if you pile on the homework. So you hate to waste a quarter of the year, or however much time you must, preparing for a test that has so little merit.

By contrast, in the wake of 9/11, it seemed to me all aspects of Islam might be worthy of attention. Yet, the first year the OAT was administered, the only question related was to name the Muslim holy book. The second year the single question was to know the name of the founder of the faith.

I was also surprised to find the state curriculum made no mention of jihad. It seemed important to address that topic if we wanted to understand current threats to the United States. The "basics" were also silent in regard to the extremist thinking propounded by Osama bin Laden. The state had no interest in Sunnis, Shiites or Kurds, central to problems in Iraq. On matters of importance after September 11, the OAT was blind, deaf and dumb.

I decided to go beyond basics and look at ideas from the Koran (Qur'an) in depth. A few examples:

The Koran/Qur'an preaches the oneness of God. God is all-knowing, merciful and forgiving. He wants men to treat others with justice and fair dealing. Man should be kind to orphans and widows. He should show charity to the poor.

Men may have sexual relations "with their wives and their slave-girls, for these are lawful to them." "You may marry other women who seem good to you: two, three, or four of them."

Jihad (or Holy War) is discussed:

When you meet the unbelievers in the battlefield strike off their heads and, when you have laid them low, bind your captives firmly. Then grant them their freedom or take ransom for them, until War shall lay down her armor...As for those who are slain in the cause of

Allah...He will admit them to the Paradise He has made known to them.

Another handout highlighted aspects of life in Saudi Arabia, a nation influenced by a very strict form of Islam, known as Wahhabism:

Keep in mind: Osama bin Laden and fifteen of the nineteen hijackers on 9/11 were born here...There are few nations more afraid of change than Saudi Arabia. The country is ruled by the Saud royal family. It is the biggest supplier of oil to the world.

Islam is against:

o   gambling
o   prostitution
o   drinking alcohol
o   portraying people in art
o   adultery (punishment can include stoning)
o   drug dealing (dealers may be executed in Saudi Arabia)
o   premarital sex (can lead to honor killing of females in several countries)

The reading went on to outline restrictions on Saudi women—not allowed to vote—drive—go shopping without a male relative—expected to cover face and hair and wear long robes in public.

We also defined polygamy. (None of this showed up on the next OAT.)

Discussion flowed in interesting directions. Most kids could see advantages to banning alcohol. One girl said we should execute drug dealers too. A friend of hers had OD'd the previous summer. In sixth bell we focused on how women were treated. Kids could see covering them reduced temptation.

"It's like when a wife hides the cookies so her husband won't ruin his diet," I noted.

Kara seemed puzzled. "Then how do they have kids?" she wondered.

"You have to go looking for the cookies," I replied.

Instantly, Kara and I, and most of her classmates caught the unintentional double meaning and burst into hysterical laughter.

"I'm going to hear from some parent on that one," I said, once the hilarity subsided.

23.

Pick Up a Broom and Sweep

"I used to be disgusted. Now I try to be amused."
Elvis Costello

Sitting across from Mrs. Kramer in her office, the only barrier between us her big gray metal desk, I had no way of knowing what my principal was thinking. Perhaps she noticed when I blanched at the news. Secretly, my dismay might have pleased her.

I couldn't tell.

Her face revealed the same emotion I'd expect from a skilled poker player, holding a kings-high full house, or, possibly running a pair-of-twos bluff.

She had just inquired whether or not I intended to return for another year in the classroom.

Including military service, I had enough time to my credit to retire in June 2007. For a variety of reasons, however, I had just answered: "Yes."

"If you do," she responded—I thought—a little too quickly, "I'll probably move you. I plan to make changes, shake up teams, get new blood in place. So I'd be moving you to eighth grade."

Surprised, to say the least, I asked, "Have there been complaints from team members, that I don't know about?"

"No," she said. There had not.

***

At that point, in January of 2007, I was halfway through my third year of Ancient World History. I still loved the kids and now had a firm grip on the material. And in the classroom, the only place that ever mattered to me, I was doing fine.

I knew what kids thought.

In June 2005, I had handed out my anonymous year-end survey to check how students felt I'd done. When asked to give opinions, 68% rated my work "excellent," 26% "good," 6% "fair."

At the end of my second year of Ancient World History, in June 2006, I passed out the survey again. In students' estimations, I performed better: 78% "excellent," 20% "good," 2% "fair."

Yet, like the Grim Administrator, Erica was pointing a fleshless finger toward the exit.

If I was still thrilled to teach, I admit my last principal and I didn't get along. I thought this was unfortunate, because when we clashed, I felt the issues were almost always trivial. If my ability to help kids was not impaired, I never worried about what my boss was doing. Besides, she ran a good building. Discipline, for example, was strong.

I told her I felt she did a good job on several occasions. That didn't help.

Who knows? Part of the problem may have been that by the time she took charge of Loveland Middle School, I no longer placed faith in "new" approaches in education, few of which were actually new, even fewer anywhere close to as effective as promised. Certainly, I had *no use* for standardized testing and made that clear during several staff discussions.

Perhaps, in her eyes, I was a pain in the ass. And why, she might have wondered, was I so skeptical when discussion turned to new plans and ideas?

I'd been around. That was part of the problem. I had been witness to the arc of modern U. S. education.

When I was new to the profession, to cite an antediluvian example, my first principal instituted a "Teacher Advisory Program" (TAP). Every teacher was assigned to work with a group of teens, meeting for twenty minutes each afternoon. The idea was to provide a place where every teen had a voice, where students felt safe and might have a little fun. Once a week we did "silent sustained reading," meant to encourage kids to get into the habit. They picked their own books—and teachers, too—but all were expected to read at the same time. Once a month we extended TAP to two hours and took groups out to lunch, museums, or bowling.

TAP was a fine idea, until you tabulated lost time. Ohio schools start with 180 days for instruction. Now we lopped off twenty minutes each afternoon. Multiply that out, add two hours for monthly outings, and we were sacrificing seventy-five hours.

A school day in Ohio is 7.5 hours long. So we were losing *two weeks* of instruction.

I hated to sacrifice time on task as a young teacher and hated it even more, decades later, long after TAP faded away. Now Mrs. Kramer brought the idea back. Once again we would carve out a block at the end of every day. Every teacher would lead a group. Silent sustained reading was back too. Now it would be twice a week.

What young teachers discovered and old ones rediscovered, was that kids often preferred to use advisory time to talk to friends or start homework. They might whine if you planned activities.

Or, on days set aside for reading, you heard: "I forgot my book."

"I have homework. Why can't I read the textbook?"

"Why do we have to *read* anyway?"

These were minor headaches. But the loss of what equaled eight days, in this case, seemed a high price to pay, particularly in an era when the Raven croaked, "Standards, Standards, Standards," evermore.

When I told Mrs. Kramer I thought we were wasting too much time I think she took my comments as proof of a churlish attitude.

On another occasion, she encouraged staff to attend a seminar called Capturing Kids' Hearts. "All the other team leaders are going," she assured me during one of our amiable chats.

"Thanks, I'm not interested," I replied. "I already know how to capture kids' hearts."

Besides, the seminar lasted three days—and that went against my taboo of cutting time for instruction, even three minutes if I could avoid it. I explained my position; but another team leader told me later Mrs. Kramer was not pleased.

What can I say? That's how I rolled.

I wasn't the smartest teacher, or prettiest, certainly not the most charming. I put stock only in working hard, in setting an example for students, and expected them to work hard, too.

Call it dedication.

Call it obsessive compulsive behavior.

Blame my Dad. Growing up, he reminded me a thousand times that a good employee put in "sixty minutes of work for sixty minutes of pay."

Fifty-nine, you say?

Nope. That wouldn't cut it.

"Find something to do," he always added. "If nothing else, pick up a broom and sweep."

There's no mystery to why I was successful in a classroom, or why so many of my colleagues did such wonderful work. As a teacher, you could always pick up a broom and find something to sweep.

***

By the time Erica and I sat down on that January day to discuss my future, I had served as a team leader for a decade. In that role, too, I was happy, having had the honor of working with a number of phenomenal educators. In 1990, our Parent Teacher Student Association (PTSA) created an "Educator of the Year" award, with one winner for each school in the district. Steve Ball, our team math teacher, won twice. Rachel Angel, who served with our team briefly, won for outstanding efforts in Special Education. Kathy Simpson, our Learning Disabilities specialist, won in 2009, after I retired. Even Pat Settlemire, our teachers' aide, was incredible, always willing to pick up a broom and sweep.

Cheri King, another great teammate, operated the same way. We used to tease her, saying she looked like Barney Rubble, motoring down the hall, legs spinning at preternatural speed. There was never a moment when Ms. King wasn't on a mission to ensure students learned as much as they could.

Fads come and go in schools, like Pet Rocks and Pound Puppies, with roughly the same impact. Still, teachers are admonished to keep up with every fad, because some expert, pushing some plan or technological toy, insists this fad—*yes, this fad!*—will change education!

And…well…hope springs eternal.

At one point, cross-curricular planning was the "Fad of the Month."

So, all team leaders were encouraged to put emphasis on cross-curricular planning.

Our team, the Olympians, did its part. Jeane Weisbrod, a Language Arts teacher, and one of my favorites, took it upon herself to introduce an NCAA March Madness research project, to get kids to think about what colleges they might one day attend. Teachers of all subjects were involved. Every student reported on daily life, degree programs and academics at a school in the tournament brackets. It wasn't Jeane's idea originally but she improved it greatly. By the time she was done our entire seventh grade, 350 students, was loaded on buses and headed south for a tour of the University of Kentucky.[18]

I know. That meant giving up a full day of instruction. But I had three "Capturing Kids" days in the bank, so to speak, and I'd have taken back eight for advisory groups too.

Besides, some sacrifices are worth it. Our kids were thrilled to visit a university—to walk across a beautiful campus—see classrooms—visit the basketball arena—scope out cute older girls and guys. Best of all, Jeane set it up for U. K. students to talk to our kids about the challenges and rewards of higher education.

If, because of lost class time, I was less than enamored with the idea of daily advisory groups, a large part of the rationale for teams at the middle school level is to help teens feel connected. That mission, our team took seriously. (I don't mean other teams didn't. I simply cannot speak for them.) One day, Pat and Kathy suggested a trip to the local bowling alley. So, after school, we piled forty-five kids onto a bus and took them bowling.

In my opinion, it was easy to avoid carving into instructional time if you made it a priority. Once every quarter we showed movies after the regular day ended, ordering pizza for twenty-six, or forty-one or however many stayed to watch. After a group of World War II veterans spoke to my classes, we sent permission slips home. Cindy Taylor, our science teacher, and Steve Ball helped chaperone thirty-five kids at a Saturday night showing of *Flags of Our Fathers*, a powerful, R-rated film about the Battle

---

[18] The other seventh grade team—also stocked with good teachers—played an only slightly less prominent role. Sally Riegler, their leader, was one of the best educators I ever met.

of Iwo Jima.

We held regular after-school "game days," as well. Steve and Chuck Battle, another fine team member, and a gentleman highly respected by students, encouraged kids to stick around and have fun.

Another time, Jeane suggested a "dress up" day for kids. We awarded bonus points to those who met sartorial standards. Now we had young men in shirts and ties and young ladies in dresses or slacks. Naturally, the kids looked and acted more mature. The next year, Jeane and Cindy and Cheri and Trish Kemen, the best young teacher I ever met, wore ball gowns. I put on my tuxedo and taught history like James Bond, minus the guns, cool cars and rugged good looks.

We tried to recognize *good kids* on our team, too, not just good students. Each spring we discussed the 175 youngsters in our charge. If a boy or girl received positive reviews from every teacher we put "Big A" posters on their lockers. The award read: ABOVE ALL, THE KEY IN LIFE IS A GOOD ATTITUDE and carried a large:

 in the middle.

We couldn't put up a "Big A" for everyone. (The only "Big A" I might have won at age thirteen from my teachers, or maybe at age fifty-eight from my boss, would have stood for something else.) We could for 145 or 150 kids in any given year and that number alone reveals something fundamental about education. It's relatively easy to teach most kids.

It can be the devil to save some of the others.

Our team lineup changed periodically, but with one exception, I never had to deal with anyone who was unwilling to sweep. Eventually, Mrs. Kemen (now: Kniskern) took a job as technology coordinator for the district and left the classroom—a great loss, I felt. Lauren Cripe took her place, impressed us greatly from the start, and only impressed us more the more we watched her in action. Michelle Serger took Ms. Taylor's spot, after Cindy left for a new school and later became a principal. Other than Mother Teresa, you could hardly find an easier person to deal with than Mrs. Serger.

I tried to be a good leader, too, and never asked anyone to do what I would not do myself. (See: Xenophon.) When team members expressed discipline concerns we adopted a collective approach. Often, we sat as a panel and called in kids who were causing trouble. Epiphanies were rare; but a panel approach had a sobering effect on even some of the "worst" kids.

Other times, if some young man or young woman was causing major trouble, I took them to the hall and rained eloquence down upon their heads. I could send 220 volts of advice coursing through any offender, with S/Sgt. Jones, my drill instructor, as model.

Still, I should be clear. I never ripped a kid because I was angry. The "anger" was part of an act.

I ripped students because I believed they needed it, because in many cases I wanted them to veer from a course likely to lead to disaster. I ripped those I thought needed to be ripped because the message had a calming effect on almost everyone who ever received a jolt.

The last few years, our team's classrooms clustered round a "pod" in a common area. "I always open my door when you yell," Mrs. Serger told me one day, "so my class gets the full effect."

She wasn't the type to want a child to suffer but she understood what I was trying to do.

***

When you're a young teacher you don't see it coming. You begin your career as one person, end as another, and maybe you're three or four different persons in between. When I was young and "cool" kids came to me for advice, like I was a wise older brother. Now, as a gnarled veteran, I felt like a therapist to parents. Whenever our team called in moms or dads for meetings to discuss a child's academic troubles, we dispensed with the litany of: "Well, he missed this assignment in English…he had an F on his math test…he didn't do his science homework." We wouldn't have been meeting if the student was doing all the work.

Issues almost always went deeper. So we tried to offer guidance and support. Often, I cited my own divorces (yes: plural) and the damage done to my two oldest children. Abby, in particular, embarked on a self-destructive path. After a long, painful struggle, her mother and I, with Abby helping, managed to get her back on a safe course. I offered up her tale as one of redemption, tried to give even the most distraught mothers and fathers reason to hope.[19]

When meetings ended, I was almost always proud of our team and felt we had done all we could to help. But you had to have *good parents* on the opposite side of the table. This was not always the case.

Consider Bethany. Her parents weren't bad people. They were simply weak.

Bethany's first year in seventh grade, on another team, she stayed home from school seventy days and failed. The next year we tried again. Now she was on our team. Attendance remained an issue. We called for a meeting with mom and dad. (We called them—they didn't call us—again, a telling detail if you hope to understand the nature of education.) On the appointed morning, there were twelve adults in the conference room, including Mrs. Kramer, the school psychologist and counselor.

Everyone had a say. I told mom and dad that when Bethany was present she had funny, creative comments. They looked relieved to hear a snippet of positive news. I liked the girl, I said.

I did.

Mrs. Liddy did the talking for the family. Mr. Liddy shrank into his suit as if he hoped the earth might split wide and swallow him up. "We try to get Bethany to counseling," Mrs. Liddy explained. "She refuses to go.

---

[19] Today, Abby is employed at the Center for Disease Control and finishing up a doctorate at Tulane. There was indeed hope.

"One day, we tricked her into the van and drove off for a session. She started screaming because she wanted to go to a movie with friends. When we stopped for a light, she opened the sliding door, jumped out and started walking."

Glancing in Bethany's direction, I saw a look on her face, equal parts disgust and embarrassment.

"We followed for half a mile," Mrs. Liddy continued. "We tried yelling. We tried pleading. Bethany wouldn't listen. So we gave up. She walked to the theater and stayed out all night."

Finally, mom admitted what was clear to every professional in the room. She and Mr. Liddy had no idea what to do. We ended up scheduling time for Bethany to meet with the psychologist and suggested to parents that they begin a round of intense family counseling.

If we had a video of that conference and one with Patricia and her parents, and a number of others, those who believe teachers are the main problem in education might glimpse a cruel truth. Parents are the issue in far too many cases. And when this is true, teachers and children may face obstacles that are virtually impossible to remove.

Patricia was a plain looking young lady at an age when Your Appearance can be paramount. Her family was poor, and she was prone to wearing mismatched clothing.

Even worse, Patricia made herself a lightning rod for mockery. Everywhere she went, she went singing. She sang loudly in the halls, so you knew she was coming. She sang as she went to the bathroom, so you knew she was going. She sang as she returned, and sang as she headed for lunch, where she sat with her only friend.

Her grades were awful. We called in mom for conference. At my suggestion, Patricia sat in on the meeting, which almost always helped. We told mom we liked the girl. Patricia had a variety of strengths. We hoped her daughter could understand our concern.

"Patricia is a very creative writer," Mrs. Weisbrod, her Language Arts teacher, noted.

Seated across the table from Patricia, Mrs. Serger gave her a "thumbs up."

A quick smile lighted Patricia's face.

Unfortunately, mom turned out to be brutal. No matter what positive remarks we offered up she sank them in a sea of bile. She wasn't mad at us. She was mad at Patricia and offered not a syllable of sympathy or support. Her input was a litany of bitter complaint. She glared at her daughter and you sensed an almost toxic hatred in words and demeanor.

Patricia's parents were divorced. At my urging, dad, the non-custodial parent, also sat in on the meeting. He didn't want to sit at the same table with the mother, but tried to offer kind words from a desk to the side.

He was in an awkward position. He lived outside the district, was down on his luck, and told me over the phone the night before his resources were thin.

Members of our team tried a dozen times to turn the conference in a more positive direction. Mom kept dragging us down. She berated Patricia.

"Something is *wrong*! I can't get her to do *anything*. She's *worse* than lazy," mom hissed. "I think she needs *psychological* help."

Mom didn't mean something was wrong, and Patricia needed love and understanding. She meant something was wrong and she was *pissed*. What she really meant was: "It's not my fault."

By now, everyone else was sorry we had asked her daughter to sit through this verbal assault. Mrs. Weisbrod caught my eye and shook her head in disbelief. I could see tears welling in Patricia's eyes. We switched to defense. I told mom, looking at Patricia, that her daughter had a good heart and college potential. Dad assured her he loved her. (Patricia told me the day before she feared switching homes and switching schools, leaving her only friend behind; and I imagine she felt she had no choice but to endure mom's abuse.)

And now we understood why she sang wherever she went. She sang, like slaves in the cotton fields, so her heart might not break.

When the meeting ended, I did something I had never done before. I took dad aside and told him, no matter what, he had to find a way to gain custody of his good-hearted girl.

***

If Mrs. Kramer and I had our problems, Jeff Sharpless and I continued our close collaboration. As part of a unit on medieval times, I created a handout called LIFE IN 1000 A.D. Jeff and I used it with success every year and followed up by inviting "visitors" from the era to speak to our classes, which we combined for the day.

For this skit we had kids in the role of serfs, and, in one class, the serf's shrewish wife, knights, nobles, priests and royals. Brian stole the show in one session, playing a leper, hands, face and arms swathed in elastic bandages. Only his eyes and mouth showed, the comic effect enhanced by a repeated need to tug at wrappings when they slipped to obscure vision or speech.

"I haven't had much luck dating," he admitted at one point, "not since my nose rotted off."

As another part of the medieval unit, I put together a CODE OF THE CHRISTIAN KNIGHT:

1. A knight must protect the Church.
2. A knight should succor (help) the poor. He stands up for the defenseless and oppressed.
3. A knight protects and respects women. He rescues the "damsel in distress."
4. A knight is loyal to his lord.
5. A knight is ready to fight the infidel.
6. A knight upholds truth and justice and never lies.
7. A knight is modest, gallant, courteous, generous, well-spoken and discreet.
8. A knight does not work with his hands. He scorns the bow.
9. A knight prefers death before dishonor.

Singing ability and clean teeth are pluses.

Tennyson describes the perfect knight. He must:
"Live pure, speak true, right wrong, [and] follow the king."

After a humorous aside about hygiene in the Middle Ages—it was considered gauche to spit across a table while eating, but a mark of sophistication to spit in a corner instead—we turned to the concept of living according to a code of honor.

This struck a chord with teens.

271

It seemed like a good idea, then, to have them draw up their own codes to live by, an assignment that turned out to be fun. Andrea, one of the hardest working students I ever had, started with this: "Always do more than is required." She added: "Love your family." "Be a friend to those who need one." "Don't be funny at someone's expense." And: "Study, study, study."

The assignment was meant to get kids to consider their values. I was pleased with what they produced. Tara had: "Don't hate. Life is too short to have enemies." And: "Show your true colors. Be you all the time, and don't pretend to be something you aren't."

Hayley provided a touch of unintentional comedy. Her code was titled: "My Mother Told Me." She had: "Don't do drugs." "Don't drink." And: "No SEX!" At the last minute, as she was passing in her paper, she noticed that her last rule needed slight alteration.

She penciled in: "Until married."

I had as many faults as any human being; but my strength as an educator was absolute faith in students, a belief all could produce good work if given a chance. That doesn't mean they *would*. School critics should keep that truth in view.

It means they *could*.

It's not usually a teacher's fault if they don't. Students, too, must pick up the broom and sweep.

So I gave star students latitude to go in directions they already wanted to go. Students in the middle might require a nudge. Shelby, for one, was putting up C's in my class, but she was an outstanding writer. I encouraged her to sign up for the school's "Power of the Pen" team, where she excelled. Kate preferred flirting to studying, but was an equally adept writer. Chelsea, her friend, was having a hard time in the wake of her parents' divorce. Her grades were shaky but I told her I was sure she had college ability.

One day, when I questioned her about a missing assignment, she melted down and I had to banish her to the hall.

The next day she apologized, saying, "I don't know what happened, Mr. Viall. This is my favorite subject."

I noticed all year that when discussion turned to world religions, Chelsea, Kate and others had excellent points to make. In my class every pupil was expected to do one project per quarter, weighted like a test. Skits were the most popular option. But students routinely came to me with creative ideas of their own.

"Mr. Viall," Kate inquired one day, "would it be okay if I did ten 'I Am' pieces as a project?"

What topic, I wondered.

"I'd like to do something about my faith, about Anne Frank and Hitler. I'd include myself."

I agreed at once and suggested she go online and find out about recent files of letters from Anne's father to various government agencies, asking for help in fleeing the Netherlands. I failed to keep a copy, but Kate, who was Jewish, turned in a masterful piece of work.

On the morning of September 11, 2001 adults arrived for a day of work as usual. Some at the Twin Towers in New York,

A pop-up page from a book on the 9/11 tragedy.

Creative stories, poetry, models, artwork, photography and video projects were other options. Elizabeth turned in an evocative series of poems, with human cruelty as a theme. Maddy's project was creative and funny—a video of "her" life as a badass Amazon warrior princess. Tara and Courtney put together a pop-up book on the 9/11 tragedy. Dave constructed a model of Auschwitz, including the German slogan over the gate: "Arbeit macht frei." ("Work makes you free.")

He clinched an A by adding a battery-operated searchlight to one of the guard towers.

Another time, we were going over the story of the early Christian martyrs when it struck me some of the kids might like to hold a debate on religion as a project option. I asked for volunteers, singled Chelsea out during fourth bell, and encouraged her to get involved.

"I don't know," she responded, "what if I get nervous up in front of class?"

"Chelsea, you know you *love* to talk," I laughed. "Besides, you have strong convictions. You'll be great."

Chelsea smiled and agreed.

The rules of the debate were simple. Participants should be ready to offer thoughts on all aspects of religion. Under no circumstances were they to insult the beliefs of others. No one would be graded on *what* they believed, only on how they expressed themselves.

The day of the presentation, Chelsea was ready. I regret that I can't recall what she said specifically—only that she was deeply committed to her faith. I know I was proud of how she and her peers handled the topic, touching on everything from Original Sin, to Jonah and the whale, to whether heaven and hell existed or not. With five volunteers in each of six classes, including Muslims, Mormons, Jews, all shapes and sizes of Christians, and an agnostic teen or two, I was happy to award thirty A's and B's for the day.

Chelsea earned an A+.

The longer you teach a subject, of course, the better you usually do. Now, in my third year, we branched off in a new direction when we discussed Carthage and Rome. I wanted to compare the demands on Roman military power and Rome's situation eighteen centuries ago with demands on U. S. military power and our situation in Iraq and Afghanistan that spring. The vast expenses of war and strains on the budgets were the same, as were the strains on the finest militaries of their eras, as they faced challenges from multiple directions.

I had already written handouts on the structure of the Roman army and Julius Caesar's campaigns in Gaul. Now I created another, focusing on fighting in Iraq, which dominated the news in 2007. As always, I looked for the telling detail that might hold the interest of teens.

This story about the attacks on Fallujah, three years before, seemed good:

Once U. S. troops watched as an insurgent raced across an empty street. They opened fire. To avoid the bullets the Iraqi did a somersault and disappeared down an alley.

"Just missed him," said a surprised Marine rifleman. Then, with a note of respect, he added: "Kind of [a] crafty move."

I included this because the gender angle might interest girls:

On June 23, 2005 a U. S. truck convoy, guarded by Humvees, was hit in an ambush. This time a suicide car bomber rammed one of our cargo trucks. The blast killed the driver instantly. Several Marines riding in the back, including three females, died. The women had been on duty at a roadblock nearby, searching Iraqi females as needed.

...The truck caught fire, rolled fifty yards down the highway, and flipped on its side. Those in back tumbled to the pavement. Ammunition began exploding in the flames. A badly burned woman kept crying, "How do I look?"

L/Cpl. Erin Liberty, a pretty blonde from Niceville, Florida, survived the blast with minor injuries. She had a hard time forgetting what she saw around her. "It was orange and black and red smoke, flames everywhere, coming at us," she said. "I didn't see my childhood, or a big white light. I just closed my eyes and I'm like, 'Wow, I'm going to die.'"

When the vehicle tipped she was surprised to find herself alive. So she jumped up and tried to drag a comrade to safety. Grabbing the other Marine's jacket, Liberty shouted, "Come on girl, we've got to go."

Another Marine told her to forget it. The woman was already dead.

To wrap the unit we set up a new skit. We had three of Julius Caesar's soldiers and three of our own, including at least one girl, "just back" from Iraq. Typically, a number of questions came up in every class related to the Roman siege of Alesia, a fortified city in Gaul. The women, Caesar had written, stood atop the wall, weeping and showing their breasts to stir pity.

In fourth period, Jake, in the role of a centurion, described the scene. "We built a long wooden wall around the city. Then we heard an army of 250,000 Gauls was marching to the rescue."

He told how the Romans built a second wall, 13 ½ miles long, facing the other way and how, outnumbered 6-to-1, they turned to face this threat. "Caesar was everywhere," he said, "encouraging us. We could see him sometimes in the thick of battle in his bright red cloak."

Finally, someone in the audience asked about the women of the town.

Jake admitted they "flashed" the Roman army. "It was Gauls gone wild!" he quipped with a grin.

The audience erupted with laughter and I was reminded, as I often was, why teaching was so much fun.

***

Jake and most of his peers might be easy to teach, but I also enjoyed helping challenging kids. When schedules were drawn up at the start of the 2006-2007 school year, the Olympians ended up with eight of the top-ten troublemakers in the seventh grade on our roster. There were two-and-a-half teams, including one split with the eighth grade, at our level. At the end of first semester, Chris Burke, our assistant principal, met with us to offer adjustment.

He and Erica would take any two students off our hands and switch them to other teams.

The next morning, my teammates kicked around prospects while I sat and listened. When Chris returned we had two names. We switched the young men in other subjects without difficulty.

I wanted to keep both. I hated to give up on any kid and wasn't having serious discipline issues. It was agreed Eric would remain in my first bell class. Only a scheduling conflict required that Gilberto be switched out of my third bell or I'd have kept him too.

I talked to Eric often in weeks to follow, assuring him I could tell he had a sharp intellect. He was lazy when it came to homework, reluctant to study for tests, but excellent in skits, and earned two STAR Awards for performances.

One evening, I had to call his dad to report that Eric had bombed another test. I wanted him to take it over.

"I'll make sure he studies," his father assured me in a tone that gave me confidence Eric would be busy.

Two days later, dad dropped him off before school. Eric tried again. Or: *tried* for the first time. His grade doubled, from a 46 F to a 92 B+ and he earned his third STAR, a positive phone call that evening.

I wasn't surprised. By this point in my career, I had been observing teens for more than three decades and my fundamental conclusions never changed. I would have bet my house and car that Cassidy, Clarissa, Emily and Reece, in seats surrounding Eric, would go on to college and make a great mark in years to come. The same was true of dozens of others who would walk through the "same rectangle" that day. Then you considered Eric's situation and knew he needed a push to move him along the right path.

I knew in my soul that I was still moving kids in a positive direction. Nevertheless, I could not move them all.

That same morning, I should have had Jarvis and Luisa in class. Jarvis behaved well enough for me, but I had to sit on him to ensure he did. He lied shamelessly, cursed other staff members, got into fights with peers in the hall, and spent the last third of the year in a lockup facility, on a long list of burglary charges.

Luisa had failed twice by the time we met her. So she was fourteen to start seventh grade. Our team rarely saw her, however, because she had crippling attendance issues. Then, in November, she had run away with her 28-year-old boyfriend—headed for Mexico, we were told.

No one on the Olympians ever saw her again.

Now, on that very morning when Eric doubled his grade, Mrs. Kramer called me in during my conference for that ill-fated meeting about my future.

After that, our troubles festered. In April, she sent me an email, saying there had been a parental complaint about one of my handouts. The mother had a child in Mr. Sharpless's class. She was upset about LIFE IN 1000 A.D., which we both used.

I asked what the complaint was about.

"Something to do with 'sexual,'" the boss emailed back.

Mr. Sharpless and I scanned the handout that morning, searching for trouble. There was blood and disease and filthy living conditions. But sex? We couldn't find anything questionable.

Erica and I met again during my conference. The "offensive" passage was in a section about Spain, in the years after the Moors, who were Muslim, wrested control from Christian rulers:

> Naturally, Christians and Muslims reacted to each other in different ways. Some fought it out in the name of God and Allah. Others lived in harmony and conducted business with the "enemy." A few even fell in love. In Moorish lands Muslim women were kept veiled and out of view. So a pretty Christian slave might have a chance to cast a spell on her master. She could sing and recite poetry—and flirt openly.
>
> One slave girl rose to the highest levels of wealth and power. Born into slavery and raised as a Christian, Subh was beautiful and brilliant. Living in the caliph's [king's] palace, she quickly caught the eye of Al Hakkim II, who ruled over Spain. Eventually they fell in love and had two sons. In later years the king rarely made a decision without asking her advice.

Two sons! You know what *that* means! After the words "flirt openly" came a footnote that sealed my doom:

> A Muslim woman who engaged in sex before marriage forever destroyed her reputation. She also brought lasting shame upon her family.

From where I stood, broom ever ready, Erica's next move was hard to fathom. From now on, she said, I would have to cite sources if I was going to write my own material.

Medieval carpenter and maidservant, from the handout.

"I've been writing my own materials since 1977, and *now* you think I should cite sources?" I said. I reminded her I had sold all my American history materials to Holt, Rinehart and Winston, a major publisher, in 1989.

I told her my sources were impeccable.

She said cite them.

Did she mean I would have to cite sources for this handout and every other one I had written? All four handouts on ancient China, all six on Judeo-Christian thought, the one on Spartan Life, and one based on Froissart's *Chronicles*? Cite sources for seventy different readings?

Cite 'em, she said.

(Holy crap, I said to myself.)

I asked if she didn't think she might back me up, asked if she knew I devoted fifty hours of my own time to produce this single reading.

She said cite sources.

That was bad enough but a few days later, she emailed about some minor matter. In offhand fashion she inquired: "Also, would you be terribly offended if I asked you not to use homemade packets of reading material next year?"

Now I cared. This cut at the bone of learning. I had worked on my "homemade packets" for decades, read a thousand books and devoted five thousand hours to writing. (That's not hyperbole.)

What could be wrong?

Mrs. Kramer responded electronically:

Every year, I get some complaints about the nature of them—whether they are too grusome (sp.), too violent, or this time, a reference to sexual. I understand their complaints, but I also understand why you write them. If the Board approved them, I could tell parents, "they are Board approved materials."

When Erica and I met again, I brought union representation. Sean Thompson, our association president, asked if anyone in the district had ever been required to list sources.

Erica wasn't sure but said from now on I must. Why, Sean wondered? "Board policy," she replied.

What policy? All materials teachers produced had to be "accurate and well-researched."

I pointed out that the recent complaint had nothing to do with accuracy or research.

Erica said we needed to follow board policy.

"What board policy?" Sean asked again.

"Materials must be 'accurate and well-researched,'" Erica countered once more.

"They *are*," I insisted heatedly. "I used eight books to write this handout!" (Again: not hyperbole.)

Sean said he had never heard of another teacher who spent so much time reading and writing original materials.

Erica replied: cite sources.

It was like a scene from *Catch-22* and I was Yossarian.

What about all those complaints? I hadn't been told about them. Well, she said, there was the *one* this year. I pointed out that that complaint was stupid.

What about the year before? Well, none.

How about the first year I taught Ancient World History, when I was spending hundreds of hours creating fresh readings? Well, one. I reminded her I solved that complaint by dropping a single sentence out of 300 pages.

It was no use. I would have to cite sources.

Rather than catalog materials used for each separate reading, I decided to compile one giant list to send home to parents. It took me an entire weekend and I made it clear I felt the entire exercise was a farce.

I began:

...I list here BOOKS I HAVE READ THE LAST THREE YEARS in order to teach Ancient World History.

My research totaled:

50,000 PAGES OF READING.

I thought that looked impressive and put it in size-28 font, hard for any administrator to miss.

I started listing:

1. *Histories* by Herodotus, translated by Robin Waterfield, 735 pp.—no serious teacher should fail to consult this work. Herodotus is "father of history."

Eleven pages later I ended with:

157. *Peoples of the Past: The Phoenicians* by Glenn E. Markoe, 189 pp.—interesting but tedious.

I admit I didn't bother to list several hundred articles from *Archaeology Today*, *National Geographic* and all kinds of newspapers and other periodicals.

No one seemed to notice the omission. In fact, I suspect no one cared.

***

In any case, if Erica had reason to be unhappy with my work, and I failed to see it, I'm sorry for being obtuse. My last year of Ancient World History, I did make more mistakes than usual. Students pointed this out when they filled out their anonymous year-end evaluations.

This time, 67% rated my efforts "excellent," 26% "good," and 5% "fair," down slightly from previous years.

In my mind, the most surprising development was that three students (2%) marked me down as having done a "poor" job. A fourth (1%) rated my efforts as "very poor," the lowest mark possible. No student had marked either of those choices for seven years.

The final complainant added a paragraph of explanation. He or she felt I had been too hard on President Bush and said I should not have been teaching about the Iraq War in the first place.

I couldn't agree about Iraq, but if one student thought I was trying to impose my political views, that was absolutely one too many.

I happen to believe Amos Bronson Alcott was right, in 1840, when he said: "The true teacher defends his pupils against his own personal influence."

(I vowed not to repeat that mistake my final year and did not.)

Having laid out my version of events, and having made myself look good, I should add something again in Erica's defense. Steve Ball once captured the essence of the trials of school leaders in the Age of the Testing Fix when he joked, "I figure, in Hell, I'll be an administrator."

I always valued his judgment. He felt, as I did, that Erica ran a good building.

Nevertheless, if I had one sentence to offer to every administrator, bureaucrat, politician and Big Fixer in the land, I'd focus on helping good teachers in every way. Prod the bad ones. Prod them for sure. Fire those who don't move despite prodding. *Your first priority, however, should be figuring out how to make it easier for good teachers to do what they already do every day.*

If they are sweeping furiously, as the great majority are, at the very least try not to tread on the broom.

24.

How to Bicycle across America

"There was nowhere to go but everywhere."
Jack Kerouac

In the end, most of my battles with Erica had little to do with the soul of education. So they didn't matter. If you want to know what matters, kids matter.

This is as good an example as any. My classroom cleared one day, as fourth bell exited for lunch. Tired after a long week at Children's Hospital, I slumped in my chair, elbows on my desk, forehead cradled in both hands. When I thought about Emily, our youngest, just diagnosed with type-1 diabetes, I felt like crying.

Some slight movement alerted me to the fact I was not alone. Under the rim of my hands I noticed two sneakered feet. I looked up to see who was there. Adam hesitated, then with great kindness said, "If you have any questions about diabetes I'd be happy to talk."

This was in the spring of 2005, and Emily had just been released to home the previous morning. Adam was type-1 himself, only thirteen, yet wise enough to offer solace to someone four times his age.

That's one of the great lessons of teaching. Give kids a chance and they almost always come through.

***

Two years had passed since. It was spring again and Erica was pushing me to retire.

I knew I had a reservoir of good will in the community. If I was going to return, perhaps kids might help raise money for a worthy cause. I made a promise to students one day, in honor of Adam and Emily and all other type-1 diabetics, including Kyle and Nicole, who passed through my classes the year before. "If you help me raise $5,000 for the Juvenile Diabetes Research Foundation, I'll bicycle 5,000 miles across the United States." [20]

Emily went on to become a diabetic nurse educator.

---

[20] That would include practice miles and a long bend north through Yellowstone National Park.

The kids laughed and predicted I'd be flattened by a tractor trailer loaded with steel beams. One young man promised to visit my grave and leave a beautiful bouquet of plastic flowers. But I was quickly overwhelmed by support. Fred Barnes, our school resource officer, and a man deeply committed to helping kids, was first in line to donate. Jillian, one of those students who make teaching a joy, handed me a check in her name and another from her parents. Anthony gave $5, explaining he wanted to honor a friend at his former school, a boy who was also type-1. Anthony was poor and his gift touched me deeply.

Good people came through with donations, including Erica and Chris Burke, our assistant principal. Steve Ball gave $110—a dollar per mile for what he figured would be a good day's ride. Jillian returned to pour out fifteen dollars in change. My two brothers, neighbors, staff and students at our high school, and strangers who read about my plan in the papers helped. Diane Sullivan, an eighth grade art teacher, and a good one, collected a quarter from anyone caught chewing gum and netted $17.50. We passed $5,000, then $10,000, and kept going.

***

That spring, I rode myself into shape, if we define "into shape" generously. Then, on June 18th, my younger brother dropped me off in Avalon, N. J. and I began my solo journey, coast to coast.

Traditionally, a rider dips a back tire in the ocean where he starts, a front tire in the ocean where he ends. I carried my heavily-laden bike across the sand and did honors in the Atlantic.

A pretty lifeguard was watching and inquired: "Where are you headed?"

"Oregon," I replied confidently. She wished me luck. After sizing me up, I imagine she was thinking: Fat chance!

And I mean *fat*.

I started my ride twenty-five pounds overweight and twenty-five years past my prime. Yet, to my way of thinking, it was a simple matter to ride across the continent, a habit of mind in which one does not allow excuses like "age" or "fat" to stand in the way. It was a way of looking at the world which I had been trying to pass on to students for decades.

I was too cheap to buy maps from reputable bicycling associations. So I charted my own course, down the coast of New Jersey, across Delaware and the Eastern Shore of Maryland. Riding in Northern Virginia, I found myself on a busy road and spent an afternoon cycling in fear. At one point, two men in a white pickup pulled alongside and slowed to speak. The passenger leaned out and observed, sage-like, "You're going to get yourself killed."

I decided it might not be wise to mention this incident when I called my wife that evening.

An hour later, with dusk descending, I rolled into Fredericksburg, Virginia. Unable to locate a campground, and too rattled to keep pedaling, I settled for lodgings at the Twi-Lite Motel. It was not the kind of establishment one chooses for a romantic honeymoon getaway. The room had three lights. Two lacked on/off switches and the third had no bulb. The dresser was Goodwill-quality but some guest had checked out, taking the drawers with him. The bathroom ceiling sagged and the towel must have arrived with the Jamestown settlers.

(Next page.)

Dogs were another hazard. I was chased six times on one back road, but learned that growling loudly kept most of man's best friends at bay. Late that afternoon, however, a German shepherd came barreling across a front yard. I was riding head down, up a hill, and had a split second to see what direction the monster was coming from. I realized he was penned in by a fence. A moment later, I saw I was headed for the roadside ditch. I stood my bike on its nose and somersaulted across the pavement.

Ah! The smell of blood and hot American asphalt! No need to mention this to my wife during nightly conversations, either.

Soon after, I struck the Appalachians. The first challenging climb of the journey came ten miles west of Charlottesville, Virginia, at Rockfish Gap, offering entry into the Shenandoah Valley. By the time I reached the top my thighs were on fire and I had to keep wiping stinging sweat from my face to see. I considered renting a car, driving home, and retiring in ignominious fashion. But I had stuck my bicycle shoe in my mouth and had no recourse except to pedal.

Passing through Pulaski, Virginia, two days later, I stopped at the library to update my blog and listened to a weather report that pegged the temperature at 96°. An hour later, after dawdling in air-conditioned comfort, I decided to push on and pedaled out of town. An African American woman was watering her garden beside the road and flagged me down to talk. I asked if I might fill my water bottles from her hose. She disappeared into her house and came back with a large chunk of ice in a zip lock bag.

"May the blood of Jesus protect you through your journey," she said and sent me on my way.

I was still working myself into shape. So fiddling over breakfast was always appealing. The locals were usually interested in what I was doing and talking about my trip was easier than pedaling.

In Justice, West Virginia one morning, I eavesdropped on four older women at a nearby table. Conversation centered on modern teens and their piercings. One member of the quartet brought up the days when they were young and first had their ears pierced. "I fainted dead away when my sister pierced my ear," her friend admitted. "But when I woke up the other one was done, too!"

The five of us, me behind my newspaper, shared a laugh.

At the cash register the owner informed me breakfast was on the house. I tried to pay. But she had heard me tell the waitress I was riding for JDRF and this was her contribution. I put the money saved aside and included it when I turned in my next batch of donations.

Asking advice at almost every stop, I bypassed some of the worst mountains in West Virginia. I made a mistake, though, when I ignored warnings and decided to ride along Highway 10. The road was narrow and twisting, with coal trucks thundering past in both directions and I made excellent time cycling in terror. Finally, a couple in a red pickup stopped and offered a lift. I gladly accepted and watched the next ten miles fly past.

Another hot afternoon, I was sitting drinking Gatorade outside a country store. An elderly couple in a beat-up blue Impala pulled into a parking space a few feet away. They asked about my trip and I explained my cause and they bought a few items before wishing me well and heading home. Ten minutes later, just as I was finishing my cold drink, they pulled back into the same spot. The old man climbed out of his car and placed a $10 bill in my hand. "Me and the missus' got to thinkin' about what you're tryin' to do and we decided we had to help."

By the end of June I had crossed into Ohio. On July 1, I pedaled 105 miles and reached home just before dark. It was a pleasure to see my wife and youngest daughter for four days. Emily was quiet the morning I left on the second leg of my voyage. Obviously, she was worried. Her mother and I were far more worried about her and her diabetes and I gave her the best hug I knew how.

On the first leg, I had ridden myself into condition and it wasn't hard getting restarted. I logged 80 miles July 6th, 83 the 7th, and 82 the 8th. One crisp morning I pedaled past a field filled with cows and noticed they were watching me as I was watching them. Cows don't get out much and I imagine they were bored. So I was something to study, to keep their brains working, like *Seinfeld* reruns for humans.

I had plenty of time to think as I chugged along at 13 mph. So, what were *they* thinking? How sophisticated is the bovine brain?

Possibly:

Cow #1: *Creature with shell on head passing. Not threat. Need to poo.*

Cow #2: *Human moving fast. Hope crash.*

Cow #3: *I envy that cyclist his freedom. These other cows are morons. Oh well, might as well chew the cud.*

I waved to my fans and kept pedaling west.

The first night out I slept behind an Indiana cornfield, where no one could see my tent. The next night I found accommodations in a graveyard. A bobcat roaming nearby woods serenaded me occasionally. The following evening I paid for a motel. I noticed there was an exercise room with an elliptical machine.

I passed and headed for bed.

A few days later I rode into Columbia, Missouri, where I picked up a bike trail running along the Missouri River. It was growing dark. So I paid for a campsite and pitched my tent close to the river. I was at peace. Fish leaped and fell back in the water with silvery splashes. Frogs croaked under the bank. V-formations of geese honked overhead.

A couple at the next campsite offered beer. They explained that their children and friends were boating. They'd soon be coming ashore. Sure enough, the vessel promptly hove into view and a dozen young men and women, the latter in skimpy bikinis, disembarked. They were towing a floating trampoline and I imagined later asking to try it out.

Bouncing babes in bikinis?

I could only hope.

The entire crew turned out to be friendly and I was offered more beer and a steak from their grill. But night soon fell and I had hard riding to do the next day. I headed for my tent.

Alas, the sounds of Nature were soon subsumed by boisterous, drunken shouting. And these drunks knew but a single adjective. "Fucking beer!" screamed one.

"Fucking frogs!" responded a second.

"Fucking geese!" whooped a third.

As tired as I was, it proved impossible to sleep. I tossed and turned and hoped the beer would soon run out.

Shortly after midnight, a storm rumbled in, bringing enough rain (I hoped) to send the alcoholics running. "Fucking rain!' shouted a drunk.

"Fucking thunder," shouted another.

"Fucking lightning," bellowed a plastered weatherman.

Only the wimps packed it in and the serious drunks kept guzzling. Finally, around 3 a.m., the beer ran out, enthusiasm waned, and everyone stumbled off to their fucking tents.

Badly fatigued, I pedaled west the next day, on into Kansas. Now I faced a five-day battle against heat, humidity and headwinds.

Trust me when I say that on the Great Plains the wind has a life of its own. On a bicycle it feels like fighting a fire-breathing dragon. First, the heat cooks your brain under your helmet. Second, the humidity soaks you with sweat and you think you're melting. (Yes, Dorothy, melting!) Third, the wind retards your forward progress. It feels like you're dragging an anchor all day.

Nevertheless, I enjoyed the stark beauty and small towns and small-town people I met. Many of these towns were dying. I passed weed-grown elementary schools and even a weed-grown church. McDonalds had shuttered its doors in Hillsboro. Twenty miles west, in Lyons, Kansas, the same was true; but Lyons was at least experiencing an ethanol boom.

At breakfast in Hillsboro an old truck driver provided a rundown of local sights. It used to be you could see the embalmed remains of Civil War veteran Sam Dingle. "When I first saw him he had a full beard and all," the driver continued. "Then I went back a few years later and the hair had all fallen out.

"The parasites or somethin' got him."

I could feel my enthusiasm for sight-seeing draining away and decided to keep on going, leaving Dingle to his inexorable fates.

I continued to meet kindness at every stop, even in motion. A motorcycle rider cruised up beside while I was pedaling one afternoon and slowed for conversation. When he heard I was raising money for JDRF he reached into his vest, pulled out a thick wad of bills, stuck out an arm and told me to peel off two tens. Then he wished me luck and roared away.

People saw my load of gear and wondered where I was going and why. A couple at a campground listened to my story, gave $50, and packed me lunch for the next day. A Kansas bakery donated coffee and two of the best cinnamon rolls I ever tasted. A bar owner paid for lunch and explained her daughter was diabetic. Then she wrote a check for $100.

East of Eads, Colorado, and again west of town, I traversed barren stretches of fifty miles with no place to find food or drink. I made it through and confidence soared. I was following the Trans-America Bicycle Trail at the time and started running into cyclists heading east. Most were young, fresh out of college, riding for adventure before settling into the workday grind.

Young legs help; but any two legs suffice.

On July 23 I picked up a tailwind and sailed along like a clipper ship. One hundred and fourteen miles later, I found lodgings at a motel in Pueblo, Colorado, across the street from a Payday Loan office. Most of the guests spoke Spanish and I doubt they could have proved legal immigration status. They had the weather-worn look of men who spent their lives in toil, "salt-of-the-earth fellows," as my father used to call them, and so had my respect.

I was sleeping quietly next morning when the desk delivered a 5:00 a.m. wake-up call.

"Juan?" inquired the voice on the other end.

"Wrong room," I mumbled.

Moments later—the phone again. "Juan?" the voice asked once more.

"WRONG ROOM!" I replied.

The line went dead.

I hope Juan made it to work on time and imagine the day ahead was filled with more arduous labor for him than for me.

The next afternoon I climbed into the Rockies and made camp a few miles from Royal Gorge Bridge. After a good night's rest, I piled out of my tent around 6:30 a.m., polished off another 2,000-calorie breakfast at a nearby restaurant, and pedaled off to see the sites. Royal Gorge is advertised as the highest suspension bridge in the world, a beautiful but nearly useless one-lane span 1,053 feet above the Arkansas River. Near the middle a sign shows where the longest free rappelling climb in history was completed. Another sign marks the spot of the world-record for a bungee jump. In a flash of weakness I wondered if this might not be the time to try for a record "bicycle drop."

The feeling passed and I kept going. You can't talk effort to students unless you give effort. I gave effort. People seemed amazed by what I was doing. I thought it was simple truth. I gave effort. It was the basic concept I had been preaching for thirty-two years.

Two legs *always* suffice.

***

I pedaled north, up the Arkansas River Valley, scenery spectacular in every direction. Eventually, I climbed to almost two miles above sea level and found a beautiful camping spot beside a mountain stream outside Leadville, Colorado. By the time I crossed Fremont Pass, the highest point on my trip at 11,320 feet, I was seeing eastbound riders daily. They warned that conditions in southern Wyoming were harsh.

One stretch, between Rawlins and Lander, was little more than 130 miles of sagebrush and sand, a treeless wasteland that had to be negotiated with care. If you were hungry or thirsty you had three choices: Grandma's

Kitchen (32 miles from Rawlins), a store at Muddy Gap (46 miles) and a café at Jeff City (88 miles). That was it. And the place at Jeff City (population: 50) closed early. When I took my break for lunch that day, eating food I carried in my bags, I had to prop my bike against a reflector by the side of the road to create a spot of shade.

Half an hour later, in the middle of the middle of nowhere, I suffered the first flat of my trip. I unloaded my bike, flipped it over, and set to work, fumbling tools and getting grease on my shorts. (I improved dramatically after suffering four flats in one day and a dozen more in coming weeks.)

Just as I was finishing, I looked up and spotted a rider in the distance. Something was wrong. I looked again. My eyes must be playing tricks in the bright sunlight. From the waist up, the silhouette appeared female. Only something was wrong.

Moments later I had my explanation when a young woman pedaled up and braked to a stop. Her name was Sarah Brigham, a free-spirited 22-year-old from Columbus, Ohio. She was outfitted in a spaghetti-strap black top and black biker shorts, topped by a red and black tutu. She told me she made it herself, said she had sold a handyman business back in Columbus and headed west for adventure. Now she was pedaling south to Durango, Colorado to meet friends. We shared hard-won lessons, each complimenting the other on an adventurous spirit, and off we went.

In this case: two attractive legs sufficed.

I continued up Route 287, pointing for Yellowstone National Park. At a Pizza Hut in Lander, where I piled three buffet plates high and cleaned them again, I met Judy and Ron Hartwigsen and their grandchildren Ryan and Beth Mitchell. Beth, 12, had been diabetic for three years. Judy called her a "little warrior" who worked hard to control the disease. Ron promised a lift into Dubois later that day. After they finished shopping they picked me up twenty miles down the road, carried me into town, bought me dinner, and added a present of Huckleberry chocolate candy for good measure.

The next day I pedaled up and over Togwotee Pass (elevation 9,649 feet). Then it was down to Grand Teton National Park. A sign warned truckers they faced a 6% grade for seventeen miles. To me that meant a sweet, swift descent, at speeds as high as fifty mph.

You can easily hit 70 mph. on such stretches; but around 40-45, I tend to start gripping the handle-bars like a Congressman accepting a fat bribe. Even at that speed you feel like you're flying.

Camping in Grand Teton that evening, I had the good fortune to share a bear box (for food safety) with the Garcia family next door. Bob

Garcia invited me for dinner and the meal turned into an evening of lively conversation and laughter. Bob and his wife Teresa had three children, Katie, 12, Jessica, 9, and Phillip, 6. The party included Teresa's sister, Dr. Lydia Rose, and her daughter Sabrina, 10. The children were well-mannered and funny. Sabrina told me she hated being shorter than Jessica, her younger cousin. "I'm the second shortest fifth grader in my *entire* school," she lamented. "And the shortest kid has a *genetic defect!*"

The next morning, when I pedaled out of camp, I could hear the family teasing Sabrina for rising late. She mumbled from deep beneath her covers, "I'm not sleeping. I'm cleaning up the tent."

With high mountains on every side and buffalo, elk and the occasional moose in the bushes to keep me alert, I headed for Yellowstone. I had driven into the park from the south several times. Looking at a road map it didn't seem that far from Grand Teton to Yellowstone. Now, on a bicycle, I discovered I would have to cross the Continental Divide in three places. By the time I entered the park I was beat. The weather turned cold and drizzly.

Then the drizzle turned to steady rain.

I managed to take in a couple of sights but afternoon was fading and all campgrounds and hotels were booked. Ignoring rules and the dictates of good sense, I pitched my tent in a grove of pines off to the side of one of the roads and out of view. I was in bear country. So I bagged my food and toiletries and hung them in a tree before turning in for the night. Around 10 p. m. some small woodland creature skittered over a corner of my tent and startled me from my dreams.

Sleep soon held me softly in its grip. Then, about midnight, a *large* woodland creature approached and I heard snuffling outside my front door. Seizing a can of pepper spray, I clicked the red button to "fire." Then I waved my flashlight about to indicate I was on the alert and kept an eye out for the first claws to come ripping through the thin nylon walls of my house.

I considered opening a window flap to see what my foe might be. But frankly I was afraid I'd be staring at a bear.

Whatever the creature was it soon wandered off and I drifted back into restless sleep. The next morning I discovered fresh "scat" two feet from my tent. I have since described this poop to experts and consulted books about the bowel movements of forest creatures. I can now say, as something of an expert, that elk and deer normally leave pellets when answering Nature's call (of the wild). This pie wasn't pellets. Then again, the books say elk don't *always* leave pellets in summer. My visitor might have been an elk.

It might have been a bear. If it was a bear I'm glad I didn't get a look. Remember that rhetorical question: "Do bears shit in the woods?" If I had unzipped my tent and looked into the eyes of a bear I assure you I know who would have been defecating in the forest.

***

After spending two more days pedaling in the park, I rolled out the west entrance and into West Yellowstone just as dusk was coming on. Motels were full and I was too traumatized to repeat my recent camping experience if I could avoid it. I began asking around and ran into another rider, Doug Toctropf, who found himself in a similar predicament. He was talking to Bill, a local fellow, whose last name I never managed to catch. Bill owned land north of town and said we could camp there.

Then he thought a moment, and added, "My boys are with their mother this weekend. You can have their beds if you want."

"I'm not much of a housekeeper," he admitted, "so the place is one step above a frat house."

Still: that was three steps above a tent in the woods, and 100 steps above being gnawed on by a grizzly.

It turned out Bill wasn't lying about his cleaning abilities. If you got past the laundry on the floor and the empty pizza boxes and missing doorknobs you could see he was philosophical and funny and a fount of information on local wildlife and environs.

Doug was equally interesting, probably 25, a young man who would have blended nicely in the 70s. He admitted mixing marijuana with pedaling. At one point he informed Bill and me, "There's nothing like coming down a mountain when you're half baked."

I decided to take his word for it.

Back home, Doug trimmed trees for a living and loved climbing. On one bicep he had a chainsaw blade tattoo. As a teen he spent two years hitching round the country. Then he got picked up by a paroled convict headed north for a stint in rehab and a meeting with an ex-girlfriend.

Unfortunately, the ex-con had the brilliant idea of stealing the car to complete his journey to rehabilitation. A police chase ensued. The car spun out and rolled. Doug rolled, too, suffered minor injuries, and decided to end his thumbing career.

The three of us parted ways the next morning and I continued north into Montana and Idaho. A few days later I crossed Lolo Pass, where history says, in 1805, Lewis and Clark nearly came to grief in deep snow. The pass wasn't difficult in summer, what with modern roads, and on the far side I ran into one of the only riders I saw heading west my entire trip. Gene Myers turned out to be a soft-spoken 47-year-old computer programmer from Pittsburgh.

We hit it off and decided to kill the afternoon and evening at a nearby camp and set off together in the morning. Part of the time we devoted to playing checkers at the lodge. Neither of us could remember the rules. I said I thought you could jump your own men. Using this novel strategy, I crushed my new companion three games in a row.

For the next few days we pedaled together through spectacular country. High mountains rose on both sides of the highway and loomed ahead, promising hard climbs to come. We spent August 8 in the Lochsa River Valley, a "wild and scenic" region, and enjoyed swimming in cold, crystal-green waters. I had been riding solo and enjoyed having someone with whom to share stories. Gene had kept company with a red-headed woman who recorded how many margaritas she downed at every stop. One night, when the count ran to eight, Gene decided it was time to part ways.

On August 9 we found a camping spot at the city park in Kooskia, Idaho. The grass was soft and lush. The Clearwater River bubbled past our tents and we were soon dreaming under the stars.

Then…what the hell….

Is it raining!

Half awake, with water battering my tent, I heard Gene swearing softly and fumbling with gear. What the hell!! Skies were clear when we went to bed. What…the…a blast of water hit my tent…HELL!!!!

I unzipped and peeked outside, to see park sprinklers blazing. Gene and I did some quick singing in the rain and moved our tents and equipment and ourselves to drier pastures.

Gene had dreamed of making a cross-country trip for twenty years. Finally, he took a leave of absence from work and began his ride in

Washington, D. C. on June 4. Like me, he had trouble believing how close we were to the finish. At one point he asked, "Will you be sorry when the ride is over?"

I realized in some ways the answer would be yes.

It was when we crossed the Snake River and saw the sign at the Washington State line that it hit us. We had said we were going to pedal across the USA.

Now we were going to do it.

On August 11—after Gene suffered an unfortunate incident involving too many prunes—we parted ways—not because of prunes, but because he was heading for Seattle and I was aiming south. I pointed my bicycle down the Columbia River Gorge, despite warnings from locals that winds came "howling up the river." It was the shortest route to the Pacific and after fifty-one days in the saddle I was ready to get home. The scenery I most wanted to see was my wife.

The first day in the Gorge the wind hit me like punches from a prize fighter and I could only average nine miles per hour. Then the winds died and I enjoyed swift sailing. At times, I used Interstate 84, legal in that area. Part of the way, I followed Historic Route 30. Built in 1916, 30 offered interesting tunnels, challenging climbs, sharp turns and gorgeous vistas.

At one point I got off the road entirely and onto a bike trail which cut through old-growth forest. Five miles later the trail sputtered to an end. I hated to backtrack, and through the trees, happened to catch a glimpse of I-84. I clawed through briars, slashing red marks across my arms and legs, stumbled up a steep embankment, cursing lustily, threw my gear over a fence, lifted my bike, and continued west.

My older brother drove up from Stockton, California and trailed me the final 150 miles, offering any assistance he could. The last night we stayed at a motel in Forest Hills, Oregon. Then we rose early and I rode over the Coastal Range and rolled down into Tillamook. I could smell the Pacific at last—or at least the cow manure *near* the Pacific. Tillamook is the heart of Oregon cheese country. So there are lots of cows and lots of pungent cow odors.

After lunch and a beer to celebrate, I discovered Tillamook sat a mile from the coast. I wobbled north, considered the ironic possibilities of getting a "PUI," found a spot at Bay City, Oregon, and dipped my front wheel in the Pacific.

Just like that: after fifty-five days and 4,088 miles, the ride was ended. I told my students I would pedal across America and did. I was twenty-five pounds lighter and thrilled to have raised $13,500 for JDRF.

And I believe in the last summer before my last year in teaching I proved a point I had been trying to make to every student since the first day of my career.

Two legs suffice.

I spent my life preaching effort and attitude to thousands of teens and believe many understood. They might not have acted immediately on this understanding. Certainly, some never acted at all. But countless others did. If I planted one seed I'm proud of, this would be it: I showed students they could do more than they thought they could.

Looking down on the Columbia River Gorge and Interstate 84.
Notice the semi-truck at lower left.

25.

Basics for Tommy, Trevor and Ryan

"I am lonesome and down hearted in Spite of my Self. I am tired of Blood Shed and have Saw Enough of it."
Private John N. Moulton

In the end, pedaling across the United States turned out to be easier than dealing with the problems I confronted my last year with Loveland City Schools. If you can have a bad year in teaching without being shot, stabbed, blown up or fired, my final year was as bad as they come. It wasn't bad because I didn't know what I was doing. It was bad because I did.

I had long feared standardized testing might do harm in education. Now, in my last nine months in the classroom, I found the danger was imminent and real. Not a staff meeting passed in 2007-2008 where we didn't focus on raising scores on the Ohio Achievement Test (OAT). Social studies department meetings had the same theme: How to teach to the test. If practicing voodoo would have helped raise scores we would have danced in circles and muttered incantations.

Preparing for the OAT became a fixation. Our district began scheduling one day per month when students were sent home at 12:30. (By law that meant they had been in attendance long enough to count as a full day.) Teachers could then devote afternoons to meetings and discussions, almost without exception focused on how to improve scores.

I always wanted to raise my hand during one of those meetings and say, "I have an idea how we can raise scores. Let's quit sending students home early and sacrificing eight half-days of instruction."

***

Now the testing imperative grabbed us like a giant squid. Members of the social studies department were taken out of class for three days to work on creating practice tests for the OAT. We spent three more days giving practice tests. In May we devoted four to administering the official Ohio Achievement Test. Finally, we rewarded students for finishing the tests by giving them a "fun day" off from class.

(That wasn't my idea.)

Should I have cared? May 8 would mark the last time any of my students took the test. I would be retiring three weeks later. It shouldn't have bothered me if the State of Ohio had ordered social studies teachers to stuff frozen fish down our pants. But I did care.

I still do.

I worry about what we're doing to education—what we're doing to kids.

My last year, I bent my principles. For that I apologize to the 175 teens who suffered through my class. Although my heart was never in it, I tried to focus on what the state required. The textbook we had, which I had never used before, numbed the senses when you waded through a chapter. On weekends I had to down a beer before diving into the dull reading. Yet I felt compelled to "go by the book." I asked students to go wading with me in hopes of raising scores on the OAT. We read, for example, an entire chapter on the Articles of Confederation, a topic I normally covered in ten minutes.

The other eighth grade social studies teachers, Debbie Pomeroy, Kelly Kuhlman and Katie Rose, had doubts only slightly less pronounced, but faced with the same dilemma, did the best they could. They decided to spend one day per week in review, using a booklet called *Mastering Ohio's Grade 8 Social Studies Achievement Test*. Each of us had been provided a classroom set.[21]

I gave the booklet a long look but was not impressed. Three years of social studies material were boiled down to 218 pages. The first eight were filled with tips on "How to Take the Test." Chapter 4 was titled "How to Answer Short and Extended-Response Questions." You were assured there would be one extended-response and two short-answer

---

[21] Like me, Debbie was about to retire. Kelly and Katie were young and had to worry about protecting their jobs.

questions on the social studies section of the OAT. Seven pages were devoted to helping students understand how to complete short essays. An "average" response provided was five sentences long, including one to restate the question. I was sick at heart to think we were preparing students to write five-sentence paragraphs and calling that "higher standards."

If you want to know why standardized testing is nuts, consider highlighted items in the *Mastering* booklet. If an item was in boldface it might be turned into a question.

Under geography, students might have to know the location of the **Irrawaddy River**, not to mention the **Salween**. (I'd never heard of that river.) And can you find the **Kunlan Mountains** on a world map?

If you planned to kill enthusiasm for learning, there could be no better way to begin than to require students to memorize information they sensed was useless. Other "basics" that might end up on the OAT included the **Proclamation Act of 1763**, and **Huang Ho**. Also: **Shih Huang-ti**, **Mansa Musa** and my favorite: the **Tariff Crisis of 1830**.

If I could not bring myself to be a good soldier, I tried not to be a coward. I did not, as I normally would, ask students to do a 1,000 word interview with an individual sixty years of age or older. What would be the point? You could never standardize that type of learning.

I skipped all sorts of long writing assignments and focused on five-sentence paragraphs. My students did *less* writing than at any time since my second year in the classroom. Nor did I spend hours trying to help them improve style. The ability to craft good prose had nothing to do with the social studies portion of the OAT.

That made me sick.

***

Even if basics were the touchstone of learning (and they aren't), we would have had to be far more skillful in determining what those basics were. Also, we might have remembered there were thousands of basics and "measuring" learning with a fifty-question test would be patently absurd.

Consider this pathetic list from the State of Ohio's official curriculum for the American Civil War:

BENCHMARK G: Analyze the consequences of the American Civil War

INDICATOR 10: Explain the course and consequences of the Civil War with emphasis on:

o   Contributions of key individuals, including Abraham Lincoln, Robert E. Lee and Ulysses S. Grant
o   The Emancipation Proclamation
o   The Battle of Gettysburg

This was a sparse collection of ideas; but I discovered to my sorrow, when the test was given in the spring, that unless a person was named or a document noted or a term highlighted in the curriculum, it *could not* be turned into a question on the standardized test.

Suppose we drilled and drilled to ensure kids knew about those three men, one document, and single battle listed by the State of Ohio. Was that all that mattered?

What else might my classes and I have covered and felt what we were doing was learning? Should I do a 250-word writing assignment I used for years, related to the First Battle of Bull Run? Young soldiers on both sides were woefully unprepared for the realities of war. Students could relate to their inexperience and youth. The girls also appreciated the story of Kady Brownell, a young woman who carried a flag throughout the fight. Should I mention Brownell, then, or even Stonewall Jackson? I skipped it all.

Even Stonewall Jackson could not end up on the test.

I've had years to think this over since retiring and still can't grasp how this makes sense. Were we wasting time if students could define "infantry," "artillery," "cavalry," "civil war," "rebel," and "casualties," which I had always included on my own Civil War test?

What value did vocabulary have if most words could not be turned into fodder for the OAT? Students would *hear* those words in real life. I knew that.

Didn't that make them worth knowing?

In the summer of 2013, during a bicycle ride in the Gettysburg area, several of my companions and I visited the national park and the stunning battlefield museum. It turned out two of my riding friends thought "casualties" meant "killed." My old students, who learned killed, wounded and missing were covered in a single word, would have known better.

In any other year I would have insisted *ideas* matter. For that reason my classes would have looked at General George B. McClellan as part of this unit. It wasn't that we needed to discuss his strategy during the Peninsular Campaign in depth. What seemed useful to me were numbers and what they showed.

In the spring of 1862 McClellan led an army of 120,000 Union soldiers in a drive to take Richmond, the enemy capital. When Joseph Johnston, the Rebel commander, was wounded, Robert E. Lee stepped in to fill his place. (At last, one of the basics!) Lee could muster only 80,000 men but immediately swung to the offensive. Again and again he struck Yankee lines. McClellan lost his nerve and begged Lincoln for reinforcements, insisting he was *outnumbered* 2-1.

Soon his army was in full retreat.

The story of the Battle of Antietam (September 1862) was even worse, or even better for my purposes. A few days before the battle a copy of Lee's orders fell into McClellan's hands. He now had knowledge that Confederate troops were badly divided. If he moved swiftly he could plant his forces between the wings of Lee's army and destroy his foe piecemeal.

McClellan moved cautiously. He always did. Lee had time to gather a few scattered elements of his army; but when the two sides faced off at Antietam, McClellan had 87,000 men. Lee had 41,000. What followed was the bloodiest single day of combat during the war, each side suffering 10,000 casualties.

That word again.

In class, in any other year—but not my last—I liked to explain the numbers briefly and ask what they meant. At first, students said the battle was a tie. Then someone would raise a hand and say: "Since both sides lost the same number, and Lee had fewer men, he's in worse shape than ever."

Correct.

That night, I normally continued, both armies held position. When the sun rose again Lee braced for attacks he was sure must come. His lines had barely held the day before and he had juggled units back and forth to meet the weight of Union attacks.

Lee knew his army had nearly shattered.

McClellan looked across the same battlefield and saw risk not opportunity. His men, he telegraphed President Lincoln, had done all he could ask. They had performed magnificently and now he dared not attack. He insisted he was outnumbered again and called for help. Students could see how ridiculous this was, which in any other year brought us to the point of discussion.

"Where did McClellan lose the battle?" I always asked.

Most kids took the question literally. Antietam? Maryland? On the battlefield?

"Where did he lose the battle?" I would repeat.

Finally, some teen would volunteer: "He lost it in his mind. He thought he was outnumbered and didn't attack."

"Very good," I would agree. "Most people are defeated, in the classroom, in life, on a battlefield in 1862, because they *think* they can't do what they can. People are most often defeated in their heads, by their attitudes."

The last time I ever addressed this topic, in the days before standardized testing began to suck the blood out of learning, I picked a student to make an example. "Trevor," I said, "on the last test, no offense, you had a 49. Then I called your mom and she made you study and take it over after school. What did you get?"

"A 96," Trevor grinned.

"Who are you?" I asked, as if we had never met. Trevor looked a bit confused. "Are you Trevor Hawley?" I continued.

"I think so," he laughed.

"Okay, were you Trevor Hawley when you took the test the first time?"

He smiled again: "I think so."

"Then how could this happen? You're still Trevor aren't you?"

"Well, I studied more and didn't give up," he responded.

"That's right. You were still *you*. The lighting in the room was the same." I walked over to the door and rapped my knuckles. "Same door." I walked over to Trevor and slid the pencil out of his hand. "You don't have a magic pencil do you?"

"I'm not telling," he replied, playing along.

"Then the only change was in your effort, in your attitude, inside your head. You could do it all the time. You just didn't know you could."

Trevor and his classmates seemed to be taking it in, a lesson I thought bore repeating with every student I ever met. He could do it. McClellan had the men. Trevor had the brains. You had to *do* it, though. You had to be determined. You had to use the abilities you possessed and not make excuses.

There it is: the *key to improving education.* We all walk through the same rectangle. There are twenty or twenty-six or twenty-nine people in every classroom in the land. All must be willing to work if we want to improve education. Every individual must carry his or her part of the burden on the road to success. You can't just say, "Let's hold teachers accountable."

That's *never* going to be enough.

As always, I had called Trevor's house to let mom know he failed the test. She was a good mom. So she did *her part* and grounded him and put him to work. When she came to pick him up Friday afternoon, after he retook the test, I told her he had doubled his score and earned an A.

"Way to go, mom!" I said.

Mom gave me a high-five.

Trevor did a little jig and hugged his mother and she said he was off grounding and, yes, his friend Mitchell could spend the night.

I *loved this lesson*—but skipped it my final year. With the new curriculum in hand, and orders to follow it like a lame script, it was no longer teaching if I brought this up.

***

If we must genuflect at the altar of "basics," I would argue at the very least we should follow the "Tommy Smith Rule." Tommy was a sweet, smart young lady in my class, twenty years ago, one of the few black students in the school then or now. When we started our unit on the Civil War I singled her out. Did she know what the flag of the Confederacy looked like? Ms. Smith did not. I chalked a picture of the Rebel battle flag on the blackboard.

She had seen it, she admitted. Yet neither she nor most of her classmates realized what the flag may mean today. I explained that it was not always intended as a racist symbol. It could be meant as a symbol of courage.

Then I cautioned: "Tommy, if I were you, and my car broke down, I wouldn't stop and ask for help at a house where this symbol was on display."

One of her classmates said he had seen the flag painted on a barn roof. Exactly. The owner placed the symbol there decades ago and you could see it (and still can), when you drove north on Interstate 71.

"Look close," I said, "and you'll see there's a burned cross in the field. The Ohio Ku Klux Klan once held a rally on the property." Discussion now turned in that direction. At moments like this you knew, whether a curriculum said so or not, that kids should know what the red flag with the blue "X" represented.[22]

That's the Tommy Smith Rule. Teach students what they *can use* in life.

There's a corollary too: Teach them *everything* you can. Fill every one of the 8,000 minutes you have with value. You're not preparing kids for one standardized test.

You're preparing them for life.

---

[22] The cross was there as late as 2013; it has since been removed.

If I was still teaching in a sane world today, I'd cover the Battle of Honey Springs (July 1863), although I never heard of the fight till I retired and read *Like Men of War,* about black Civil War soldiers. As I see it, the matter of Honey Springs encapsulates the dangers of a standardized curriculum. A standardized curriculum is lifeless and inert. It cannot adapt. It cannot expand. Worse, a teacher risks being penalized for going beyond narrow confines since all that matters are the "standards" that end up on the test.

The Battle of Honey Springs is unimportant in and of itself. But the lessons the fight offers might prove invaluable. Both North and South deployed regiments of Native American troops, the 2nd Indian Infantry in blue on one side, Creeks and Cherokees in gray on the other. Members of both those tribes owned slaves, an irony well worth discussing.

At the center of the Yankee line the 1st Kansas Colored Infantry took a stand. It was a hot day and soldiers on both sides stripped off unnecessary equipment. The 1st Kansas fellows went further, removing their shirts so their "black skins glistened in the sun."

If it were left to me, I would skip the **Proclamation Act of 1763**. I would ask kids instead why they thought those 1st Kansas boys took off their blue shirts and stood ready to shed red blood for a country that denied them equality. I know students would see the point—see points I don't see myself. If Tommy or someone like her was in my class today, I'd hope they might sense the pride those men felt in 1863. I'd like every kid of every color to know brave Southern boys, flying that Rebel banner, advanced within twenty-five yards of the Kansas line. Then black and white and red Yankees poured in fire and drove them back.

I'd like to stand in front of a class again and challenge students to examine their ideas of race and courage and patriotism and ask how patriotism can be good if it is found in equal measure on both sides.

I'd like students to *think*.

Indeed, we might make the Civil War memorable if we taught it right. I'd throw in Tillie Pierce's story as she tended wounded at Gettysburg. Pierce was fifteen when she visited a field hospital one evening to offer help. A soldier keeping vigil by the bedside of a badly wounded comrade asked the girl to take his place while he got a bite to eat.

Tillie explained:

I then took the candle and sat down beside the wounded man. I talked to him and asked if he was injured badly. He answered:

"Yes, pretty badly."

I then asked him if he suffered much, to which he replied:

"Yes, I do now, but I hope in the morning I will be better."

I told him if there was anything I could do for him I would be so glad to do it, if he would only tell me what. The poor man looked so earnestly into my face, saying:

"Will you promise me to come back in the morning to see me."

I replied: "Yes, indeed." And he seemed so satisfied, and faintly smiled.

The man who had been watching him now returned, and thanked me for my kindness. I gave him the light and arose to leave.

The poor wounded soldier's eyes followed me, and the last words he said to me were:

"Now don't forget your promise." I replied:

"No indeed," and expressing the hope that he would be better in the morning, bade him good night.

The next day she hastened down to the basement again, "and as I entered, the soldier lay there—dead…I had kept my promise, but he was not there to greet me. I hope he greeted nearer and dearer faces than that of the unknown little girl on the battlefield of Gettysburg."

It would be interesting, if I still taught, to ask teens to write an essay, and not some lousy one-paragraph essay, about what that soldier was thinking his last night on earth. Or they might make up a different ending and have a chance to be creative. If it was up to me, I'd ask every student to write at least 250 words—extra credit for longer stories—and no "things" or "stuff."

***

When Ken Burns' documentary on the American Civil War aired in 1990, forty million viewers watched. One source was *Co Aytch*, a memoir by Sam Watkins, who survived four bloody years of combat. Once Burns alerted me to Watkins' story, I headed for the bookstore to find a copy. As soon as I read it, I knew students would be interested in what Watkins had to say.

All I had to do was stitch together parts of his tale and hand it over to teens. The first time I used this handout, A REBEL SOLDIER'S WAR, I let students begin in class, to gauge reaction. Every student, all day, read quietly. No one asked, "What do we have to know this for?"

I put good material in good hands and let Sam do the rest:

He was born in Columbia, Tennessee on June 26, 1839. Twenty-one years old when shots were fired at Fort Sumter, he enlisted as soon as he heard the news. "In my imagination, I am young again tonight," he wrote twenty years later.

I hear the fife and drum playing Dixie...I see our fair and beautiful women waving their handkerchiefs and encouraging their sweethearts to go to war. I see the marshaling [gathering] of the hosts for "glorious war." I see the fine banners waving and hear the cry everywhere, "To arms! To arms!"

Like all young men, Watkins was blind to what lay ahead. When news came that the South had crushed the Yanks in the first fight at Bull Run, he and his comrades were disappointed. "We felt that the war was over, and we would have to return home without even seeing a Yankee," he explained. "Ah, how we envied those who were wounded. We thought at the time that we would have given a thousand dollars to have been in the battle."

I threw in details, as below, because I knew I had to make history meaningful at the human level if I expected anyone to remember what they were taught after all the tests ended:

Not long after, the eager soldier had his first taste of combat. It came one night as he was standing guard. "While I was peering through the darkness," he remembered, "my eyes suddenly fell

311

upon the outlines of a man." The more he stared the more certain he was that a Yankee was closing in. "I could see his hat and coat—yes, see his gun." Sam found himself in a "cold sweat" but called out, "Halt, who goes there?" When the shadowy figure failed to answer he advanced. With a sudden lunge he drove his bayonet "through and through" the enemy.

Too late he realized: "It was a stump."

Sam and his comrades had their first chance to shoot at targets that shot back when they played a minor role at the Battle of Shiloh (April 1862). Even when that battle ended, Sam found life as a soldier less glamorous than he had hoped:

> "War had become a reality," he admitted, and the men "were tired of it." During a winter march freezing rain fell on the troops and "icicles hung from their clothing, guns and knapsacks." Many suffered from frostbite. Sam's feet froze. Later his skin "peeled off like a peeled onion." Another time he told about marching on a hot day in Georgia. Dust in the road was so deep it was "like tramping in a snowdrift, and our eyes, and noses, and mouths, were filled with the dust that arose from our footsteps."

That fall, Rebel forces moved north into Kentucky, headed for a savage fight at Perryville (October 1862). Both armies were mauled. Watkins described the fearful cost:

Joe Thompson, Billy Bond, Byron Richardson, the two Allen boys—brothers, killed side by side—and Colonel Patterson, who was standing right by my side. He was first shot through the hand, and was wrapping his handkerchief around it, when another ball struck and killed him. I saw W. J. Whitthorne, then a...boy of fifteen years of age, fall, shot through the neck and collarbone. He fell apparently dead, when I saw him all at once jump up, grab his gun and commence loading and firing...I heard him say, "D—n 'em, I'll fight 'em as long as I live." Whit

thought he was killed, but he is living yet. We helped bring off a
man by the name of Hodge, with his under jaw shot off, and his
tongue lolling out. We brought off Captain Lute B. Irvine. Lute
was shot through the lungs and was vomiting blood all the while,
and begging us to lay him down and let him die. But Lute is
living yet. Also, Lieutenant Woldridge, with both eyes shot out. I
found him rambling [wandering] in a briar patch.

Like Burns, I wanted students to feel what it was like for those
who fought this terrible war. We followed Sam through four years of
service, the South reeling ever closer to defeat, no matter what sacrifices
Watkins and his comrades were willing to make, no matter how much
courage they displayed, no matter how high the price for soldiers and their
families.

We finished the reading with something Sam said about the
sorrows of war. Looking back, every death, he said, had lost its glory. All
he saw was "broken homes and broken hearts."

In fact, if you want to refute the idea that testing is the be-all-end-
all of education, Ryan's story is beyond price. For thirty-three years, one
rule I followed was never, ever tell a student, "No, I don't think you can."
Only once did I come close. Ryan was a pleasant young man in one of my
afternoon classes, many years ago, but afflicted with a terrible stutter.

Despite his handicap he was a pleasure to deal with in every way.
Ryan loved history and could add good comment to any discussion. If I
called on him, though, I had to have extra time. Words came slowly,
painfully, and classmates and I had to listen closely to follow his logic.

Occasionally, if I was in a hurry, I pretended not to see his raised
hand.

One day, I was seated at my desk, while students started the
Watkins handout. I reminded anyone who needed to do a project that this
would be a good time to come back and talk. Ryan approached. For
obvious reasons he had never volunteered to get up in front of class. Now
he said he would like to do a skit on the life of a Civil War soldier, a
subject that clearly interested him. I held doubt in check, asking only,
"Who will be working with you?"

Stumbling over every syllable, he replied that he would go it alone. "I…I…I wa…wa…wan…wan…want to bu…bu…be a Rebel sol…jer," he stammered.

It was in my blood to have faith in teens, to assume each young man and young woman could do more than they knew. Now I wanted to say, "No. You can't." I could only imagine how awful his experience would be, exposed in front of an entire class, trying to talk for forty-five minutes.

The tip of my tongue touched my palette to form the word "no." I didn't want this kind-hearted young man to be cut up by the verbal knives of peers. But I couldn't tell him to lose faith.

I caught myself and nodded approval.

A week later Ryan stood at the front of the room dressed in gray jacket and battered, gray slouch hat. For all intents and purposes he was naked emotionally at age fourteen, risking being stripped of his dignity if he failed.

It was immediately apparent he had studied long and hard. Ryan wove details from Watkins' story and half-a-dozen sources into a cohesive narrative. What surprised everyone was the clarity with which he spoke. Perhaps because he was so intensely focused on what he had to tell, his stuttering was less profound. He still stuttered; but his classmates and I sensed we were witnessing something great. Ryan told us about battles in which he played a role, talked about seeing friends die, and mentioned love letters his girl sent from home.

When I asked what she looked like he said she was "b..b..beautiful, with d..dark hair and dark eyes." He handled every question, stumbled over syllables, but never faltered in his tale, and held center stage the entire period.

When he finished, his class did something I'd never seen before. They rose and gave him a standing ovation.

I don't think I was ever prouder of a student—or a class—or happier to be a teacher.

***

You see: in a sane world, I would argue that a standing ovation trumps the **Tariff Crisis of 1830**. I would argue that Tommy Smith needed

314

to know about that flag, that Trevor and everyone else needed to think about how their attitudes might be the cause of their defeats in life.

I would also argue that *true learning* can't be measured with five-sentence paragraphs.

In 2011, three years after I laid down my grade book forever, Kim, who passed through my class in the early 80s, sent me this message via Facebook, on the death of her grandmother, "a strong woman," as she said:

> I have mentioned this to you before but I want to thank you again for it. Your famous 1000 word essays that anyone who had you in school had to write. I wrote about grandma and grandpa. I learned so much about them doing that essay. I know more about how they lived and who they are and where they came from, the hardships they had to endure in the 1930's and 1940's from that essay. I remember writing that they were one of the first people on their block to own a TV. Neighbors would come to the house and ask to see the new TV. Thanks again, Mr. Viall.

It reminded me once more what I had done—and not done—my final year in the classroom. I bent my principles, and apologize again to students who had me that year and might read this book. I wish I had asked them to do that interview.

I wish I had asked them to do less reading in that mind-numbing text.

I wish we had covered the Civil War the right way.

I know B. J., who impressed me with his incisive thinking, and Nick and Ken and Grace, always so diligent in their studies, might have learned about their own families had we done that essay.

Craig, who loved history, and Stelanie, always polite and pleasant, would have done the creative essay on the dying soldier and done it with flair. Anna and Megan, Mike and Michael, Logan and Jarron, Brooke and Michelle, John and Jillian, Charlotte, Emma and Erik, Austin, Rachel and Sadie, and all the other fine young people I had in my classes that year would have benefitted if we had worked more on writing with clarity and style.

Aaron, who had true acting ability, would have been great if we had done all the usual skits.

M. K. and Colleen, Natalie, Eric, Ashley, Abby and Matt—we could have done so much more *worth doing* had I not wavered from my course and tried to teach to the test.

26.

Roger is the Key

"I do things like get in a taxi and say, 'The library and step on it.'"
David Foster Wallace

Deep into a second decade of sweeping school reform, the average American should expect great gains across the board. Starting with passage of No Child Left Behind in 2002, the Big Fixers sounded the charge and sent millions of educators and students storming down the path to victory. The Fixers said we had to "grade" schools. We graded schools. They said we needed charter schools. We created charter schools. They said we had to hold teachers accountable. We held teachers accountable. They said we needed more and more standardized tests.

We developed a shitload of standardized tests.

Test scores became the Alpha and Omega of learning and the Fixers promised scores would rise.

***

First, a caveat: We all know you can prove anything with statistics. Yet, with that in mind, evidence is grim. We did as the Big Fixers ordered. Frontline teachers and principals charged when they said charge and students followed. Scores on the Scholastic Aptitude Test (SAT) didn't rise. They fell.

The drop wasn't large, but a drop it was, when gains had been guaranteed. From 2002 to 2014 math scores fell from 504 to 497. Reading scores inched down, 516 to 513. Scores on the writing test, first added to the SAT in 2006, slipped from 497 to 487. The College Board, which designs and administers the SAT, responded "boldly" to halt the slide. They simply decided to dump the writing portion of the test in 2016.

(Higher standards, indeed!)

Meanwhile, American College Test (ACT) scores were as flat as the Kansas prairie. In 2014 the average composite score was 21.0, exactly the same as the average in 1997, before the testing mania in grades K-12 took hold.

As for Program for International Assessment scores (PISA), routinely used to put a point to demands for school reform—because U. S. students scored "badly" on PISA tests—those slipped too. The drop was not precipitous; but if you looked at results from 2000 to 2012, our kids appeared to be falling farther behind, not gaining ground. Math scores dropped from 493 to 481, science from 499 to 497, reading from 504 to 498.

If these declines were not necessarily cause for panic, they were certainly nothing to brag about. True, in 2012, we beat the Russians badly in two out of three categories and lost by one point in math. So: take that Vladimir Putin! And if the Germans and French beat us in reading, and British kids outscored America's fifteen-year-old readers by a point, we did thump the Spanish and Italians.

Well, then, what went wrong? Why didn't test scores rise?

Setting math and science aside, because I have no experience in those subject areas, we might consider reading results from the National Assessment of Educational Progress. When scores were released for 2013 you could see a promising bump for nine- and thirteen-year-olds. Yet the trend line for high school seniors, the "finished product" of school reform, was flat and depressing. The average reading score in 1992, before all those billions were wasted on high-stakes testing: 292.

The average score in 2013: 288.

Even racial gaps, which were supposed to close as a result of increased focus on disadvantaged kids, refused to close. White 17-year-olds scored 24 points higher than African Americans in 1992, 30 points higher in 2013. Asian Americans continued to thump Native Americans and every other group every time NAEP tests were administered.

Since I taught half my life, I wasn't surprised. In fact, I'm so sure my "plan" to raise reading scores will work I hereby notify our current president and all those thinking of running in 2016 that I *will* accept an offer to become tenth U. S. Secretary of Education.

"Mr. President," or perhaps, "Madame President," I plan to say in our first sit down together, "I know why scores aren't rising. The plan is not the key.

"You have to reach *people* with books."

***

From the first day, when I walked into a classroom as a young man, until the final day, gray-haired, when I walked out, going the other way, I could see one wide path to follow if I wanted to help students improve reading skills. If I could convince them to *read more* they'd improve the same way athletes gain strength by going to the gym. For that reason I required students to read books.

I admit my plan is pretty simple.

Still, there it is.

It was my goal to turn as many teens into lifelong readers as possible. So I tried to make my requirement palatable. Books were not assigned. Students could choose from a list of hundreds, or might substitute options they discovered on their own. I also told them to keep searching till they found books they enjoyed.

The first year I set up the program I asked students to turn in written reports. Book reports are tedious to write—tedious to read—and not that difficult to fake. I soon dispensed with the requirement and started asking pupils to come back to my desk whenever we had time and give oral reports.

Never once, in thirty years, did I mean to trick a teen. I allowed the broadest possible latitude in reporting. "Tell me what you read about," was how I started every session. Usually that was enough. Most teens were happy to talk about what they'd learned and I had the satisfaction of doing the Lord's work, opening up wide horizons in literature. But students had to do their part too.

As a boy I enjoyed *To Hell and Back*, Audie Murphy's World War II memoir. So that was on my list.

During study hall one day Scott approached and said he was ready to report. I asked what book he'd read. He said he finished *To Hell and Back*. I asked if he liked it. He said he did.

"Tell me what you read about," I began.

"I don't remember," he replied succinctly.

I waited for him to flesh out his report. Nothing. I tried again: "You said you liked the book. Why?"

"It was......exciting," he replied in a wavering voice. I waited for details.

Nothing.

"What was Murphy's childhood like?" I tried, by way of a hint. Despite the passage of forty years, I remembered Audie Murphy had grown up poor.

"I don't remember."

"Okay, why did he join the army?"

Despite a second hint, Scott could not recall. "I read the book. I just don't remember."

Two boys seated nearby were listening in on our exchange. I think they wanted to get a close look at the car wreck and see if anyone had been killed or maimed.

Another hint: "Audie Murphy joined the army when he was a teen. What's the book about?"

"War?"

"Right." I tried again: "What was it like fighting in World War II?"

"Dangerous?" Scott replied. Behind him, I noticed the two boys shaking their heads.

"Murphy won more medals than any American during World War II," I tried. "How?"

"Killing people...."

With that, I smacked my forehead with the palm of my hand. Someone in a seat behind Scott burst out laughing. Ten minutes down the drain and he waved the white flag.

"Okay, I didn't read it," he said.

I felt like snapping, "I already knew that!" but bit my tongue and pointed him to his seat.

Over the years, I did everything I could to get kids to read. In the end what I did was never the sticking point. At first, every student was required to finish four books. If you've ever taught you know what's coming. Even some of the best students went looking for the four shortest books. *Jonathan Livingston Seagull* was wildly popular for several years.

I started asking everyone to read four books *and* total 1,000 pages. This raised a host of issues. "If we start a book we don't like," students wondered, "will the pages count if we don't finish?"

It defeated my purpose to have them plow through a work they hated. I said yes.

Then the big one: "If we read a book, like a biography, for another class, can that count for history too?"

Every year, we talked about why the answer was no. "If you go to the gym once a week you don't gain strength as fast as you do if you go twice. Three times is better. If you read the same book for history and another subject it's like going to the gym once. You just don't need a shower," I laughed.

The bibliophiles laughed with me.

For other students, the "college argument" hit home. Most Loveland kids were going to give higher education a try, especially those who sat in my classes the second half of my career, as the community grew in affluence. I made the case accordingly. I told them, whether they were ready or not to go on to that level, their success or failure would have no bearing on my happiness. I *prayed* my children would be strong readers, ready for college. I only *hoped* my students would be.

Familiarity with the written word would be critical at Boston College, Ohio State or Tulane. Yet nearly half of all freshmen failed to finish.

On which side of that equation did my pupils wish to stand?

When it comes to improving the reading abilities of ordinary students, school reformers overlook the critical factor. They call for more rules and regulations. They form committees—write standards—design tests to measure progress—and ignore human nature. You can't get in shape if all you have is an exercise *plan*. The great variable is *motivation,* the willingness to pound the weights, or pound the books.

In my class, with the 1,000-page rule in force, too many students were "falling behind." This meant the requirement was killing grades. Not everyone needs to go to college, I reasoned. Bowing to realities, I halved the figure for anyone content to keep a C average in history for the year. If a boy or girl was okay with a D they need finish only one book and 250 pages.

Even this modest requirement struck some parents as too stiff a price to pay for a quality education. I called Mrs. Pim one evening to talk about her son and a string of missed assignments. The boy was satisfied to bump along with a D average. Mom still felt I was asking too much. "Why does he have to do a book report in history anyway?" she grumbled.

Therein lies a second problem. We hear a thousand times *schools* must set higher standards. That's not where the battle is waged. A school is bricks and mortar. The battle we must somehow win takes place in the minds of teachers, parents and students, all equally involved.

In the final week of school one year a father called me at home to say my 1,000 page requirement, still in force for A and B students, was "ridiculous." He used that word repeatedly during our conversation.

I jotted it down.

His daughter was an honor roll student; but she had come up 300 pages short. Now she was two days away from the end of the year and what would be a major hit to her average. I defended the requirement, using the same arguments we covered in class. Dad wasn't listening. He was spouting. Or, to be fair, he was trying to save a daughter he loved.

Julia "needs time to be a kid," he insisted. Then he added: "I could understand if this was reading class."

No. It was "only history." I was taking notes.

I told him his sympathy was misplaced. Julia had been warned on May 1 she was 300 pages short. That meant she let a month slip when she should have been busy. She could have read ten pages a day and finished with time to spare.

Dad insisted this was "far too much."

I told him parents *said* they wanted high standards. If you *set* high standards you had to deal with a bunch of "friggin' complaints." He didn't like my use of a term clearly meant to replace a pungent Anglo-Saxon word.

I apologized for that.

In almost every way that mattered, he sounded like a good father. His daughter was proof he probably was. She was polite and pleasant and normally hardworking. Yet, when she ran into a standard and failed to meet it, dad turned out to be like too many modern parents. He called for a lower standard of excellence, not a higher standard of effort.

We talked for half an hour, but made no headway. Finally, I said in disgust, "I'll tell you what I'll do. I hope you never complain about standards again. You want a lower standard? You've got it. I'm going to give Julia an A+ for the grading period and an A+ on the exam, without even grading it, because you don't care about learning. All you care about are grades."

I told him I hoped Julia would be a success in the future and said I was pretty sure she would be. In the same situation, I said, I would never ask a teacher to lower requirements for my children and hoped my kids would push themselves to excel.

He spluttered a response.

I cut him short, told him he had what he wanted, a grade that signified nothing, and hung up the phone.

Putting frustrations aside, I remained a missionary for books. I added to the list whenever I came across anything students might like. We also cut choices if teens agreed they weren't good.

On weekends I haunted garage sales, estate sales and used book shops, spending a dollar or fifty cents for copies of works I thought students might enjoy. For years I had a fruitful connection with Goodwill Industries. On one occasion I walked out happily with sixty books crammed into large shopping bags. Another day I was thrilled to pick up nineteen copies of *Night*, fifty cents each, the most popular book on my list.

For twenty years, until the cartilage in my right knee wore out, I also ran an "open gym" on Sunday nights at our school. I charged players, including some of my favorite former students, a dollar to play basketball. I loved the game, chipped in my dollar, too, and over the years raised several thousand dollars. Then we used the money to buy books for the school library and my classroom reading program.

In fact, if I was still teaching today I'd add all kinds of works I've read since retiring. *Matterhorn*, a brilliant Vietnam War novel, and *The Absolutely True Diary of a Part-Time Indian* would be on my list. My wife would want me to include *A Tree Grows in Brooklyn*, which now sits atop a tall stack of books I hope to read before I go to the Big Library in the Sky.

***

Over the decades students read 10,000 works for my class. Jason polished off *Lonesome Dove* in two weeks, faster than I read it myself. Brian knocked off all 1,143 pages of *The Rise and Fall of the Third Reich*. One day I noticed Jodi hunched over a book during study hall. I asked what she was reading so intently. A story about Frederick Douglass, the runaway slave, she said.

"I love it," Jodi added, and thanked me for getting her into the reading habit.

On another occasion, Roger informed me he was ready to report. The biography of General Custer, he admitted, was the first book he ever read in his life. I don't know who was happier when he completed his oral report successfully, him or me.

You see: the plan is never the key.

Roger is the key. What matters is his motivation, his willingness to tote the book. We're off on an epic goose chase if we focus on rules and regulations to fix schools. If you're a teacher you design the best *plans* you can; but it's far more important to convince students to *work as hard as they can*. The plan is a blueprint. You must still build what's been designed.

My role was to get good books into good hands. If I could do that I knew we would reap benefits of all kinds. An e-mail from Mollie's mother reinforces my point:

> I want to say kudos for your assignment…Mollie selected a rather intense novel, *Night*, [actually a memoir] about a young Jewish boy's experiences during the Nazi occupation of Europe in WWII. Because it was pretty gruesome…I decided we should read it out loud to each other. We ended up enjoying our time together…and I was glad I could be with her to explain the historical background of the Holocaust.
>
> I realized she really did "get it" when she said, "Mom, the thing I learned is that we can't be naïve about evil and we really have to stop it as soon as it starts." Thanks again for pushing the envelope and making the kids go the extra mile to learn.

Betsy, a former student (and by then assistant professor of religious studies at Marymount Manhattan College), contacted me via Facebook. She thanked me for convincing her in eighth grade to read more—and choose more challenging works. She forwarded two photos, showing crammed shelves in her library at home, volumes overflowing to form stacks on the floor.

I could take partial credit, or blame, she said, for her bookish obsession.

Betsy's library neatly stacked with books.

A third message also arrived via Facebook. "You may not remember me," Robert wrote. "I had you for history in the 8th grade. I had long red hair, and was a lazy smartass at times. I just wanted to thank you for being a great teacher, and somehow holding my interest at times."

We exchanged messages and he explained what he'd been up to for twenty years. He'd had his ups and downs after dropping out of school. Eventually he earned a GED.

"I actually read *To Kill a Mockingbird* for a book report for you even though I had seen the movie," he added finally.

When a "lazy smartass" remembers what he read two decades earlier, and read a classic novel at that, it bolsters my case. All the focus on standardization distracts us from the truth. As a teacher, I can help Robert, and should do everything I can; but Robert holds the key to success.

He has it in *his* hand.

***

The last few years I taught it was clear No Child Left Behind was a Frankenstein creation, a threat to much of what matters in education. I tried to hold the line on books, even my final year. I still insisted A or B students read four and total 1,000 pages, C students read two and total 500, D students finish one and 250. But time spent discussing options and listening to reports cut into time to devote to improving scores on the Ohio Achievement Test.

I brought this up during one staff meeting. "Erica," I asked my principal, "I have a girl named Kate Farmer first period. She's reading *Gone with the Wind*. Do you want me to stop worrying about reading, which has nothing to do with the official social studies curriculum, and focus on a fifty-question test?"

The boss didn't have a good answer, probably because there isn't one. When I pressed the issue she felt I was baiting her and made sharp retort.

Mrs. Kramer was good enough to apologize later, but in the meantime, I earned my first poor classroom evaluation in twenty-five years. I think Chris Burke, who sat in to observe, felt bad, like he was kicking an old man who was fumbling for his dentures. Under general notes he added:

John, during Friday's [meeting] you asked questions regarding writing and reading in social studies. I encourage you to find ways in which you can encourage students to go beyond the curriculum in their side time, but you are ultimately responsible for only the 8th grade standards and benchmarks. If it is not in the curriculum you don't need to be teaching it.

I know our administrators' hands were tied. The state was going to judge them according to test scores, too.

Nevertheless, I couldn't offer a better summation of what was wrong with standardized testing if I pounded away at my keyboard for a hundred years. Kate could read *Gone with the Wind* or go to the moon for all it mattered. She could pick up a hundred vocabulary words and improve her writing style by exposure to masters. I also warned her to pay attention to the racism that runs like a thread through the book. None of this could be measured on a social studies test.

So, none of it counted as learning—as far as I was to be judged. A thousand pages of reading, twenty-five hours of intellectual growth if she's a fast reader, would amount to nothing, unless Rhett Butler ended by saying, "Frankly, my dear, I don't give a damn about the Kansas-Nebraska Act."

Yes, Scarlett, that *was* in the curriculum.

Think about it: Reading *for* history might help on the *reading section* of the Ohio Achievement Test. Yet for insisting on reading *in* social studies, I was called to atone for my sins.

Daredevil that I am, I kept pushing books. Most students kept pace as the year progressed. Kate polished off four, totaling 2,000 pages. Dave read *Night, Band of Brothers* and *Black Hawk Down,* all works I would have happily read at his age. Katelyn, the funniest girl I had in class, read *Night* as one option. For once, when she reported, she had nothing humorous to add. The story, she said, had moved her to tears.

Even Carlotta, who hated my class and hated me, but clearly had potential, read *Go Ask Alice.*

(I'm sorry she had a tough home life and sorry I failed to reach her all year.)

Kenji's case is particularly telling. Kenji's family had come to the United States only five years before. In seventh grade I had him for Ancient World History and while he struggled with English, he worked hard to improve.

Now I had him in eighth grade and he was making great strides. His writing style—in English—improved greatly and neither he nor his parents complained about his having to read 1,000 pages in a second language. By spring he had finished *Night, Gone with the Wind* and *Pudd'n'head Wilson,* a lesser Mark Twain classic.

By the end of March my 144 students had read 400 books.

True, some were getting shut out. There always are and always will be kids who don't do assigned work—unless God gets a teaching degree and decides to keep tabs on all His reading creatures. But I could never see where my requirement was onerous.

Kids and parents knew the score. We talked about the reading in class regularly and I sent multiple letters home to remind parents. Darla, for one, was falling behind and talked to me several times about books she might try, telling me how much she wanted to go to college. Personally, Darla was one of my favorite kids, but I couldn't convince her to read a single book.

***

Friday morning, April 4, 2008: One month till the Ohio Achievement Test. Less than two months till I retire.

I could put it on autopilot and cruise.

It comes up during our team meeting that students are complaining to Sue Lundy, our team leader (and, I should again add, a truly wonderful educator). A book is due for history by year's end. Another is due for Language Arts. In Language Arts students are reading a novel about the Holocaust. Kids want to know why they can't count it for history. Sue asks the team what we should do.

"I'm not about to change my rules," I responded. I'd been fighting this battle for decades. "The kids have known about the reading all year and have two months to read two books."

Monday morning, before our regular team meeting, Sue informed me that Erica wished to see me in her office. I knew this wasn't going to be an awards ceremony but when I entered was surprised to see Erica, Chris, and our team Language Arts teacher, Scott Sievering, seated at a round table.

It turned out all three felt we had a problem with the reading. I didn't. So the problem was me.

I don't mean my colleagues were unkind. Erica was a good principal. I don't deny that and you can torture me and I won't. (Well, maybe if it hurts a lot, I will.) Chris always treated me with absolute fairness and had my respect. Scott was a good young man with an excellent rapport with students.

Still, they hit me with so many questions it was hard to keep track. Someone put this proposition: "What will parents say if they hear the Discovery Team [our team] makes children read an extra thousand pages? Won't they want their kids on a different team?"

Scott, I think, asked: "What if kids learn to hate reading?"

Wasn't it "unfair," one of them suggested, to make students on one team read more than students on the other eighth grade teams?

I put up every defense I could, but it was 3-1, and I was old and closing in on retirement, and they were young, and I couldn't prove I was right.

"So are you telling me I have to let kids count the book they read for Scott for history?" I finally asked.

"Basically…yes…that's the idea," Chris responded.

"Why didn't you tell me that in the first place so I didn't have to waste my breath?"

I rose and left the office in disgust.

***

Thirty-nine work days until I retired. With exercise and proper diet, after that, I began what I called the "7,000-day weekend." A wiser man might have let it go. But this incident troubled me more than anything that happened during my career, even more than the young man who brought the gun to school.

I fought a rear-guard action in class, trying to convince the last teens I would ever teach not to take the easy path, suddenly thrown open. I insisted learning required real effort.

In every bell opinion was divided. Some students saw my point. Others didn't. When Kyle told me during fourth period my requirement was "stupid" I boiled up and kicked him out of the room. I liked Kyle, too;

329

funny kid. In sixth period, Elle, a fine student, said she didn't like to read and didn't see why I cared. I bristled again. I just couldn't believe we had come to this. Half my students had completed the reading. Most were closing in on their goals. Now we were going to let those who had fallen behind give up and quit.

I emailed my oldest daughter to outline developments, knowing she'd understand. Abby was the kind who read *War and Peace* in eighth grade. Later she worked as a tutor for one of those companies that promised to help students raise their scores on the SAT and almost always did.

"How depressing!" she replied via email. "No wonder Americans are falling behind. That sort of workload is exactly what the Korean and Indian parents of kids I tutored were paying 1000s of dollars to ensure their kids received!"

At night, I couldn't sleep. Exhaustion caught up with me as I was heading home from work one afternoon. At a stoplight not far from school I zoned out and rear-ended an SUV driven by Katie, a favorite former student. Luckily, no one was hurt, including Parker, her younger brother, who was sitting in the back and had been seated in my third bell earlier that day.

I liked Parker, too. I'm glad I didn't squash him.

That night I tossed and turned again. Finally, I arose to write my colleagues a letter. I said we were looking at a tragedy which had nothing to do with me. I was going to be gone in a month, whether every student read fifty books or every student read fifty words.

Or none.

I mentioned that Sarah, my 20-year-old, had just called to ask about applying for medical school. I wrote from the heart, saying my third child always pushed herself and this was what I had tried to convince all my children and all my students they must do. I ended with this: "I think you do great harm when you make no demands on students…You show, inherently, you do not respect their talents. You expect less than they can give."

With that, I fell into bed and slept for an hour and when I rose again, felt calm. I was dealing with people I liked or respected, or both. I knew none of them would ever intentionally harm any student—and the sentences quoted do not perfectly capture my intended meaning—though they point in the direction I always felt we must go.

I put the note aside and in class that day told kids the matter was settled. I would drop my requirement by the equivalent of one book.

Even some students wondered if we weren't caving in too soon. When I told first period the book everyone was reading for Language Arts would count for history, Kate, who had already met her requirement, asked with studied sarcasm, "Why don't we just read the same book sixty times?"

Exactly, I wanted to say, exactly.

Later that day, as I explained the situation to sixth period, Emily asked: "Isn't this like writing the same essay and using it twice?"

Again, I wanted to tell her she was correct.

I felt that day, for the first time in my career, that I had been totally defeated in the classroom. I had given up the ground I believe educators must hold and allowed students to do less than I *knew* they could.

Since that day seven years ago, I've read all kinds of articles and books about American education. Almost all stress the need for better teachers—smarter teachers—improved ways to train teachers—ways to take tenure away from all the "lousy" teachers we have.

At the risk of stating the obvious, I found, as a teacher, I was not *alone* in the room. I was surrounded by teens. If they weren't willing to work, what I did wouldn't much matter.

POSTSCRIPT

A telling survey in 2010 found the average American was watching 34 hours of TV a week. By contrast, 46% of adults admitted they hadn't read a single book not required for work or school in the last year.

Meanwhile, researchers at the University of Tennessee discovered a simple way to raise reading scores. It was found that "giving low-income children access to books at spring fairs—and allowing them to choose books that most interested them—had a significant effect on the summer reading gap."

Typically, with few books in the home, low-income children saw a decline in reading skills of two months each summer. A control group of 500 children was not given books. A second group of 500 received twelve books and the change in reading scores for this group was equal to a child "attending three years of summer school."

In other words: put books children like in children's hands and they improve their reading. They do it themselves.

Want to raise reading scores? Then focus on Roger. Roger is the key.

Parents, you are the key. Take your child to the library. Visit the book store as often as you can.

Young person, you are the key. Put away your cellphone. Turn off the TV. Grab a good book.

Two eyes suffice.

You'll see.

27.

And His Soul Left His Body

"War is a crime. Ask the infantry and ask the dead."
Ernest Hemingway

If I got one idea right in a classroom it was this. It's something the non-teaching-advice-giving-school-reforming types miss. I found learning could be advanced and enhanced in a thousand ways.

After the attacks of 9/11, I renewed efforts to bring guest speakers in to talk to my classes. If we were at war, students should be clear about what that meant. In the spring of 2002, Pat Settlemire, our excellent aide, told me her father-in-law would be happy to speak to our kids. Jim Settlemire was 76 at the time of his visit. In 1945, at age 20, he had commanded a B-17 Flying Fortress over Nazi Germany.

During one mission, he told us, a waist gunner (he showed crew positions on a model he brought) radioed warning to the cockpit. A strange craft was fast approaching from 3 o'clock high. A moment later a German jet flashed by and blasted a sister bomber out of the sky. It was the first time Settlemire or just about anyone in the world had seen a jet in combat.

On another mission his B-17 was rocked by a burst of flak. At first there appeared to be no damage. "The ball turret gunner called on the radio," Settlemire told the class. "We had some kind of oil leak. Fluid was splattering the turret glass. My copilot and I checked gauges but pressure was normal. The gunner radioed again. The fluid was blood. It turned out our navigator had been struck in the throat by a shell splinter and killed."

When Mr. Settlemire was too ill to return in 2003, I turned to staff and students for help. Mark, in fourth period, said his grandfather belonged to an organization for retired Marines. I made the call that night.

"I can get you speakers," Tom Bravard, the group commandant assured me. "How many do you want?"

***

That spring we picked a date when the district had already cut a day in half so staff could devote the afternoon to discussions about how to prepare for the OAT. Seventh grade teachers agreed to divide the remaining four hours into equal blocks, one for eating. The remaining blocks would be scheduled so all 350 students could hear three speakers.

The lineup was incredible. Mark Adams, an F-16 pilot, and father of one of my pupils, talked about what it was like in January 1991 in skies over Baghdad. He described maneuvering to avoid an Iraqi missile that locked onto his aircraft and watching it rip past his cockpit and explode. "The muscles in my rear end kind of puckered," he admitted.

Naturally, that brought a round of laughter from his audience.

On another mission a call came in to provide cover for a five-man Special Forces team pinned down in the desert by 150 Iraqi soldiers. Adams was low-key about his role in driving off enemy troops but admitted there were "camel parts flying in all directions" once he opened fire.

Bravard was a hit, as well, though only a peacetime Marine. He talked about enlisting in 1956, stubborn at 17, picking the Marines because "everybody told me not to." He brought along a friend, Paul Walker, who drove a tank for the U. S. Army in the early 60s. The kids loved listening to the two old-timers poke fun at one another and enjoyed handling the equipment they brought to show. Tom had an M-1 rifle in mint condition, .45 pistols, bayonets, and an MRE (Meals Ready to Eat). He could also demonstrate, with requisite volume, how Parris Island drill instructors ordered recruits about.

Ace Gilbert, a Vietnam veteran, proved to be an eloquent speaker. I expected as much, having interviewed him by phone prior to his visit. I placed him in the auditorium and let him talk to seventy-five kids in each of four sessions. [23]

At first, I stuck around to be sure he could handle a crowd. Ace started off by telling the kids he wanted questions and then launched into

---

[23] Veterans ate together at the end of the day.

his story. After five minutes I knew he'd be fine. So I snuck out the back to see how other speakers were faring.

I came back later that day to listen. It was obvious kids felt they were "in" on something, and they laughed repeatedly, because Mr. Gilbert used salty language to make several points. He talked about nights spent in the jungle, posted for ambushes, senses so attuned to noise, "You could hear a mosquito fart." Naturally, 13- and 14-year-olds loved that line.

Ace wanted students to understand there was no glory in war. "The Marine Corps trains you to kill," he told them, "but you never train for the fact your best friend might die in your arms."

On November 11, 1969, his unit launched an assault against dug-in North Vietnamese troops atop a hill the Marines wanted. Sometime during the day, Bobby Hamel, his buddy, was wounded and fell into a deep shell crater in a position too exposed to reach. That night, Ace was finally able to help carry Bobby back down the hill, but it was clear the young Marine might not last. Ace told him to hang on. Medevac helicopters were coming.

His friend grimaced and said, "If you really like me, get some help."

Around 6:30 a.m. on the 12th the sound of choppers gave them brief hope. "Bobby turned his head for a look and his soul left his body," Ace explained.

An auditorium filled with teens was silent, save for the sound of one young lady weeping.

Mr. Gilbert had been a machine gunner. On his first night ambush he told listeners how he cut down nine enemy soldiers at close range in one burst of fire. He knew what it was like to see men die and told students, "I still think about those men I killed." He spoke of dead friends as "forever nineteen" in his mind and the kids knew it wasn't easy to explain.

He had to be prompted to say he had two Purple Hearts. One came when Ace stepped on a land mine. "It felt like I got kicked in the ass by a supersonic mule," he laughed. Again he had the rapt attention of the audience.

When we finished the program we asked students to write thank you notes to the veterans they heard. Ace told me he was stunned his first year to receive hundreds of heartfelt notes. He and his wife sat on their bed, reduced to tears by the outpouring of sympathy and support.

Two Legs Suffice

***

We ran variations of the program for several years, always with success. In May 2008, with retirement looming, I brought in fourteen speakers, the best lineup ever. Adams, Bravard and Gilbert were back. We added Ron Walton, a second Vietnam combat veteran, and Rob Shoftall, who served with the U. S. Air Force in Iraq. (He called it the "Chair Force.") We had Dave Volkman, a colonel in the U. S. Army Reserves and a high school teacher in our district, just back from Afghanistan. We invited Lt. Colonel Tony Capetillo, who led Marines during the invasion of Iraq, and he brought along Sgt. Jason Faust, one of his men.

Jonathon, one of my star students, helped line up another young veteran to speak. Seth Judy talked to kids about how he enlisted after 9/11 because he "loved this country." He deployed to Iraq in March 2003 and was wounded six months later when a suicide car bomber rammed the Humvee in which he was riding. He mentioned temperatures as high as 130° and blinding sand storms. But he had to be coaxed to discuss his injuries and the ten surgeries to follow.

Joe Whitt had always been part of our program, as good a speaker as we could hope to find. "I was serving aboard the *USS San Francisco* the morning the Japanese bombed Pearl Harbor," he said. "I had paid a buddy to teach me how to play the guitar and we were just starting our first lesson when the call to battle stations came over the ship's intercom."

Whitt raced topside. "Another sailor stuck a rifle in my hands and told me to start shooting. Low-flying enemy planes would zoom past, so close you could see the pilot's faces and the big red meatball on the side." He didn't hit anything, but he was "mad as heck." Shooting made him feel better.

I knew Joe was a Pearl Harbor survivor when I first asked him to visit but did not realize he had seen action in the waters off Savo Island, near Guadalcanal. Joe was there on the night of November 13, 1942, when Japanese and American forces tangled in a savage fight. His ship suffered forty-seven hits and barely remained afloat. Joe watched another U. S. vessel take a direct hit, explode, and sink within seconds, taking most of her crew with her.

"It just took your breath away, all those poor American boys," Joe said with immeasurable sadness, as imagination carried us all across the decades. It was a powerful story, and a roomful of teens was stunned.

I thought of all those young boys, and choked up myself, and had to struggle to hold back tears.

Joe never had trouble keeping kids' attention, but in 2008 we had a second World War II Navy vet. So we paired them up. Alvie Taylor was born in Pine Knot, Kentucky, enlisted at eighteen, and served aboard a destroyer in the Pacific. "One day," he explained, "an officer gathered the crew and asked if anyone had cooking experience. I said I was from a large family and could cook in an emergency. So they made me a ship's baker."

His battle station, though, was a 20 mm anti-aircraft gun and he saw action at Leyte Gulf and Okinawa. Taylor was as thin at age eighty-one as he was at eighteen, and cackled at his own tales, except when discussion turned to kamikazes. "I used to see them swarming overhead," he said, "and it was 'get them before they got you.'" Alvie had never forgotten the fear he felt at such moments.

Joe rejoined the conversation. He said he still had bad dreams about Savo Island. "I see that U. S. warship explode. I see bodies go flying in the air." In his dream he's one of them. He's sailing across the sky. "I start coming down and I'm scared. At the last moment, I put my feet together and lock my arms at my sides and prepare to hit the water.

"Then I always wake up."

Last but not least, we had three old Marines scheduled in our library with a hundred students in each session. One was Milt Rooms, who looked like the kindly grandfather he was. At nineteen, Rooms was married with a one-month-old son when he joined the Marines. Milt had been out to school before. I knew he was hard of hearing, so we hooked him up with two new guests. Tom Thomas signed up at seventeen, with his parents' permission, five months after Pearl Harbor. John Neal enlisted in 1943. Rooms, Thomas and Neal had seen great slaughter and seemed apologetic about surviving when so many others did not.

I asked Milt if he had any close calls.

"Sure," he smiled broadly. "One time a Jap came up behind me with a mattock. By the time I turned he was only six feet away." Milt crouched slightly and pretended to raise an M-1.

"Pow, pow, pow, I dropped him."

337

The three old veterans shared a quiet laugh, remembering how lucky they had been.

I had to stop a speaker occasionally and ask them to explain a term—what a "mattock" was, for instance. I scanned the audience now and then for signs of rudeness or trouble. Teens weren't poking each other or writing love notes or staring into space. Hands were up all over, waiting to ask questions, and a hundred students were engaged.

Thomas smiled when a girl asked if he was afraid the first time he went into combat. "We were a bunch of teenagers," he told his teen audience. "We didn't know what was coming."

Neal had his first taste of war at Saipan in '44. "It seemed unreal," he said, "like playing cowboys and Indians." Then he heard bullets thudding into flesh and saw bodies bobbing on the waves.

He landed at Iwo Jima in February 1945 and survived that battle without a scratch. A boy asked how he did it. Neal laughed and said, "I was jumping from hole to hole a lot, to avoid being hit. I guess somebody up there likes me." To illustrate another point he unsheathed a samurai sword, picked up from the side of a dead enemy officer. One of the girls volunteered to come forward and he let her handle it.

On a day like this, learning could hardly be more basic. We put fourteen veterans from five wars and 700 teenagers together and let them interact. That's how you educate the young.

You reach them in meaningful ways.

Unfortunately, by 2008 schools across the nation were fixated on standards and testing. I remember asking Mrs. Kramer, if all we cared about were A, B, C and D answers, then wasn't this day technically a waste? In the Age of the Testing Fix every syllable the veterans uttered, unless they brought up mercantilism or Shay's Rebellion, was irrelevant, time ill spent.

Erica was a good principal, as I've said, but shrugged and seemed at a loss for an answer.

Again: probably because there isn't one.

***

When I retired, Dave Fletcher, who served more than a decade in the U. S. Army before going into teaching, took my place. He continues the veterans' program and improves it every year. Each spring he invites me back and I do my part, sharing harrowing tales of my time as a supply clerk, seated in a revolving chair, filling out paperwork in triplicate.

In the spring of 2014 he gathered together nineteen veterans, including two of my former students, who talked about their time in Iraq. To top it off, he added a Holocaust speaker.

Dave limits the program to eighth graders and when speakers finish for the day, asks everyone to head for the auditorium. After all the teachers and students were seated, and all the guests stood to be recognized, 400 teens rose and gave a thunderous ovation. I knew what that meant to the other veterans—almost all of whom had seen combat—and got chills listening.

Next, Mr. Fletcher called up Bill Mansfield, an infantryman in World War II, and handed him an award. He got another standing ovation.

Dave called forward a second veteran, William Sutton, also an infantryman during World War II. He too got a standing ovation.

Werner Coppel, the Holocaust speaker, talked for the next thirty minutes and when finished received the fourth standing ovation of the day. It turned out he had ten minutes left to take questions and when he was done the student body rose once more and applauded for two minutes.

I got chills again and knew this day of learning mattered on every level that counted.

I'd also like to mention two former students and give full names: Mark Jacquez, USMC, and Chuck Garrett, U. S. Army. Both served their country bravely and came back to their old school to speak.

Mark talked about his time in Iraq and told listeners about a friend who deployed to Afghanistan (after Mark's time in the Marines was almost up) and lost both arms and both legs when an IED exploded. "He's one of only two men to survive those kinds of injuries," he explained.

Chuck talked about a Humvee from his unit that was hit by an IED and caught fire while he was in Iraq. His best friend was inside and wasn't able to get out. Chuck described opening the door after the flames were put out. "I wish to god I had never looked inside," was all he said, and every person in the audience could sense his terrible pain.

That's how you reach students in a way they'll never forget. That's what true learning is about.

Veterans in 2008: Volkman, Shoftall, Walton, Faust, Taylor, Bravard,
Rooms, Judy, Whitt, Thomas, Adams, Neal and Capetillo.
(Gilbert not shown.)

28.

Gone, Test, Gone

"Infinite effort and ingenuity went into accomplishing very little."
Christian Meier

Was I right to be so adamant in opposition to standardized testing? To the very marrow of my bones, I believe I was.

In May 2009, the State of Ohio gave the social studies section of the OAT one last time. Scores across the state remained dismal, though good at my old school. Complaints about content were multiplying. Printing, distributing, administering, collecting and grading the tests cost money. The state budget was tight. So, scattering benchmarks and indicators to the winds, the state did away with the social studies portion of the OAT.

Counting state standardized testing in the late 80s and early 90s we're deep into the third decade of the Age of the Testing Fix. Yet nothing has been fixed, almost nothing gained. What do we have to show for all the time and money spent? A strait-jacket has been placed on good teachers. Much of what makes education special has been lost or circumscribed. The paperwork burden on frontline educators grows, metastasizes and threatens to kill the host. Bureaucrats tighten their grip on schools.

The IRS model comes to education.

By 2010, it was obvious NCLB had failed. Policy makers decided new Common Core standards would work where old standards had not. All tests then in use would be scrapped.

Fresh billions would be spent to devise and implement a new testing regimen. Forty-two states and the District of Columbia jumped aboard for the latest merry-go-round ride.

Experts promised. This time testing was *going* to work.

Five years later, many states are backing out. Politicians who care ten times more about remaining in office than students or learning still argue over what teachers must do.

How nutty does this seem? The Ohio General Assembly voted in 2010 to implement Common Core. Ohio educators began gearing up to meet the newest testing challenge. Vast amounts of time and effort were invested, only to discover in November 2014 that lawmakers were shifting position once more.

In 2015, tests tied to Common Core were used for the first and only time. The Ohio General Assembly decided to drop out of Common Core.

So *another* set of tests was dead.

Brand new tests, possibly based on the pre-Common Core standards used by the Commonwealth of Massachusetts, would be created for 2016. If lawmakers had their way, these standards would remain in place for three years. Then they, too, would be phased out and Ohio would develop some really cool standards of its own. Frontline educators, increasingly fed up with political idiocy, could only rub their weary eyes in disbelief.

The merry-go-round continued to spin. Every June, it stopped in pretty much the same place.

***

In the meantime, we continued to use standardized tests to "measure" what students knew and held teachers alone accountable. Molly Hinker, a dedicated young Language Arts teacher, was shocked one year when a young lady turned in her standardized test two minutes after receiving it. She had colored in the bubbles at random and left every essay question blank.

A teacher may not supply answers, but Ms. Hinker did ask if she might not like to take her test booklet back and try doing *something*.

She replied astutely, "It's not my grade, it's yours." And with that she headed happily for her seat.

In terms of accountability, we still blame teachers for low scores even if a student fails to show for class sixty-five days in a single school year.

We still blame teachers when kids are homeless and have to worry about their next meal.

We still blame teachers when teen girls get pregnant and lose interest in school.

We blame them when teen boys smoke marijuana daily.

We blame them when parents abuse or neglect kids, who must cope and take tests the following day.

We fault teachers and fail to help children.

And that's a tragedy and a crime.[24]

---

[24] At this final writing Congress is *still arguing* over reauthorization of No Child Left Behind—a process that has dragged on for eight years. In July 2015, the House of Representatives passed its own reauthorization version, 218-213, with almost no Democratic support. Meanwhile, the Senate put forth a different version. And President Obama was threatening a veto.

Call me a cynic: but I don't think politicians on either side of the aisle know what's best for children. Even if they did, I'm not sure they'd care. Not unless the children hired lobbyists and donated heavily to their reelection campaigns.

29.

Nuns and Runners

"Before the gates of Excellence the high gods have placed sweat."
Hesiod

When I informed my oldest daughter I was writing a book about education, Abby asked what I thought we should do to fix America's schools. I replied succinctly, "I don't know."

"Dad," she groaned, "that's the one chapter people will want to read."

If that. If that.

***

Before taking a stab at an answer allow me to focus on attitude one final time. Societies, like individuals, are marked by different attitudes. Or, as T. S. Eliot put it, "Cultures get what they deserve." Schools are mirrors in which a society sees reflected attitudes it inculcates in its young. Some societies, like Korea and Japan, honor education. We honor sports.

In May 2009, ninety-six reporters showed up to watch Tom Brady *practice* after he sat out the previous season with injury. You couldn't get ninety-six reporters to watch one teacher unless that teacher was Gisele Bundchen, Brady's supermodel wife, grading papers in Victoria's Secret lingerie.

(I'd watch that, myself.)

In the spring of 2012, a thousand reporters traveled to Hoover, Alabama, to attend Southeastern Conference Media Days. Hard-hitting investigative journalists wanted to know what Louisiana State coach Les Miles thought about his football team's chances to repeat as SEC champions. They listened like acolytes as Nick Saban explained how his

Alabama squad might capture a national title. They quizzed officials from Missouri and Texas A&M about why their schools switched conferences and joined the SEC. The one word answer was "money," but no one cared to say.

If fans couldn't wait to read what the coaching gurus were saying, the SEC Digital Network was streaming live coverage. Safe to say, few reporters were there to pursue stories about higher education, to focus on the "student" in student-athlete.

Oh no. We honor sports.

Consider, then, the power of attitude to shape *societies*. Those of us who grew up in the 50s remember an era when girls were warned it was unladylike to sweat. That meant, for most, serious involvement in sports was out of the question. In 1964 Dale Greig, a German runner, ignored convention and set a world record in the women's marathon. Her time was 3:27:45—what today would be considered a pedestrian eight-minute-per-mile pace.

It wasn't just in sports we could see different attitudes in play. In 1965 there were 180,000 nuns serving the Roman Catholic Church in the United States.

Times were changing, however. In spring 1967, an announcement came over the PA system at Revere High, my school. A girls' track team was being organized: an idea which struck male students dumb. Neither I nor my friends could imagine what a girls' team might look like. Apparently, neither could most girls. Two showed up for tryouts and plans were scrapped.

Yet the ladies at Revere *could* have run. They weren't paraplegics. It was attitude that mattered, more than physical realities. Attitudes turned out to be more limiting than shackles.

That same spring, Katharine Switzer decided to do a little unladylike sweating and set out to become the first female, albeit surreptitiously, to run the Boston Marathon. At the two-mile mark race officials were informed a *woman* was on the course. They pinpointed Switzer, in a hooded sweatshirt, and decided she had to be ejected from the field. Only a body block on a race official, delivered by her boyfriend, allowed her to continue.

As attitudes changed so did the choices women made and the demands they made of themselves. *You can repeat that sentence and apply it perfectly if you want greater success in any classroom in America today.* With the hold of religion weakening and the appeal of a life of celibacy fading, only 57,500 U. S. nuns now remain. By contrast, Revere High fields a girls' track team and female marathoners proliferate. When the first New York City Marathon was held in 1970 not a single woman crossed the finish line. Three did in 1971. Thirty-six made it in 1975. By 1980 the number had swelled to 1,621, a decade later to 4,500. In 2003 there were 11,715. Maybe even a couple of nuns.

Three years later, Deena Kastor set a record for U. S. women in the marathon. Her time, 2:19:36, represents a blistering 5:19-per-mile pace.

The question is: "What changed?" Not anatomy. Nuns still had the same working parts. Female runners still had two legs and ten regulation toes. The difference was the thinking that made those legs pump. In the end, attitudes changed.

Nothing else really mattered.

Two legs, once women realized it, sufficed.

The question, then, is how do we change attitudes that matter when it comes to education? We hear all the time about the need to raise test scores in schools. What if the way to raise scores is right in front of us? What if it's both easy and yet hard to do?

***

When I was teaching, I never missed a day with students if I could avoid it. If I had to be out for some reason, I usually knew in advance. I had business to attend to one Friday. So, I scheduled an open-book test for a substitute to give.

On Monday a note the sub left indicated William had turned in a blank paper. You might know what I'm going to say: I liked William.

When asked what happened, he replied, "I don't care. Just give me a zero."

It was time for what drill instructors at Parris Island referred to as an "attitude adjustment."

I took the young man across the hall to an office used by another faculty member. The blinds were down, but there was light enough for William to see the fury (feigned) in my face when I banged the door shut. I told him I wasn't going to let him waste his talent. I said I ought to kick him in the butt. Or I was *going* to kick him in the butt. After all these years, I'm not sure of the semantics. I do know I chewed William's ass. Then I told him to get back to class and get busy. *Or else.*

Something in the young man's attitude shifted that day, if only for an hour. He motored back to my room and buckled down to work. He did not earn a zero the second time around. He scored 100%.

Same test.

Same kid.

Same teacher.

New attitude.

We all enter by the same rectangle. Teachers and students walk in the same door every day.

That's what I mean.

One William stepped through on Friday and settled for a zero. A second William hustled through Monday and scored 100. The results differed, as they do for female runners today, because attitudes are *the* great driving force, inside education as well as out.

So, here it is: my prescription for improving schools. Since no bag of tricks, no matter how deep, can fix humanity, the surest line of attack is to focus on attitudes. If we don't change the way students think, and parents and educators, too, everything else is shuffling paperwork and moving our lips.

***

The non-teaching types rarely glimpse this fundamental truth. In six years spent banging away at a keyboard to finish this book, I read every article on education I could find. On April 22, 2009 Thomas L. Freidman weighed in with a typical column in *The New York Times*:

There are huge numbers of exciting education innovations in America today—from new modes of teacher compensation to charter schools to school districts scattered around the country that are showing real improvements based on better methods, better principals and higher standards.

Most of Friedman's commentaries are spot on, but here the missing link was still missing.

His focus was mostly structural.

Structural change isn't irrelevant—but has never been the keystone and never will. Imagine you could go back to the spring of 1967 and give the young ladies at Revere High the best 2015-quality running shoes and offer modern training seminars. Those girls would remain rooted in one spot. You could build a new track and name it Deena Kastor Stadium. The fundamental question would remain. *Did those girls want to run?*

It is the desire to run—to run hard—to run harder—that matters most.

In Friedman's case, he focused on structural change wrought by Wendy Kopp, the non-teaching founder of Teach for America. The Teach for America model is designed to steer top college graduates through the certification maze and into classrooms across the land. The premise is solid. Smart teachers are better than dumb teachers any school day of the week.

Still, you had to wince when Kopp explained a dramatic rise in applications for the year. Freidman wondered if it had to do with the battered state of the economy. Kopp said no. Idealistic young men and women were "responding to the call that this is a problem our generation can solve."

Intelligence helps. Idealism—an attitude, after all—is highly important in any classroom. But the self-righteousness of reformers can take your breath away. Teach for America recruits make up 0.2% of all teachers in this country and just because they graduated from Harvard or Yale, that doesn't mean they have a corner on idealism or that they can solve problems that have daunted millions of educators who have gone before.

We all enter through that rectangle. So the question isn't who has the bigger brain when they pass through the door. What matters is attitude once you step into a room filled with kids, and your willingness to expend rivers of sweat. The Big Fixers continue to focus, wrongly, on the color, width and design of the door.

Progress in education for individuals and nations hinges on great effort sustained over time. It's not a sprint, it's a marathon; and everyone involved needs to be willing to lace up the shoes and run.

We don't need 40-hour-per-week teachers. Nor will we be saved by two-year wonders, which is all the commitment Teach for America asks. We need 55- and 60-hour-per-week teachers. We need people willing to step through the rectangle and battle down the decades and never quit.

***

Some people will say: That's it? Then you have no plan, no solution to fix the schools.

That's true. I don't believe in grand plans.

There is no *solution*.

First, we need to understand that what works for one teacher cannot always work for another. You can train all your soldiers one way—force all your teachers to follow an increasingly scripted and narrow curriculum—but in the end it comes down to courage on the battlefield. The tools and tactics of war change. The tools and tactics of education change as well. The machine gun puts an end to massed infantry attacks in 1918. The use of computers allows students to correct first drafts in writing, a century later. Soldiers still die and kids still struggle to find the telling phrase.

Teach for America teachers aren't *the* answer.

Computers in the classroom aren't *the* answer.

Standardized tests aren't *the* answer. In fact, they distract us from following a trail of obvious clues.

Even shoveling money at problems isn't *the* answer. That only means you've paid for a more expensive door.

Leaders in education reform have been seduced by a belief charter schools are *the* answer. That's like taking the door off one room and moving it to a different building. Our focus must be on what happens *after* people pass through the rectangle—through that door.

We also need to be clear about the role teachers play. The idea they alone must shoulder the burden is the essence of nonsense. Unless we demand greater effort from our young, and unless parents and society accept that premise, education reform boils down to sliding sideways, but at huge additional cost. If all we plan to do is test every child for the next thousand years and blame teachers when scores are low we can expect to end up just about where we are today with another millennium gone to waste.

Students do not control the facilities they attend, run-down inner-city schools or suburban brick-and-mortar palaces. They do not control the weather outside during spring gym class or the quality of textbooks inside after they shower and head for science. They have no power to write curriculum and may enter the classrooms of great, middling, and poor teachers all the same day. They have no way to alter the abilities with which they were born, the odd lottery of God. Yet, they have the power to dramatically affect their own outcomes every day.

This is *their* key variable. They determine how much they are prepared to work to earn a quality education.

***

According to a January 2013 article in *U. S. News and World Report*, Americans spend $60 billion annually on diet plans, home exercise equipment and health club memberships. This was only slightly less than the budget for the U. S. Department of Education that year ($67.8 billion). Still, we're fat and getting fatter, including me.

Almost every adult is trying to lose weight. But diet advice is like education theory. Everyone agrees Americans need to lose weight and every expert has a plan that *can't* fail.

Yet they *fail*.

Kelly D. Brownell, a psychologist and director of the Yale Rudd Center for Food Policy and Obesity, notes that if your goal is to lose weight, "What matters most is your level of motivation and your willingness to change."

The treadmills, stair-climbers and stationary bikes await you at the gym. But you have to *get* to the gym. You have to get off the couch, walk through that rectangle, and climb aboard. If you want to lose weight you don't need another plan. In fact, if you want to lose weight buy a bunch of diet books and carry them around. There's your first workout right there.

Want to lose weight? Take your hand out of that Frito's bag. Drop those corn chips!

(I need to follow that advice, myself.)

Want to lose weight? Strap on your tennis shoes and head out the door right now. Take a walk. And, no: you can't take the Frito's with you. If you want to be thin eat less and sweat more.

Shortest diet plan ever.

The same premise is true when we consider what happens in schools.

A non-teacher friend once asked if I thought it was more important to work "harder" or "smarter." In my mind both approaches are good. They aren't mutually exclusive. Every teacher and student can work smarter and should. I figured out a way to ensure that kids always got to class on time. One of my star students told me she liked to stick different colored post-it-notes up all over her bedroom to help her study for tests.

Once you learn how to work smarter you have to work harder too. You can change and improve methods, but I never cycled across country because I pedaled in a smarter way.

Methods didn't make me a good teacher, either, though they made it easier to do good work in the end. You reach your goals in education exactly the same way you pedal a bicycle from one coast of the United States to the other.

Give me thirty-five kids of any race, creed, color, or background, if all are ready to work. Pack them in my room. Take away all computers. Make us use old books. Cut my pay 10%. Or, if you prefer, raise it the same. Cancel the standardized tests. Close down the U. S. Department of Education. Feel free to send all the big-talking-do-nothing-keep-talking Big Fixers to the remotest corners of Tibet. If *all* thirty-six people in that room are ready to work, we'll be fine without any other help and better off without all the petty interference.

The true engine of success is, always has been, and always will be, individual effort.

Focus on that if you expect improvement in the schools. It's all simple truth. Two legs suffice.

Ready to go: Atop Cadillac Mountain in Maine, June 2011.
Most people think they could never bicycle across the country.

The author tried to teach students, figuratively, that they could.

30.

Clean Underwear Standards

"...though of real knowledge there be little, of books there be plenty..."
Herman Melville

Before sitting down to write, I looked at what was available in the "Education" sections at local bookstores. I wanted to see if some teacher had already explained what I thought should be said.

It turns out there aren't many books written by classroom veterans. *Teach like Your Hair is on Fire* looked interesting, but the author worked in the lower grades. So his perspective was different.

I tried the main public library in downtown Cincinnati. There were a thousand education-related titles, but offerings by experts outnumbered writings by teachers 50-1. You could read *The Devil in the Classroom: Hostility in American Education* or choose *Multiple Perspective Analyses of Classroom Discourse* instead. If behavior was your bag you had *The Acting-Out Child* and *Preventing Classroom Discipline Problems*. The *Trouble with Boys* seemed canceled out by *Failing at Fairness: How American Schools Cheat Girls*.

Education was going to be fixed in all kinds of ways: *Inventing Better Schools, Accelerated Leaning for the 21st Century, Winning the Brain Race, Overcoming Inertia in School Reform* (I probably needed to read that) and *Culturally Responsive Teachers*.

Sometimes experts baffled rather than edified. Editors of *Teaching Every Child Every Day* included this nugget: "Most teachers agree that an emphasis on algorithmic applications in an unauthentic environment with a lack of social interaction defeats the very educational objectives that we seek to promote."

Yeah. I guess.

353

***

Honestly, I *wanted* to believe. I wanted to think solutions to timeless problems could be found between the covers of a book. I wanted to imagine that if we fixed schools we could fix the world.

So I slid *The Tracking Wars* from the shelf and read a few pages before setting it aside. Teach long enough, and you see every kind of tracking tried except stacking. Here is what you discover. No matter how you track, you solve one problem and create another.

When I began teaching, Loveland tracked the lowest-performing students in one class. This concentrated kids with discipline issues. So we gave that system up.

Later we tried a gifted program for a dozen kids. The parents of #13 and #14, who missed the cut, had fits. The next year we had twenty-five gifted students. The third year we had fifty. We gave that up, too, before the parents of #51 and #52 could come after us with chainsaws and picks.

Next we tried tracking everyone in high, middle, and low groups. No affluent parent wanted a child in a low group. Half the kids in the middle had parents who felt they belonged in the high. We returned to heterogeneous grouping. When that failed to solve all problems we tried heterogeneous grouping in most classes, tracking high, average, and low in science and math.

In the 90s, the federal government began ordering schools to mainstream children with special needs. One day I glanced in the direction of a special needs student in my second bell class. He was looking at *Clifford the Big Red Dog,* a book my wife read to our children when they were in pre-school. I didn't mind that he was ignoring the lesson. The point of inclusion in his case was almost entirely socialization and we had two special education teachers, Kathy Simpson and Rachel Angel and several aides, like Kathy Bruening, who did amazing work integrating all kinds of youngsters into regular classes.

I will never forget the day Katie, a Down syndrome teen, turned in her history project. She had pasted bits of colored paper together to create a large poster of Mona Lisa. Mrs. Simpson coaxed her to stand in front of her peers and answer a few questions. When Katie finished, classmates did what I'd only seen that one time before. They gave her a standing ovation.

At the same time, Congress passed laws ordering schools to integrate students with "severe behavior problems" in regular classes, while simultaneously creating pull-out programs for gifted pupils. In other words, in one door came kids with serious emotional and psychological problems, because "inclusion" was a positive good. And out the other went kids with great gifts, because mixing students of different abilities slowed the gifted down.

If you were an average kid—and the gifted kid just disappeared—and now a kid with behavior problems took the vacated seat right beside you—well, you might wonder.

What was going on?

If tracking wasn't exactly the answer, what was? In Loveland we changed from a "junior high" to a "middle school" configuration. We tried a Teacher Advisory Program. Then we gave it up. A generation later the concept rose from the dead. We tried all-positive-reinforcement-all-the-time and reaped limited results. We tried corporal punishment, discipline plans, created an in-school suspension room, and set up the SPARK class. We added a school resource officer, which basically meant we had a cop in the school.

In the 90s, experts assured us computer literacy would revolutionize education. Faster than you could say *McGuffey's Readers*, teachers found themselves seated at seminars, listening to speakers tout the virtues of Power Point. Every educator learned to use Power Point, like members of some electronic cult.

Instead of writing on the board: AMERICAN CIVIL WAR (1861-1865) and telling students to remember those dates for the next test you put it in Power Point. Letters and numbers flew out of a corner of the screen. They lined up in cartoon fashion to say: AMERICAN CIVIL WAR (1861-1865). You could even add sound effects like horses whinnying and cannon blasts. No one seemed to notice that students would still have to memorize the same *fact*.

Computers helped a little and hurt a little. Students gained access to a wealth of material. Yet they often preferred surfing the net to find pictures of hot young movie stars or played solitaire when teachers weren't vigilant. They turned to Wikipedia, instead of visiting the library, proving adept at cutting and pasting, substituting plagiarism or paraphrase for original work. You could even go to YouTube and find creative new ways to cheat. (Check the inside of labels on bottled water, teachers.) The essence of education remained the same.

Meanwhile, the states turned to proficiency tests as cure-alls in the late 80s and 90s.

When that didn't work the federal government stepped in with No Child Left Behind, which failed.

What else changed? When I began my career I had four classes every day and worked with 110 pupils. By the time I left the profession, Loveland Middle School staff members were carrying six classes and up to 175 students. In theory, this load should have killed test scores. It didn't—although that kind of load can kill teachers.

I worked for four principals and eight assistants and we had all kinds of school board members and superintendents. We had Democratic and Republican presidents and we're on our ninth U. S. Secretary of Education. Almost nothing fundamental really changed.

Success was never a matter of systems. Success did not come mainly as a result of improved means. Success turned out to be a result of grinding effort, and not by teachers alone.

Victory still had to be won by the soldiers and the battlefield was still inside the same four walls. Students and teachers had to do almost all the fighting, with parents and administrators and everyone else helping (or, if not careful, hindering) from the rear or the wings.

So, the inescapable question remains. Why, despite the promises of a thousand Big Fixers, haven't we seen tremendous progress across the land?

Consider one example from the early 80s, when leaders in education fastened on student-teacher ratios as the linchpin to improvement. A highly-regarded Tennessee study in 1983 showed a student-teacher ratio under 20-1 was critical in grades K-3. Yet when states reduced class sizes in an attempt to boost results they found no consistent improvement.

This baffled researchers. It wouldn't baffle my friend. She teaches third grade in a poor inner city school and could tell you more about student-teacher ratios than a hundred bureaucrats and theorists. Five years ago her principal said she would be getting a new boy in class.

On paper, her student-teacher ratio went from 23-1 to 24-1 but there was more to the story than +1. Until then, Tony had been on home instruction. Now, under court order, he was returning to school and would be in her care. Tony had been staying away because he had all kinds of problems, including "bowel issues."

Researchers who study student-teacher ratios don't study children like Tony. Bureaucrats don't take such kids into account when charting test data. Experts who write about education describe the process in an antiseptic sense. In the real world, where my friend had to try to save the boy, Tony refused to wear a Depends, as was the plan when the decision to bring him back to school was made.

For Tony, the words "school reform" had no meaning. A victim of sexual abuse by his father, he suffered from what medical people call encopresis, leakage from the anus, round partially-formed stool. It's a common problem in abuse cases. In class he soiled himself daily, never asking to go to the bathroom. Nor did he admit he had a bowel movement when he did. He sat at his desk, working distractedly, stewing in feces, until someone noticed the smell. When asked, "Did you have an accident?" he denied it. The odor gave his story the lie and a classroom aide led him away and she or the school nurse cleaned up the mess.

The boy's behavior was a "control issue" related to the abuse. Sometimes the school called and asked mom to bring clean clothes. Or she could drop by and wash up her son. Most days she said there was nothing she could do. She was poor and lacked transportation.

One day she brought in fresh clothing. Normally, she failed to make provision.

Mom was only 24, a confused, unprepared fifteen-year-old on the day her son was born.[25]

So try a different ratio. Try a different tracking system. Pass out the proficiency tests. Tony still soils himself daily. In his world the basics are clean underwear and shorts.

***

---

[25] Some teen mothers do a fine job. Some mothers who wait until thirty do half as well. Generally speaking, waiting is better than getting pregnant at fifteen.

If you want to know how much good the "standards" movement will probably do in the end you could do worse than consider changes made at Prospect Hill Elementary School in Pelham, New York. I have not visited Pelham and do not mean to cast aspersions on the motives of anyone involved. I only think we can predict with some certainty where cosmetic reforms will lead.

According to an article in *The New York Times* in 2009, traditional grading at Prospect Hill was dead, house-landing-on-the-Wicked-Witch dead. All those A's, B's, C's, D's and F's had been replaced with 4's, 3's, 2's and 1's.

"Standards" were going to save education. So Pelham schools made the switch to standards-based report cards, "part of a new system flourishing around the country as the latest frontier in a 20-year push to establish rigorous standards and require state tests on the material."

Well, what did such standards *measure*? At the second grade level there were 39 different standards. Some of those mentioned at various grade levels in the story included:

Basic computer skills
Communication skills
Comprehension
Decoding strategies
Fluency
Number sense and operations
Presentation skills
Publishing skills
Reading engagement
Research skills
Vocabulary development

Even standard "learning behaviors" were measured:

Engagement
Organization
Respect
Responsibility

How do you measure "respect?" With a meter stick? Well, it doesn't matter. Thomas R. Guskey, a Georgetown professor, told reporters standards-based report cards were *the* solution. He insisted they measured progress against a stated set of criteria. It was all right there in his new book!

You wondered, though, if Guskey ever dealt with a college student who soiled himself and sat silently in class, steeping in filth.

This is America, though, and where there was reform there was reaction. According to reporters educators loved the change. (I didn't believe that.) Only parents had qualms. A "4" meant the child was "meeting standards with distinction." You could not earn a "4" till the end of the year and so the highest possible marks till then were 3's.

Since 4's were best, parents were furious. What! Are you saying my child is not a "4" student!

In the San Mateo-Foster City district, near San Francisco, where similar reforms had been instituted, hundreds of parents signed a petition to bring A's and B's back. They were angry because top students stopped working once they found they could earn 3's with ease and couldn't earn 4's till year's end.

"Parents were beyond livid," one mother explained.

In Pelham, it depended on who touched the education elephant and where. One parent liked the new system because students were no longer compared. (I didn't believe that either.) Competition, she said, had no place in fifth grade. Another parent discovered the new reports were bargain-basement versions of real report cards. Her second grader was "crushed" to earn 2's in English second marking period even though she read nightly at home with mom and dad.

As far as I could ever tell education was straightforward business. If you read every night at home with mom and dad that was a plus, no matter what mark might be assigned to "measure" effort the following day. Suppose you wanted every third grader to learn 200 new vocabulary words by year's end. Knowledge is the objective. Grading systems are means to an end. If a boy or girl knows 9/10 words on the first vocabulary quiz you give them a 90% or a B under a traditional grading system. Or you look at the new standards-based criteria and 9/10 means they receive a "3" for "vocabulary development." You could design a system where a "3" was a ♥ instead. The child knows nine words in any case.

Knowing nine words is good.

It's better than eight.

Tony is a third grader. Suppose he moves to Pelham with his mom. His dad, of course, is long gone and from what my friend has been told ought to be in jail for what he did to his son. The boy still trails crippling emotional issues in his wake. His mom is still 24. She still doesn't have money to get him professional help and might not be interested if she could. If Tony gets 7/10 right and you give him a D or he gets 7/10 right and you give him a "1" his problems are the same.

At Pelham we have a glimpse of the hardest truth of all, a hint at the efficacy of all the Big Fixers' audacious plans. On the "basic" level, no matter how you grade or what you call your school, or whether or not your students are in teams, the nature of education is inalterable. You want students to know that $7 \times 7 = 49$. You can call it "number sense and operations."

Or you can call it "math."

Imagine we force all the Tonys at all the grade levels in all the fifty states to take more standardized tests. You still can't reform the world outside of school and Tony will still have a terrible rash. Only a good teacher or counselor or nurse or psychologist or an involved administrator is ever going to help Tony, as far as education goes, to have a better life.

So that's the fight the non-teaching types ignore, through naïveté or arrogance, it hardly matters which.

Never once in all my years in a classroom did I doubt that what I did mattered tremendously. I had to bring passion to my work every day—really, every minute of every day—if I expected to foster greater learning. I've argued at great length, though not too great, I hope, that attitudes are the key variable when it comes to improving academic outcomes. And I include student attitudes, parent attitudes, educator attitudes and societal attitudes, too. I would focus more on changing attitudes, where necessary, than almost any other factor in U. S. education.

Yet, I also saw what every frontline educator sees.

I saw that what I had it in *my power* to do would never be enough to help every child. I saw that in my school, and in every other, there were kids like Tony who were suffering terribly.

I saw that the idea we could "fix schools" and somehow save every child was a grotesque fraud and that in following this false path we did a disservice to the young who needed help most.

Here was a fight I knew that we—as a society—should be waging—and waging with all hands on deck. We had to stop talking about fixing schools and holding teachers accountable and start focusing on human beings with *individual* needs.

We, *as a society*, had to help Tony.

We had to help Ted (page 194), who lived in a rusted out automobile with Uncle Buster, the pothead.

We had to do something about Mike (page 163), who missed 106 days of class in one year, and his mother who allowed it.

We had to realize schools needed help with 14-year-old Luisa (page 277), before she ran off with a boyfriend twice her age.

We had to figure out some good way to work with Drew (page 222), who threatened to kill his science teacher, and the poor child (page 196) whose schizophrenic mother chased the principal out of the school with a knife.

We couldn't just dump the problems of millions of children on educators and then *complain* when they failed to solve them all.

I saw, and every educator sees it every day, that we needed to do far more to help children.

We needed to focus a great deal more of our efforts on what happened outside of schools.

***

I know people expect authors of books about education to offer neatly packaged plans and promise solutions. I don't believe fallible human beings ever solve all problems. I can, however, offer hypotheticals. I'd start by beefing up children's protective services in every state and city and corner of the land.

Raise taxes if you must. But get children help. Invest in America's young.

If you don't like higher taxes, stop paying college football coaches $7 million annually. Pay them a pittance. Make them struggle to get by on

361

$500,000 per year. Use that extra $6.5 million to hire 130 drug counselors, at $50,000 each, to work with teens that badly need help.

Put those counselors directly in schools.

Speaking of taxes, start by telling major league sports teams: "Hey, build your own stadiums!" And all the cities and states band together and say, "If you threaten to move, no one is going to take your carpet-bagging teams." The State of Minnesota, for instance, is footing half the bill for a new, billion dollar palace for the Vikings of the NFL. The state has agreed to pay $348 million outright. A hospitality *tax* of $150 million will also support the project.

Okay, I know. Americans—including me—love sports. And guys like Alex Rodriguez might have to take pay cuts to pick up part of the slack. But he'll get by. In 2008 he signed a ten-year deal, worth $275 million. So he can afford a few truckloads of cement and still purchase all the steroids he wants. The owners can pitch in too! After all, when Donald Sterling embarrassed himself with a series of racist rants, he still managed to sell the Los Angeles Clippers for $2 billion. So, yes, owners can pay for their own steel girders.

What else might we do, if we don't want to raise taxes, but do want to help children? We could do what Finland does—to circle back to that first question posed by the humble Harvard professor, to start this book.

No. I don't mean hire smarter teachers.

I mean…just maybe…spend a little less on defense. From 2010 to 2013, 1.3% of GDP in Finland went to the military. During that period, the United States spent $850 billion annually, 4.3% of GDP. In other words, each 0.1% spent by the U. S. = $19,767,441,860.

A 0.1% percent drop, to suggest one possibility, would allow us to provide $10,000 worth of medical and psychological services to 1,976,744 kids, or parents, as the case might be.

And Tony or his mother could use help.

Or: consider the cost of one F-35C fighter jet. Lockheed Martin promises you can pick one up for $116 million. So cancel the order for one jet.

Then hand out ten books ($10 each), to 1.16 million kids from low-income families. (See page 331, for the efficacy of such an approach to improved reading scores.)

If you don't like any of these ideas, you can reprioritize spending in a thousand ways, if children are your focus. According to Fox News, in 2013, members of Congress forced the U. S. Navy to keep ships in service the Navy no longer needed or wanted—all for political reasons—at a cost of $4.3 billion over two years. You could sink those ships for free and hire 43,000 new social services workers ($50,000; two years each) to go out to homes—or rusted out station wagons—and try to help a million kids like Ted who suffer every day.

You could pass a series of new laws and implement policies to strengthen the American family. Start by offering tax credits to couples who marry, since children living in two-parent homes are much less likely to drop out of school.

What else might we do? Provide good day care for all preschool children. Dump the "abstinence only" policy when it comes to sex education in schools. Keep teen girls from getting pregnant and they, too, are far less likely to drop out of school. Their children would then be less likely to represent the next generation of young with problems that start in the home.

(I'm sure our representatives in Congress can tackle these problems successfully. Motto: We keep getting reelected even though our approval rating is 17%!!!)

Last but not least, make me, or any other man or woman who has spent a lifetime working with kids, the next U. S. Secretary of Education. I promise if appointed, on my first day, to eliminate the posts of several thousand bureaucrats.

I will send them out to work directly in the schools. Instead of conducting studies, tabulating data and shuffling paperwork, I will task them with using their talents and skills to ensure that unfortunate kids like Tony have a chance for a good education and a better life.

If nothing else, they can clean him up whenever he makes a mess of himself.

Come to think of it, just shut down the whole Department. Devote the $70 billion saved annually to college scholarships to help the nation's young.

Hand out full rides to state colleges, four years, at, say, $100,000. You could provide for 700,000 high school seniors every year; and you'd do a hell of a lot more good.

- Diogenes

Nuts

"Now, as to myself, I have so described these matters as I have found and read them; but if anyone is inclined to another opinion about them, let him enjoy his different sentiments without blame from me."
Josephus

In all the years I toiled over this book, I searched land and sea and air for someone who could answer one question correctly. I would ask every educator I met: "Do you think all the standardized testing and recent changes in education have enhanced learning, hurt learning, or had, basically, a neutral effect?"

I would ask in as affectless a tone as possible, rather than telegraph my sentiments.

What would be the "correct" answer? I would know when I heard it.

On a plane, coming back from a wedding in California, I ended up sitting next to a retired elementary school principal. When I put the query to her, she didn't allow me finish.

"Hurt!" she replied empathically. "Does anybody say anything else?"

"Well, not really," I had to laugh.

"Hurt," of course, is not the correct answer. It is simply a variant of the answer I always receive—and I've asked hundreds of educators this question. At a birthday party one day, I ran into a veteran kindergarten teacher. She called the push for more and more testing "terrible for children."

It turned out her husband taught high school band. He chimed in with an answer, too. "The changes have had a stunting effect on music education," he said.

Sadly, I agree with these responses. But the correct answer, if I ever hear it will be something along these lines: "Yes, testing has allowed us to form a clear picture of what students are learning, and not learning, has helped us form a picture of the 'whole child' that we never had before. It has allowed us to devote more *time and resources* to helping students in a direct fashion.

"Testing has enhanced learning in a thousand ways. Testing has allowed us to reach young people in a manner that matters to each boy and girl, as individuals."

(I've heard nothing like that.)

I suppose the most "ringing" endorsement of testing came from Mike White, a respected school psychologist, who said he thought testing helped the bottom 20% of schools. But he went on to admit testing might hurt the other 80%, too.

So, like Diogenes, only looking for a frontline educator who firmly believes testing enhances learning, I wander the world in an unending quest.

In May 2015, at a retirement ceremony for friends at Loveland Middle School, I asked a dozen educators to provide their answers. Sue Lundy, twice "Educator of the Year" for LMS, called the testing mania "crazy." Hillary Pecsok, another winner of the "Educator of the Year" award, sneered at the idea testing and collecting data was doing any good. She said the process reminded her of "a really bad Saturday Night Live skit." Jane Barre, my old principal, who went on to serve as assistant superintendent for another local district, called the changes "lunacy." When she started as assistant superintendent in 2003, testing took up 10% of her time. By 2009, it was 50%, and that "made it hard to get anything else done."

The burden for her successor, she added, was much worse.

Jeane Weisbrod, and Diane Sullivan, both retiring that day, were scornful. "What bothers me most," Jeane said, "is all the valuable instructional time lost." I think Diane, who taught art, wanted to use a colorful word in reply, but caught herself. "Are you kidding? Of course it hasn't helped." Lauren Cripe, a very fine teacher, now a ten-year veteran, and team leader, nodded sadly.

I was asking people who I knew cared. I wasn't asking "stupid educators" who wanted to loaf—inept men and women anxious to avoid "accountability." I was asking those who were skilled in their craft and deeply committed to helping teens.

They weren't "experts" spewing theory—or shills for the big testing companies that didn't care if testing worked so long as more and more tests could be sold. They weren't politicians pandering for votes. These were combat veterans—people intimately involved in the "bloody" fight for knowledge.

Finally, I put my question to Chris Burke, now principal at Loveland Middle School. He's a gentleman I respect, concerned with what's best for kids. Testing didn't help students, he said. "It's all about compliance, John. We had to spend nineteen days on testing this year." Then he admitted 35% of LMS seventh graders simply "opted out" in 2015.

That's a growing phenomenon too. Across the country, parents are telling their children not to take the tests.

Katie Rose and Jenn Ramage, two good young teachers, were listening in on what Mr. Burke had to say. "Can you believe it?" Katie said to me. "Nineteen days!

"Forget covering Reconstruction," she noted, "I had *one day* left for the Civil War! How sad is that!"[26]

"You thought it was bad before," Jenn assured me. "You'd really hate it now. It's nuts!"

Meanwhile, the "education generals" keep ordering teachers and principals to take their students and charge the hill. They keep getting mowed down by machineguns and little or no ground is gained. So you start asking, "Do the people who are designing all these plans of attack really know what they're doing?"

Those of us who have served or still do serve in the front lines— who have charged that hill—we have no doubt about the answer to *that* question.

They don't.

---

[26] In Ohio, the eighth grade American history curriculum indicates that a teacher should cover the years from 1492 to 1877, ending with the Era of Reconstruction.

31.

Was Your Father a Teacher?

*"There is but one question in this world: How to make man better;
and but one answer: Education."*
Francis W. Parker

I take pride in what I accomplished as a teacher. If nothing else, I worked hard for thirty-three years. That's not unusual. There are hundreds of thousands of educators out there right now, working just as hard, or harder, every day.

I felt like I was mining diamonds in my classroom, never knowing what might turn up. I was an optimist where the young were concerned, believing that with proper polishing any teen might shine.

I worked on this book for six years—obstinacy, I suppose—but nothing in all that time surprised me more than this: Almost no one bothers to ask frontline educators what they think. Wendy Kopp, founder of Teach for America, is routinely quoted in newspapers like the *Wall Street Journal* and *The New York Times*. She never taught. Arne Duncan took his post as U. S. Secretary of Education at the same time I started this book. I don't believe that poor man has uttered two sentences in succession since to indicate he has any idea what really happens in classrooms across the land. Like Mayor Bloomberg and virtually all the other Big Fixers, Duncan has no classroom experience at all.

So, I thought I should write a book.

I actually *know something* about teaching. I should stand up for good teachers and do my best to explain what it is they try to do. I should reveal the false construct that is the call to "fix the schools" and focus attention on the iceberg. I should point out the damage done by the fetish for standardized tests, the futility of such an approach, the criminal waste of time, money and resources involved.

Finally, I should reveal the "hidden path" to higher scores—and—a hundred times more important—the path to true learning. This path is not actually hidden, though all too frequently ignored. It's the path all teachers and almost all students have it in their power to take. (I employ that modifying, "almost," because Tony and others like him will always need help, outside of the classroom, before they can travel down any path to success.)

Want to follow this all-important route? Well, then, go on, no one is stopping you.

Two legs suffice.

***

What do I know? I know teaching the way Herman Melville knew whaling. That is, he sailed on whaling ships and learned the risks and rewards of such voyages firsthand.

Speaking of artists who produced inaccurate paintings and drawings of whale species, Melville warned against the hopelessness of forming a true picture of Leviathan from afar:

> So there is no earthly way of finding out precisely what the whale really looks like, and the only mode in which you can derive even a tolerable idea of his living contour, is by going a-whaling yourself; but by so doing, you run no small risk of being eternally stove and sunk by him.

I went a-whaling, so to speak. But don't call me Ishmael.

I devoted my life to helping kids. Like Melville, I knew where to find the ambergris.

If I hadn't been adept at striking the harpoon, I'd never have had the audacity to write this book. In 1990, when our Parent Teacher Student Association instituted an "Educator of the Year" award for each of the five schools in the district, a member of the committee stopped by my room to say I had won. I wasn't a member of PTSA and by rule would have to join to be eligible. It didn't seem right to enlist just to collect a medal. So I declined. I won again—or won for the first time, in 1997—and repeated in

2002. And I believe I was probably a better teacher in 1979 or 1988, when I was more intense.

Some of my best work came from 2004 to 2007, when I switched to Ancient World History, and read 50,000 pages of material to teach a new subject.

I have sources, too, if you want them.

I wasn't some "Medal of Honor" type in the classroom. But I know what it's like to be part of the fight. I don't think they're going to turn my story into a movie, either. And I have no doubt you could send teams of reporters out across this great land and discover countless educators with better stories to tell, if only they weren't too busy actually trying to help the young.

The problem is that no one bothers to ask these combat soldiers what fighting in the trenches is like. So I have tried, in my own puny fashion, to speak in their stead.

If I haven't made this clear, knowing nothing about teaching hasn't stopped all kinds of people—Kopp, Joel I. Klein, Steven Brill, and even Glenn Beck—from penning books about U. S. education. For all they add to the ordinary reader's understanding they might just as well have written about whaling.

Me? I wrote about the only subject I knew.

I believe I did my job well, even though no one ever left class knowing about mercantilism. Wendy invited me to her wedding locally, Dave to his wedding in Maryland. Ali asked me to attend her Bat Mitzvah. Jill and Megan requested I stop by their high school graduation parties. Former students have paid for several meals in restaurants. Sadly, none has ever stepped up to make my mortgage payment. (Hey, it's never too late!) Josh stopped me in a bar one Saturday evening and insisted on matching shots of tequila. I felt honored he asked.

On another occasion, my wife and I were walking past an outdoor basketball court when a young man called out, "Hey, Mr. Viall!"

We stopped to chat.

Jerry asked how I was doing. He told me about high school, girls, and plans for the future. Before we walked away he remarked, "You were always my favorite teacher."

"He must have been a good student," Anne commented when we passed out of earshot.

"No," I replied, "I flunked him in seventh grade."

***

I look at notes and letters students gave me and I'm proud of what they discovered in my class. I should thank them all, instead. These kids I have mentioned, and many, many more, filled my life with joy and I never once regretted choosing the profession I did. I killed a whale or two, just like every good teacher I knew.

Kris added her name and a brief paragraph to the year-end evaluation in 1983: "Also, in your class I've learned that if I try and work hard, as you do, I can succeed at anything I do. This is the most important lesson I've learned and I'd like to thank you for giving that to me."

Katie hit the same note a few years later: "You also have taught me to always try my hardest and not look for the easy way out all the time."

A teacher leaves a mark in many ways. These marks cannot be standardized.

Nor should they be.

John's year-end evaluation from the late 90s is one of the most touching I received:

Mr. Viall has a fun class I think. I'm not just sucking up. I have enjoyed his class the past two years. I may have failed if it weren't for him caring about kid's grades enough to call parents and give so much extra credit and chances to pass. He does fun issues and tries to make his class fun. Some days when I came in I'd be depressed and leave happy again. Sometimes not. Like today I was depressed because a friend of mine died last night cause a car smashed and totaled his head. I feel a little better now. It has to be the better humor Mr. Viall has.

Another year-end evaluator wrote: "You've really made me think and evaluate myself. I think I have a better understanding of what I believe in and stand for now."

Kelly weighed in with a wonderful, non-standardized letter after she and her family moved to Derby, Kansas:

You taught me so much, not just about history, but also other aspects of life. I can never ever write a paper without thinking about "things" and "stuff." No other teacher has ever had a complaint about those words, but how could they when I never use them?! Your "training" has made me think, actually think…It would be so easy to slip into writing "things" instead of what I really mean, or "stuff" because I cannot think of a better, more appropriate word. But no, I take the extra time to get it right because Mr. Viall once told me that "things" and "stuff" were the weakest words in the American language. Thank you! You have made me a better, more articulate writer.

Or I look at this note from Tammy, a young lady who badly needed advice:

Dear Mr. Viall,

This letter is to say thank you for everything you've done for me in the last two years. This year and last you lended your support to me.

When my ex-boyfriend broke up with me. That was a major problem to me. You helped me through it. You said the right comments and cheered me up when I was down. Thanks.

This year when one of my closest friends moved away, that wasn't half the battle, that came when I found out he was doing drugs.

The toughest decision there was should I tell his dad. You help me make the right decision. I would rather have a person hate me for ever than to die permanentally.

I told his father. He thanked me for the information.

Two weeks later Bryan moved back home. Still to this day he doesn't know it was me.

I don't regret that, what I regret is that I didn't do it sooner.

Now it's the last day of my eighth grade year and I'm still alive. I made it through those problems. There is going to be millions more. In my opinion I don't think I could have made it through those without you.

So thank you for everything you've done.

Brandee stopped by my room in the fall of 2005. Classes had ended for the day and I had already headed for home. So she left a note and email address.

I quickly responded, saying I remembered her long hair and Star Wars obsession.

"Honestly," she replied, "you are the most memorable teacher I had in middle school...You made history human, about people. I loved your class and wanted you to know you made an impact on my life."

She noted that she had married recently. Her husband had been to Iraq and returned safely. She also denied seeing Star Wars 58 times, as I thought she once told me. The figure was more like 22, she claimed. But I think that was simply denial.

Another kind note came from Karen, several years after she passed through my class:

Before I had you as a teacher, history was just another subject I had to take in school. You changed all that by teaching me that history is living and life itself....

Truthfully, I can say you taught me what work was, and it was such a pleasure, because I learned. Even today I find myself applying the concepts you taught to different situations. Discrimination, equal rights, the never-ending revenge cycle, the humanness of *all* people—everything remains with me today.

I appreciated what parents said too. Sarah's mom sent me this kind note at year's end:

I think your approach to history is fantastic and will serve them through the years. Thank you for opening Sarah's eyes, challenging her mind, and encouraging so much writing...In the days of Sarah's diminishing communication at home, she elaborates about your lessons, the way you give tips on life and help them prepare for their future...These kids appreciate being treated as intelligent, capable beings...[They] will remember you and your class for life.

Matt's mom had this to say:

Instead of trying to catch children in what they don't know, you do everything possible to give them credit for what they do know...[Matt] has learned a greater social conscience in your class—something we have tried to instill in him through our love, teachings, and church.

Even now, via Facebook, I get the kind of reactions that tell me what I did mattered. Fortunately, Jenny harbored no grudge. She forgave me for drilling a hole in the center of her textbook. (I just happened to have a drill in my hand on a day in May, when she complained about how dull the book was—and I knew—and she didn't—that the text was to be phased out in June.)

When she heard I was writing a tall tale about teaching she responded, "Maybe you should include the fact that, despite the difficulties brought on by trying to read through a hole in the center of my book, I did finish it. And, the fact that your history class made me want to become a writer."

Harlan sent another one of my favorite messages:

You were my favorite teacher in Jr. High because I got more out of your class than any. I guess I was just more focused by the way you taught. At times it was hard though with Robin [his dream girl]...sitting right next to me. Ha ha...I would have to say that you personally helped jump start me to play basketball. After getting cut by Mr. Battle, I was crushed. Thought I was good enough to make the team but I was the last one to be cut. After what happened you asked me to play on Friday's after school [with a group of kids]. That time made me a better person and a better player and I want to thank you for that time and attention.

If a former student (in the Braves jersey) invites you to the ballgame you should go.

And there are comments like these:

Eric: "It's funny I was just talking about you because a passenger on a plane saw I was reading *People's History of the U. S.* and we got to talking and I told him how you turned me on to history, but most importantly to a love for continuous learning and truth seeking."

Melissa:

I still remember that Holocaust packet. You told me I could stop reading because it was upsetting me but I knew the importance of it and didn't want to. Mr. Viall, you were definitely one of the best teachers I ever had. You always made class interesting and fun and engaging.

Shawn: "sir im not sure after all these years if you remember me I wouldn't be upset if you didn't...I was a pain and sometimes to stubborn for my own good but you never gave up on me and I wanted to thank you for that."

I'm also proud of comments Loren made when he heard I was writing this cursed book.

"That's awesome!" he said. "As a Company Commander I try to model some of the ways I teach soldiers off your methods."

Becky posted on my wall another day:

You taught history to me in middle school. All I have to say is...thing, thing, thing, stuff, stuff, stuff and you are a DOLT. You were a SPECTACULAR teacher. It is good to see you are still riding. I am working on my personal training license and moved back to Loveland a year ago after 10 years in Georgia. I would love to know how you are.

We exchanged messages. She mentioned other teachers who inspired her or now helped her son. Mr. Bauman and Ms. Rodier, educators I didn't know, were two she mentioned.

I've had former students tell me about scores of educators who changed their lives and only wish I could list them all.

In the end, perhaps this message from Mark sums it up best: "Through the years I've often thought back to your teaching...Everything you did in the classroom, discipline included, was geared to help us become better thinkers, better writers and better citizens."

In an era when the Big Fixers and critics who never taught insult frontline educators at every turn, insisting that they know what real teachers should do, and how they should do it, I'm content to say I did my best to stand on that ground.

I say that also knowing that what I tried to do was not standardized in any way.

***

Sometimes, recognizing our unusual last name, former students stop my wife or one of my children to say how much they enjoyed my class. One night my son ran into one of my old students at a local pool hall.

"Was your father a teacher in Loveland?" his opponent inquired on hearing his last name.

Seth said I was.

His challenger took a sip of beer, set the bottle down on the edge of the table and offered quick assessment: "I hated that fucking dick." Then he struck the cue ball, sank the seven, and took another swig.

Okay, not everyone was a fan.